EMERSON loved the good more than he abhorred evil ⁊ Carlyle abhorred evil more than he loved the good. If you should by chance find anything in this book you do not especially like, it is not at all wise to focus your memory on that, to the exclusion of all else—bless my soul! —*E. H.*

To My Darling
Daughter
From Mother
Jan. 1978

"To Forget is
Rare
To Forgive
Divine "

Always with my
Eternal Love
mother.

ELBERT HUBBARD

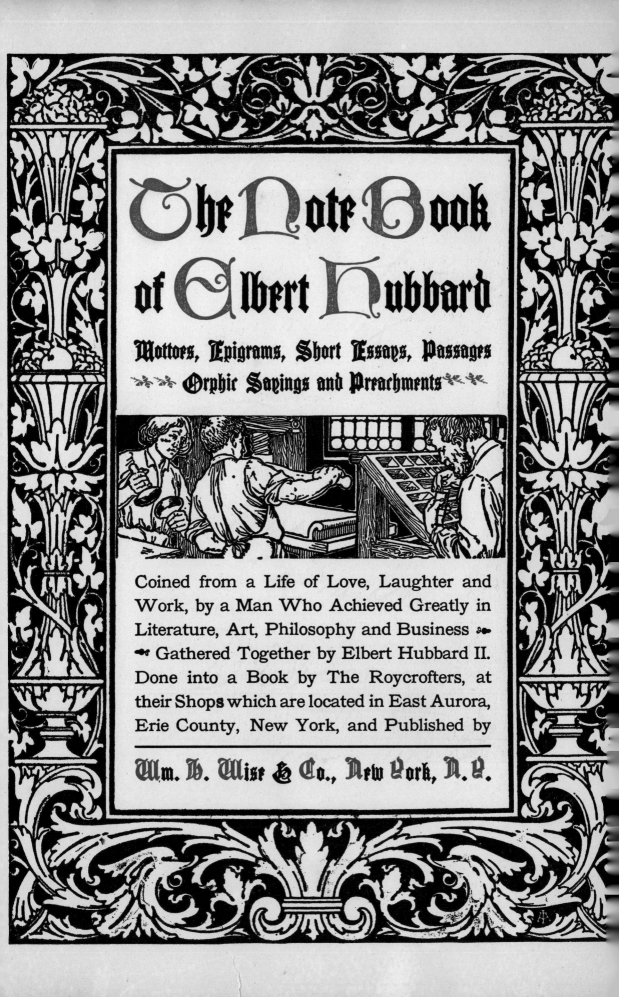

The Note Book of Elbert Hubbard

Mottoes, Epigrams, Short Essays, Passages
Orphic Sayings and Preachments

Coined from a Life of Love, Laughter and
Work, by a Man Who Achieved Greatly in
Literature, Art, Philosophy and Business
Gathered Together by Elbert Hubbard II.
Done into a Book by The Roycrofters, at
their Shops which are located in East Aurora,
Erie County, New York, and Published by

Wm. H. Wise & Co., New York, N. Y.

PRINTED IN U. S. A.

 # *Introduction*

BY ALICE HUBBARD

LBERT HUBBARD, the most positive human force of his time, is a man of genius in business, in art, in literature, in philosophy. He is an idealist, dreamer, orator, scientist. In his knowledge of the fundamental, practical affairs of living, in business, in human interests, in education, politics and law he seems without a competitor. ❡ He is like Jefferson in his democracy, in teaching a nation to love to govern itself and to simplify all living. He is like Paine in his love for liberty and in his desire that all shall be free to act in freedom and to think in freedom.

❡ He is like Lincoln in that he would free all mankind. He, too, knows that there can be no free man on the earth so long as there is one slave. Elbert Hubbard sees, too, that just so long as there is one woman who is denied any right that man claims for himself, there is no free man; that no man can be a superior, true American, so long as one woman is denied her birthright of life, liberty and happiness.

He knows that freedom to think and act, without withholding that right from any other, evolves humanity. Therefore he gives his best energy to inspiring men and women to think and to act, each for himself. He pleads for the rights of children, for so-called criminals, for the insane, the weak, and all those who having failed to be a friend to themselves, need friendship most. The Golden Rule is his rule of life.

His work is to emancipate American men and women from being slaves to useless customs, outgrown mental habits, outgrown religion, outgrown laws, outgrown superstitions. He would make each human being rely upon himself for health, wealth and happiness.

Elbert Hubbard is like Emerson in seizing upon truth, embalmed and laid in pyramids of disuse. Into these truths he has breathed the breath of life and they have become for many of us living souls. From the thoughts of Moses, Socrates, Solomon, Pythagoras, Loyola, Jesus, Buddha, Mohammed, he has brought to us wisdom that applies to the art of living today.

Elbert Hubbard is a unique figure in history. The strength of his individuality comes from his having lived much and intensely. He lives his philosophy before he writes it, proves his theory before he announces it. Like Shakespeare he has access to universal knowledge, and from his storehouse he draws the vital fact whenever he needs it. Without effort, his mind seizes upon the important part of any subject, scene or situation, and he presents the few parts which will suggest the whole. He knows psychology, the needs of humanity at large, the needs of races, the needs of classes in races, and individuals in a class.

He knows men and women, American men and women, their hopes, their fears, their strength, their weakness, their possibilities, and he deals with them, having ever before him the ideal. He, too, is looking for a Hapi, a Messiah, a Superman. He is never discouraged, never tired, never depressed. Eternal hope is in his heart, so every morning brings to him a New Day, and ushers in a New Year of the Better Day. Work, laugh, play, think, be kind, is the day's program he lives and recommends.

Economic freedom is the first necessity in human happiness. So Elbert Hubbard's first lesson is industry, producing wealth, using it wisely, distributing it. He knows, too, that food, shelter, clothing, fuel, are not enough to fill man's needs.

Man has a soul to be fed and evolved as well. Love, beauty, music, art, are necessities, too. Had he but two loaves of bread he would sell one and buy *White Hyacinths* with which to feed his soul. He loves all animal life, and believes that men should spend a part of every day in the garden, on the farm, with horses and animals, which are the civilizers of man.

Elbert Hubbard is a businessman and a philosopher. He is a wise man in the use of his time, his energy. The law of his life is action. He knows that to focus his mind on the development of man is to degenerate into something less than a man. Man is developed, quite incidentally, through his work. Work is the exercise which develops brain, nerve, muscle.

Work is the means which man uses to accomplish the end, the superman who shall understand Nature. He knows that creed is the subjugation of the individual, so his desire is to give every person about him equal opportunity with himself. He loves humanity. He believes in man, of the ultimate triumph of the noblest qualities in man. He is brother to all mankind and kindred to every living thing. He lives as a nobleman, every day without fear. All days are holy days.

All natural phases of human life are sacred, and he respects them all. Through the power of his imagination he has lived all lives, and he condemns no man. Content to live in one world at a time, he has the genuine faith which does not creep into the Unknown, but lives to the full today, assured that "the power which cares for us here will not desert us there."

—From *An American Bible*, May, 1911

The Note Book of
Elbert Hubbard

THE NOTE BOOK OF ELBERT HUBBARD

AN! I wonder what a man really is! Starting from a single cell, this seized upon by another, and out of the Eternal comes a particle of the Divine Energy that makes these cells its home ✒ ✒ ❧ Growth follows, cell is added to cell, and there develops a man—a man whose body, two-thirds water, can be emptied by a single dagger-thrust and the spirit given back to its Maker in a moment.

SIXTY generations have come and gone since Cæsar trod the Roman Forum. ❧ The pillars against which he often leaned still stand. The thresholds over which he passed are there. The pavements ring beneath your tread as they once rang beneath his. ❧ Three generations and more have come and gone since Napoleon trod the streets of Toulon contemplating suicide ✒ Babes in arms were carried by fond mothers to see Lincoln, the candidate for President. ❧ These babes have grown into men, are grandfathers possibly, with whitened hair, furrowed faces, looking calmly forward to the end, having tasted all that life holds in store for them. Yet Lincoln lived but yesterday ! ❧ You can reach back into the past and grasp his hand,

THE Supreme prayer of my heart is not to be learned, rich, famous, powerful or even good, but simply to be radiant. I desire to radiate health, cheerfulness, calm courage and good-will. ❧ I wish to live without hate, whim, jealousy, envy, fear. I wish to be simple, honest, frank, natural, clean in mind and clean in body, unaffected — to say "I do not not know," if it be so, and to meet all men on an absolute equality, to face any obstacle and meet every difficulty unabashed and unafraid. ❧ I wish others to live their lives, too, up to their highest, fullest and best. To that end I pray that I may never meddle, interfere, dictate, give advice that is not wanted, or assist when my services are not needed. If I can help people, I'll do it by giving them a chance to help themselves; and if I can uplift or inspire, let it be by example, inference and suggestion, rather than by injunction and dictation. That is to say, I desire to be Radiant—to Radiate Life!

and look into his sad and weary eyes. A man! ❧ Weighed with the sins of his parents, grandparents, great-grandparents, who fade off into dim spectral shapes in the dark and dreamlike past. ❧ No word of choice has he in the selection of his father and mother; no voice in the choosing of environment. Brought into life without his consent, and pushed out of it against his will — battling ✒ striving, hoping, cursing ✒ waiting, loving, praying ✒ burned by fever, torn by passion, checked by fear, reaching for friendship, longing for sympathy, and hungering for love, clutching—nothing.

MY heart goes out to you, O man, because I can not conceive of any being greater, nobler, more heroic, more tenderly loving, loyal, unselfish and enduring than you are ✒ ✒ All the love I know is man's love ✒ ✒ All the forgiveness I know is man's forgiveness. ❧ All the sympathy I know is man's sympathy. ❧ And hence I address myself to man —to you—and you I would serve. The fact that you are a human being brings you near to me. It is the bond that unites us. I understand you because you are a part of myself.

You may like me, or not—it makes no difference. If ever you need my help I am with you. ⟨ Often we can help each other most by leaving each other alone; at other times we need the hand-grasp and the word of cheer.

I am only a man—a mere man—but in times of loneliness think of me as one who loves his kind.

What your condition is in life will not prejudice me either for or against you.

⟨ What you have done or not done will not weigh in the scale.

If you have been wise and prudent I congratulate you, unless you are unable to forget how wise and good you are—then I pity you.

If you have stumbled and fallen and been mired in the mud, and have failed to be a friend to yourself, then you of all people need friendship, and I am your friend.

I am the friend of convicts, insane people and fools—successful and unsuccessful, college-bred and illiterate.

You all belong to my church.

I could not exclude you if I would. But if I should shut you out I would then close the door upon myself and be a prisoner indeed.

The spirit of friendship that flows through me, and of which I am a part, is your portion, too.

The race is one, and we trace to a common Divine ancestry.

≈ ≈

I OFFER you no reward for being loyal to me, and surely I do not threaten you with pain, penalty and dire disaster if you are indifferent to me ≈

You can not win me by praise, promises or adulation.

You can not shut my heart toward you, even though you deny and revile me.

⟨ Only the good can reach me, and no thought of love you send me can be lost or missent.

All the kindness you feel for me should be given those nearest you, and it shall all be passed to your credit, for you yourself are the record of your thoughts, and no error can occur in the count ≈

You belong to my church, and always and forever my friendship shall follow you, yet never intrude.

I do not ask you to incur obligations nor make promises.

There are no dues. I do not demand that you shall do this or not do that. I issue no commands.

I can not lighten your burden, and perhaps I should not even if I could, for men grow strong through bearing burdens.

If I can I will show you how to acquire strength to meet all your difficulties and face the duties of the day.

It is not for me to take charge of your life, for surely I do well if I look after one person.

If you err it is not for me to punish you. We are punished by our sins not for them ≈ ≈

Soon or late I know you will see that to do right brings good, and to do wrong brings misery, but you will abide by the law and all good things be yours. I can not change these laws—I can not make you exempt from your own blunders and mistakes ≈ ≈

And you can not change the eternal laws for me, even though you die for me. But perhaps I can point you the pathway that leads to love, truth and usefulness, and this I want to do because I am your friend.

And then by pointing you the way I find it myself.

You belong to me—you are a member of my church. All are members of my church. None is excluded nor can be excluded ≈ ≈

So over the plains and prairies, over the mountains and seas, over the cities and towns, in palaces, tenements, moving-wagons, dugouts, cottages, hovels, sleeping-cars, autos, day-coach, caboose, cab, in solitary cells behind prison-bars, or wandering out under the stars, my heart goes out to you, whoever you are, wherever you are, and I wish you well. Only love do I send and a desire to bless and benefit.

≈ ≈

Our admiration is so given to dead martyrs that we have little time for living heroes ≈ ≈

≈ ≈

The Ideal Life is only the normal or natural life as we shall some day know it.

...nders! O, Mystery!!

...the pain and travail
...there is distilled
...allembic of...
...wds finer products.
...safely
...ping
...un free
...one

He was so rich that he could only get into Heaven by a Suspension of the...

His religion was that of his priest, and his political views were acquired from his patrons.

¶ This book is a life of Jesus of Nazareth, as the author sees the man, viewing him across the centuries. No contemporary writer mentions Jesus, although it was an age of writing men. The alleged references to Jesus...

Man becomes like the thing he hates, just as inexpert bicyclist riding into that which ... makes to avoid. Let carry that thought one step farther: man is like the thing he hates and through hating it he becomes the identical thing he once despised.

Where men continually confirm with oaths a certain number of individuals will cease to own at all.

GRAND HOTEL
AND
NEW ANNEX
FIREPROOF
BROADWAY & 31ST STREET
THE HURLBERT GRAND HOTEL CO.
PROPRIETOR
THE NEW GRAND
New York.

write play with Robert Owen as central figure.

Elbert Hubbard jotted down notes on every conceivable subject whenever an idea came to him. Here is a handful taken at random

IN San Francisco lived a lawyer—age, sixty—rich in money, rich in intellect, a businessman with many and varied interests. Now, this lawyer was a bachelor, and lived in apartments with his Chinese servant, " Sam."

Sam and his master had been together for fifteen years.

The servant knew the wants of his employer as though he were his other self. No orders were necessary. If there was to be a company—one guest or a hundred—Sam was told the number, that was all, and everything was provided.

This servant was cook, valet, watchman, friend. No stray, unwished-for visitor ever got to the master to rob him of his rest when he was at home.

If extra help was wanted, Sam secured it; he bought what was needed; and when the lawyer awakened in the morning, it was to the singing of a tiny music-box with a clock attachment set for seven o'clock.

The bath was ready; a clean shirt was there on the dresser, with studs and buttons in place; collar and scarf were near; the suit of clothes desired hung over a chair; the right pair of shoes, polished like a mirror, was at hand, and on the mantel was a half-blown rose, with the dew still upon it, for a boutonniere. Downstairs, the breakfast, hot and savory, waited.

When the man was ready to go to the office, silent as a shadow stood Sam in the hallway, with overcoat, hat and cane in hand. When the weather was threatening, an umbrella was substituted for the cane. The door was opened, and the master departed. When he returned at nightfall, on his approach the door swung wide. Sam never took a vacation; he seemed not to either eat or sleep. He was always near when needed; he disappeared when he should. He knew nothing and knew everything.

For weeks scarcely a word might pass between these men—they understood each other so well.

The lawyer grew to have a great affection for his servant. He paid him a hundred dollars a month, and tried to devise other ways to show his gratitude; but Sam wanted nothing, not even thanks. All he desired was the privilege to serve.

But one morning as Sam poured his master's coffee, he said quietly, without a shade of emotion on his yellow face, " Next week I leave you." The lawyer smiled.

" Next week I leave you," repeated the Chinese; " I hire for you better man."

The lawyer set down his cup of coffee. He looked at the white-robed servant. He felt the man was in earnest.

" So you are going to leave me—I do not pay you enough, eh? That Doctor Sanders who was here—he knows what a treasure you are. Don't be a fool, Sam; I 'll make it a hundred and fifty a month —say no more."

"Next week I leave you—I go to China," said the servant impassively.

GENIUS is only the power of making continuous efforts. The line between failure and success is so fine that we scarcely know when we pass it: so fine that we are often on the line and do not know it. How many a man has thrown up his hands at a time when a little more effort, a little more patience, would have achieved success. As the tide goes clear out, so it comes clear in. In business, sometimes, prospects may seem darkest when really they are on the turn. A little more persistence, a little more effort, and what seemed hopeless failure may turn to glorious success. There is no failure except in no longer trying. There is no defeat except from within, no really insurmountable barrier save our own inherent weakness of purpose.

"Oh, I see! You are going back for a wife? All right, bring her here—you will return in two months? I do not object; bring your wife here—there is work for two to keep this place in order. The place is lonely, anyway. I'll see the Collector of the Port, myself, and arrange your passage-papers."

"I go to China next week: I need no papers—I never come back," said the man with exasperating calmness and persistence ﹏ ﹏

"By God, you shall not go!" said the lawyer ﹏ ﹏

"By God, I will!" answered the heathen.

❦ It was the first time in their experience together that the servant had used such language, or such a tone, toward his master. The lawyer pushed his chair back, and after an instant said, quietly: "Sam, you must forgive me; I spoke quickly. I do not own you—but tell me, what have I done—why do you leave me this way—you know I need you!"

"I will not tell you why I go — you laugh."

"No, I shall not laugh."

"You will."

"I say, I will not."

"Very well, I go to China to die!"

"Nonsense! You can die here. Have n't I agreed to send your body back if you die before I do?"

"I die in four weeks, two days!"

"What!"

"My brother, he in prison. He young—twenty-six, I fifty. He have wife and baby. In China they accept any man same family to die. I go to China, give my money to my brother—he live, I die!"

Next day a new Chinaman appeared as servant in the lawyer's household. In a week this servant knew everything, and nothing, just like Sam. And Sam disappeared, without saying good-bye.

He went to China and was beheaded, four weeks and two days from the day he broke the news of his intent to go. His brother was set free.

And the lawyer's household goes along about as usual, save when the master calls for "Sam," when he should say, "Charlie." At such times there comes

a kind of clutch at his heart, but he says nothing.

﹏ ﹏

THE desire for friendship is strong in every human heart. We crave the companionship of those who understand. The nostalgia of life presses, we sigh for "home," and long for the presence of one who sympathizes with our aspirations, comprehends our hopes, and is able to partake of our joys. A thought is not our own until we impart it to another, and the confessional seems to be a crying need of every human soul.

❦ One can bear grief, but it takes two to be glad.

We reach the divine through some one, and by dividing our joy with this one we double it, and come in touch with the Universal. The sky is never so blue, the birds never sing so blithely, our acquaintances are never so gracious, as when we are filled with love for some one else ﹏ ﹏

Being in harmony with one we are in harmony with all. The lover idealizes and clothes the beloved with virtues that exist only in his imagination. The beloved is consciously or unconsciously aware of this, and endeavors to fulfil the high idea; and in the contemplation of the transcendent qualities that his mind has created, the lover is raised to heights otherwise impossible.

Should the beloved pass from this earth while such a condition of exaltation exists, the conception is indelibly impressed upon the soul, just as the last earthly view is said to be photographed upon the retina of the dead.

The highest earthly relationship is in its very essence fleeting, for men are fallible, and living in a world where the material wants jostle, and time and change play their ceaseless parts, gradual obliteration comes and disillusion enters. But the memory of a sweet affinity once fully possessed, and snapped by Fate at its supremest moment, can never die from out the heart. All other troubles are swallowed up in this; and if the individual is of too stern a fiber to be completely crushed into the dust, time will come bearing healing, and the memory of that once ideal condition will chant in his heart a perpetual eucharist. And I hope the world has passed forever from the nightmare of pity for the dead; they have ceased from their labors and are at rest.

But for the living, when death has entered and removed the best friend, Fate has done her worst; the plummet has sounded the depths of grief, and thereafter nothing can inspire terror ✺ ✺

At one fell stroke all petty annoyances and corroding cares are sunk into nothingness ✺ The memory of a great love lives enshrined in undying amber. It affords a ballast 'gainst all the storms that blow, and although it lends an unutterable sadness, it imparts an unspeakable peace. Where there is this haunting memory of a great love lost, there are also forgiveness, charity and sympathy that make the man brother to all who suffer and endure.

The individual himself is nothing: he has nothing to hope for, nothing to lose, nothing to win, and this constant memory of the high and exalted friendship that was once his is a nourishing source of strength; it constantly purifies the mind and inspires the heart to nobler living and diviner thinking. The man is in communication with Elemental Conditions ✺ ✺

To have known an ideal friendship, and have it fade from your grasp and flee as a shadow before it is touched with the sordid breath of selfishness, or sullied by misunderstanding, is the highest

I BELIEVE that no one can harm us but ourselves; that sin is misdirected energy; that there is no devil but fear; and that the universe is planned for good. We know that work is a blessing, that Winter is as necessary as Summer, that Night is as useful as Day, that Death is a manifestation of Life, and just as good. I believe in the Now and Here. I believe in you and I believe in a power that is in ourselves that makes for righteousness ✺

good. And the constant dwelling in sweet, sad recollection of the exalted virtues of the one that is gone, tends to crystallize these very virtues in the heart of him who meditates them.

✺ ✺

THE old and once popular view of life that regarded man as a sinful, lost, fallen, despised, despicable and damned thing has very naturally tended to kill in him enthusiasm, health, and self-reliance. Probably it has shortened the average length of life more than a score of years ✺ When man comes to realize that he is part and particle of the Divine Energy that lives in all he sees and feels and hears, he will, indeed, be in a position to claim and receive his birthright ✺ And this birthright is to be healthy and happy.

❐ The Religion of Humanity does not seek to placate the wrath of a Non-Resident Deity, nor does it worship an Absentee God.

It knows nothing of gods, ghosts, goblins, sprites, fairies, devils or witches. I would not know a god if I saw one coming down the street in an automobile ✺ ✺

If ever a man existed who had but one parent, this fact of his agamogenesis would not be any recommendation to us, nor would it make special claim on our reverence and regard. Rather, it would place him outside of our realm, so that what he might do or say would not be vital to us. He would be a different being from us, therefore his experiences would not be an example for us to follow.

❐ The Religion of Humanity knows,

nothing of a vicarious atonement, justification by faith, miraculous conception, transubstantiation, original sin, Hell, Heaven, or the efficacy of baptism as a saving ordinance.

It does not know whether man lives again as an individual after he dies or not ૭ ૭

It is not so much interested in knowing whether a book is " inspired " as whether it is true.

It does not limit the number of saviors of the race, but believes that any man or woman who makes this world a better place is in degree a " savior" of mankind. It knows that the world is not yet saved from ignorance, superstition and incompetence, nor redeemed from a belief in miracles. And hence it believes that there must be saviors yet to come.

It believes that the supernatural is the natural not yet understood.

૭ ૭

COMMERCE is no longer exploitation. It is human service, and no business concern can hope to prosper which does not meet a human need and add to human happiness.

The indiscriminate giving to the poor was a mistaken policy. It tended to make poverty perpetual. Now we aim to give just one thing, and that is opportunity ૭ ૭

Business aims to render life safe and secure. To supervise wisely the great corporations is well; but to look backward to the days when business was polite pillage and regard our great business concerns as piratical institutions carrying letters of marque and reprisal is a grave error, born in the minds of little men. When these little men legislate they set the brakes going up hill.

❦ Charity and piracy are things of the past. They were always closely akin, for pirates were very charitable, and ever in their train were troops of sturdy beggars ૭ ૭

Business will yet do away with graft and begging. Reciprocity, cooperation and mutuality are the important words now ૭ ૭

Laws for the regulation of trade should be most carefully scanned. That which

hampers, limits, cripples and retards must be done away with. That which gives freedom, security, and peace must be encouraged. We are moving toward the rising sun; and no man can guess the splendor, and the riches and the beauty that will yet be ours. Let America lead the way!

૭ ૭

THE word business was first used in the time of Chaucer to express contempt for people who were useful. The word was then spelled " busyness."

In those days the big rewards were given to men who devoted their lives to conspicuous waste and conspicuous leisure. He who destroyed most was king by divine right. And everybody took his word for it ૭ ૭

Even yet we find that if you would go in " good society " you had better not lift a trunk, sift ashes, sweep the sidewalk or carry a hoe upon your shoulder.

૭ ૭

THERE is a common tendency to cling to old ways and methods ૭ Every innovation has to fight for its life, and every good thing has been condemned in its day and generation ૭ Error once set in motion continues indefinitely, unless blocked by a stronger force, and old ways will always remain unless some one invents a new way and then lives and dies for it.

And the reason men oppose progress is not that they hate progress, but that they love inertia.

Even as great a man as John Ruskin foresaw that the railroads would ruin England by driving the stages out of business and killing the demand for horses, thus ruining the farmer.

Thomas Jefferson tells us, in his autobiography, of a neighbor of his who was " agin " the public schools, because, " when every one could read and write, no one would work."

Governor Berkeley thanked God there was not a printing-press in Virginia. ❦ In the time of Mozart, musicians were classed with stablemen, scullions and cooks. They ate below stairs and their business was simply to amuse the great man who hired them.

EACHING things out of season is a woful waste of time. It is also a great consumer of nerve-force, for both pupil and teacher ❧ ❧

For instance, the English plan of having little boys of eight study Latin and Greek killed a lot of boys, and probably never helped a single one to shoulder life's burden and be a better man.

Knowledge not used, like anything else not used, is objectionable and often dangerous ❧ ❧

Nature intends knowledge for service, not as an ornament or for purposes of bric-a-brac ❧ ❧

" Delay adolescence — delay adolescence!" cries Stanley Hall. The reason is plain. The rareripe rots. What boy well raised, of ten or twelve, can compare with your street gamin who has the knowledge and the shrewdness of a grown-up broker! But the Arab never becomes a man.

The awkward and bashful boy from the country—with mind slowly ripening in its rough husk, gathering gear as he goes, securing knowledge in order to use it, and by using it, making it absolutely his own, and gaining capacity for more —is the type that scores.

The priestly plan of having one set of men do all the thinking, and another set all the work, is tragedy for both ❧

To quit the world of work in order to get an education is as bad as quitting the world of work and struggle in order to be " good." The tendency of the classical education is to unfit the youth for work. He gains knowledge, like the gamin, in advance of his needs.

The boy of eighteen who enters college and graduates at twenty-two, when he comes home wants to run his father's business. Certainly he will not wash windows ❧ ❧

He has knowledge, but no dexterity— he has learning, but no competence ❧

He owns a kit of tools, but does not know how to use them. And now, if his father is rich, a place is made for him where he can do no damage, a genteel and honorable place, and he hypnotizes himself and deceives his friends with the fallacy that he is really doing something.

❊ In the meantime the plain and alert young man brought up in the business keeps the chimes on the barrel, otherwise 't would busticate.

Use and acquaintance should go hand in hand. Skill must be applied. All great writers learned to write in just one way —by writing. To acquire the kit is absurd—get the tools one at a time as you need them ❧ ❧

College has just one thing to recommend it, and that is the change of environment that it affords the pupil. This is what does him good—new faces, new scenes, new ideas, new associations. The curriculum is nil—if it keeps the fledgling out of mischief it accomplishes its purpose ❧

But four years in college tends to ossification instead of fluidity—and seven years means the pupil gets caught and held by environment: he stays too long.

❊ Alexander von Humboldt was right —one year in any college is enough for any man. One year gives him inspiration and all the spirit of good there is in it; a longer period fixes frats, fads and fancies in his noodle as necessities.

Men are great only as they train on. College may place you in the two-thirty list, but you get into the free-for-all only by letting the Bunch take your dust ❧

❊ Happy is the man, like Ralph Waldo Emerson, who is discarded by his Alma Mater, or like Henry Thoreau, who discarded her ❧ ❧

In any event—God's name, get weaned!

❧ ❧

M Y father has practised medicine for seventy years, and is still practising.

❊ I, also, have studied the so-called science of medicine.

I am fifty-five years old; my father is ninety ❧ ❧

We live neighbors, and daily ride horseback together or tramp through the fields and woods. Today we did our little jaunt of five miles and back across country.

❊ I have never been ill a day—never consulted a physician in a professional way; and, in fact, never missed a meal except through inability of access.

The old gentleman and I are not fully agreed on all of life's themes, so existence for us never resolves itself into a dull neutral gray.

He is a Baptist and I am a Vegetarian. ❧ Occasionally he refers to me as " callow," and we have daily resorts to logic to prove prejudice, and history is searched to bolster the preconceived, but on the following important points we stand together, solid as one man:

First—Ninety-nine people out of a hundred who go to a physician have no organic disease, but are merely suffering from some functional disorder, caused by their own indiscretion ❧

Second—Individuals who have organic diseases nine times out of ten are suffering from the accumulated evil effects of medication ❧ ❧

Third—That is to say, most diseases are the result of medication which has been prescribed to relieve and take away a beneficent and warning symptom on the part of Nature ❧ ❧

Most of the work of doctors in the past has been to prescribe for symptoms, the difference between actual disease and a symptom being something that the average man does not even yet know. And the curious point is that on these points all physicians, among themselves, are fully agreed, what I say here being merely truism, triteness and commonplace.

❧ ❧

A RELIGION of just being kind would be a pretty good religion— don't you think so? But a religion of kindness and useful effort is nearly a perfect religion. We used to think it was a man's belief concerning a dogma that would fix his place in eternity ❧ This was because we believed that God was a grumpy, grouchy old gentleman, stupid, touchy and dictatorial. A really good man would not damn you, even if you didn't like him; but a bad man would. As our ideas of God changed, we ourselves changed for the better. Or, as we thought better of ourselves we thought better of God ❧ It will be character that locates our place in another world, if there is one, just as it is our character that fixes our place here. We are weaving character every day, and the way to weave the best character is to be kind and to be useful. Think right, act right; it is what we think and do that makes us what we are.

❧ ❧

To know the great men dead is compensation for having to live with the mediocre.

❧ ❧

It is easy to get everything you want, provided you first learn to do without the things you can not get ❧ ❧

❧ ❧

Love goes to those who are deserving— not for those who set snares for it and who lie in wait. The life of strife and contest never wins.

❧ ❧

We are under bonds for the moderate use of every faculty, and he who misuses any of God's gifts may not hope to go unscathed.

A Prayer

POWERS that be, make me sufficient to my own occasions ❧ Teach me to know and observe the rules of the Game. Give me to mind my own business at all times, and to lose no good opportunity of holding my tongue. Let me never lack proper pride or due sense of humor. Preserve, Oh, preserve me from growing stogy and unimaginative.

❧ Help me not to cry for the moon or over spilled milk; to manage my physical constitution and my practical affairs discreetly, never to dramatize my spiritual discomfort. Grant me neither to proffer nor to welcome cheap praise; to distinguish sharply between sentiment and sentimentality, cleaving to the one and despising the other.

❧ Deliver me from emotional excess. Deliver me from atrophy of

COURTESY in every line of life is now the growing rule. ❡ No strong man lowers himself by giving somebody a lift, no matter who that " somebody " is. It may be an ignorant foreigner, unversed in our ways and language, but there is a right way and a wrong way, even in pantomime. And to the clerk who would succeed, I say, cultivate charm of manner. Courteous manners in little things are an asset worth acquiring ✍ When a customer approaches, rise and offer a chair. Step aside and let the store's guest pass first into the elevator ✍ These are little things, but they make you and your work finer ✍ To gibe visitors, or to give fresh and flippant answers, even to stupid or impudent people, is a great mistake. Meet rudeness with unfailing politeness and see how much better you feel. Your promise to a customer is your employer's promise always hurts; and it shows weakness in the character of a business organization, just as unreliability does in an individual. ❡ If your business is to wait on customers, be careful of your dress and appearance. Do your manicuring before you reach the store. A toothbrush is a good investment. A salesman with a bad breath is dear at any price. Let your dress be quiet, neat and not too fashionable. To have a prosperous appearance helps you inwardly and helps the business. ❡ Give each customer your whole attention, and give just as considerate attention to a little buyer as to a big one. ❡ If asked for information, be sure you have it before you give it. Do not assume that the location or fact is so now because you once thought it so. Don't misdirect. Make your directions so clear that they will be a real help. ❡ And the more people you direct, and the higher the intelligence you can rightly lend, the more valuable is your life. The most precious possession in life is good health ✍ Eat moderately, breathe deeply, exercise outdoors and get eight hours' sleep ✍ And cultivate courtesy as a business asset.

✍ ✍

the emotions. When it is appointed me to suffer, let me, so far as humanly be possible, take example from the well-bred beasts, and go away quietly to bear my sufferings by myself.

Let me not dwell in the outer whirlwind of things and events; guide me rather to central calm and grant that I may abide therein. Give me nevertheless to be always a good comrade, and to view the passing show with an eye constantly growing keener, charity broadening and deepening day by day.

Help me to win, if win I may— and this, O Powers, especially— if I may not win always, make me at least a good loser. Vouchsafe me not to estrange the other me at my elbow; suffer not my primal light to wane; and grant that I may carry my cup, brimming, yet unspilled to the last. Amen.

A broken promise

IT requires two to make a home ✍ The first home was made when a woman, cradling in her loving arms a baby, crooned a lullaby. All the tender sentimentality we throw around a place is the result of the sacred thought that we live there with some one else. It is our home. The home is a tryst—the place where we retire and shut the world out ✍ Lovers make a home, just as birds make a nest, and unless a man knows the spell of the divine passion I can hardly see how he can have a home at all; for of all blessings no gift equals the gentle, trusting, loving companionship of a good woman ✍ ✍

✍ ✍

We help ourselves only as we help others.

ROM being regarded as The Book, the Bible is now looked upon as one of many books, and is only worthy of respect as it instructs and inspires. We read it with the same reverence that we read Emerson and Whitman.

The preacher was once a commanding figure in every community. Now he is regarded as a sort of poor relation. The term "spiritual adviser" is only a pleasantry. We go to the businessman for advice, not the priest. If a book is listed on the *Index,* all good Catholics read it in order to know how bad it is.

¶ Those who institute heresy trials have no power to punish—they only advertise ❧ ❧

Christianity was evolved, as all religions have been—it was not inspired. It grew in a natural way and it declined by the same token ❧ ❧

Whether it has benefited the race is a question which we need not discuss now. That it ministered to poverty and disease is true, and that it often created the ills which it professed to cure is equally a fact.

Poverty, ignorance, repression, superstition, coercion, disease, with nights of horror and days of fear, are slinking away into the past; and they have slunk further and further away the more Christianity's clutch upon the throat of the race has been loosened.

The night is past—the day is at hand! The East is all aglow! Health, happiness, freedom and joy are all calling to us to arise and sing our matin to labor. Our prayer is, "Give us this day our daily work, and we will earn our daily bread."

¶ Our religion is one of humanity. Our desire is to serve. We know that we can help ourselves only as we help others, and that the love we give away is the only love we keep.

We have no fears of the future, for we have no reason to believe that the Power which cares for us in this life will ever desert us in another.

❧ ❧

THAT is good which serves—man is the important item, this earth is the place, and the time is now. So all good men and women and all churches are endeavoring to make earth, heaven, and all agree that to live now and here the best one can, is the finest preparation for a life to come.

We no longer accept the doctrine that our natures are rooted in infamy, and that the desires of the flesh are cunning traps set by Satan, with God's permission, to undo us. We believe that no one can harm us but ourselves, that sin is misdirected energy, and that there is no devil but fear, and that the universe is planned for good. On every side we find beauty and excellence held in the balance of things. We know that work is a blessing, that Winter is as necessary as Summer, that night is as useful as day, that death is a manifestation of life, and just as good. We believe in the Now and Here. We believe in You, and we believe in a Power that is in Ourselves that makes for Righteousness.

These things have not been taught us by the rich—a Superior Class who governed us and to whom we paid taxes and tithes—we have simply thought things out for ourselves, and in spite of them. We have listened to Coleridge, Emerson, Brisbane, Charles Ferguson and others, who said: "You should use your reason and separate the good from the bad, the false from the true, the useless from the useful. Be yourself and think for yourself; and while your conclusions may not be infallible they will be nearer right than the conclusions forced upon you by those who have a personal interest in keeping you in ignorance. You grow through exercise of your faculties, and if you do not reason now you will never advance. We are all sons of God, and it doth not yet appear what we shall be. Claim your heritage."

❧ ❧

Mankind is moving toward the light, and such is our faith now in the Divine Intelligence, that we do not believe that in our hearts were planted aspirations and desires that are to work our undoing.

❧ ❧

The heroic man does not pose; he leaves that for the man who wishes to be thought heroic.

ORK to please yourself and you develop and strengthen the artistic conscience. Cling to that and it shall be your mentor in times of doubt; you need no other. There are writers who would scorn to write a muddy line, and would hate themselves for a year and a day should they dilute their thought with the platitudes of the fear-ridden people ♨ Be yourself and speak your mind today, though it contradict all you have said before ♨ And above all, in art work to please yourself—that other self which stands over and behind you, looking over your shoulder, watching your every act, word and deed—knowing your every thought ♨ ♨ Michelangelo would not paint a picture to order ♨ "I have a critic who is more exacting than you," said Meissonier, "it is my other self." ♨ Rosa Bonheur painted pictures just to please her other self, and never gave a thought to any one else; and having painted to please herself, she made her appeal to the great common heart of humanity—the tender, the noble, the receptive, the earnest, the sympathetic, the lovable. That is why Rosa Bonheur stands first among the women artists of all time; she worked to please her other self. That is the reason Rembrandt, who lived at the time Shakespeare lived, is today without a rival in portraiture. He had the courage to make an enemy. When at work he never thought of any one but his other self, and so he infused soul into every canvas. The limpid eyes look down into yours from the walls and tell of love, pity, earnestness and deep sincerity. Man, like Deity, creates in his own image, and when he portrays some one else, he pictures himself, too —this provided his work is art.

If it is but an imitation of something seen somewhere, or done by some one else, or done to please a patron with money, no breath of life has been breathed into its nostrils, and it is nothing, save possibly dead perfection—no more. It is easy to please your other self? Try it for a day. Begin tomorrow morning and say: "This day I will live as becomes a man. I will be filled with good-cheer and courage ♨ I will do what is right; I will work for the highest; I will put soul into every hand-grasp, every smile, every expression — into all my work. I will live to satisfy my other self." You think it is easy? Try it for a day.

♨ ♨

HE Busy Man's Creed: I believe in the stuff I am handing out, in the firm I am working for, and in my ability to get results. I believe that honest stuff can be passed out to honest men by honest methods ♨ I believe in working, not weeping; in boosting, not knocking; and in the pleasure of my job. I believe that a man gets what he goes after, that one deed done today is worth two deeds tomorrow, and that no man is down and out until he has lost faith in himself. I believe in today and the work I am doing; in tomorrow and the work I hope to do, and in the sure reward which the future holds. ❧ I believe in courtesy, in kindness, in generosity, in good-cheer, in friendship and in honest competition. I believe there is something doing, somewhere for every man ready to do it. I believe I'm ready—RIGHT NOW!

Man's business is to work—to surmount difficulties, to endure hardship, to solve problems, to overcome the inertia of his own nature: to turn chaos into cosmos by the aid of system—this is to live!

♨ ♨

There is no such thing as success in a bad business ♨

OT long ago, in a Western town, I was invited by a district judge to sit on the bench with him and listen to the evidence in a certain case that he was sure would interest me.

¶ It was a divorce suit, and everything had been conceded except the question of alimony. In determining this, the value of certain property held by the parties jointly was under consideration.

¶ The Northampton Tables of Mortality had been cited as authority. To back up these tables an insurance actuary had been called in. Sure enough, the evidence of this actuary struck a cosmic chord in my consciousness.

In the preliminary examination, to show his fitness as an expert witness, the actuary was asked this question:

" Can you make a close estimate on the average length of human life? "

And the answer was, " Yes, if numbers are taken into consideration."

" Can you tell the probable length of the life of an individual? "

And the answer was, " No."

When asked why, the witness said, "The element of chance enters into single lives, and where large numbers are considered chance is eliminated, so we get the law of average."

The next question was, " But suppose we bar the element of accident, can you then tell how long an individual will live? "

And the answer was, " No."

Being pressed for a reason, the actuary expressed himself in a little speech that impressed every one in the courtroom. I can not recall the exact words, but the gist of it was as follows:

There is an element in longevity that can not be ascertained or passed upon by any one except the man himself.

My opinion is that every man should be his own physician, and he should be wise enough and sane enough to make a diagnosis of his own case—spiritually, mentally, physically—much closer than any one else ever possibly could.

The one thing in human life that no one but the man himself knows, is, how long does he expect to live.

It is a pretty good general rule that, barring accident, the man will live as long as he expects to, or, if you please, as long as he wants to, or hopes to.

Many people are obsessed with the fallacy that the age of man is fixed at the limit of threescore and ten; and so, with a vast number of people, when they are around sixty-five they begin to prepare to shuffle off. They quit business, retire from active work, close up their affairs, and when they do these things, death and dissolution are at the door. There are other men who work on until they are eighty, and then they do exactly what the other man did at seventy, with a like result.

Great numbers of very strong, active, earnest men, reach the age of eighty, and die at eighty-two, eighty-three, eighty-four. And the reason for this passing is not so much a physical one as it is a mental. These men have fixed this age limit in their minds, and their entire life and death conform to the idea.

¶ As a general proposition I would say the way to live to be one hundred is, not to consider the question of time, but simply to continue an active, earnest interest in human affairs, and not overeat ·

The individual who looks for ease and rest, and bodily gratification, be he young or old, is in a dangerous position. To eliminate the toxins which accrue in the human body, activity is positively necessary. The activity of the mind reacts on the organs of the body. So thought is a physical process, and to gain this elimination which insures health, no man should ever think of retiring from business and quitting the game ·

If you retire from one thing you must take up something else that is more difficult ·

Change of occupation is a great factor in human health; but the one thing that makes a man live long is an earnest vow early in life, well kept, to "never say die! " ·

Only such a one can make a century run, and the death of the centenarian is almost without exception a painless process. ❨ And no physical examination can probe these inner facts and attitude of the man's mind.

The individual himself knows and can determine how long he will live, better than any one else possibly can; and I believe he can himself, if he is honest with himself, size up his case, and, barring accidents, figure the day of his death, as Moses did on Mount Horeb.

❧ ❧

CHRISTIANITY supplies a Hell for the people who disagree with you and a Heaven for your friends.

The distinguishing feature of Christianity is the hypothesis that man is born in sin and conceived in iniquity: that through Adam's fall we sinned all, and to save us from eternal death or eternal damnation, the Son of God died on the cross, and this Son was God, Himself. These things are still in its creeds and confessions of faith. Has the Roman Catholic Church or any of the orthodox Protestant churches officially repudiated its creed, and made a new one founded on industry, reciprocity, sweetness and light? ❧ ❧

Christianity is not a unique religion. It has traits in common with many other religions ❧ It is a conglomeration of Judaism and Egyptian mythology, with the protests of Jesus and the ideas of Paul fused in the pomps and pride of Rome. It is a combination of morality and superstition, and they never form a chemical mixture. Man is the only creature in the animal kingdom that sits in judgment on the work of the Creator and finds it bad—including himself and Nature. God, personally, we are told, looked upon His work and called it good. There is where the clergy of Christendom take issue with Him.

No greater insult was ever offered to God than the claim that His chief product, man, is base at heart and merits damnation.

❧ ❧

MAKING men live in three worlds at once—past, present and future has been the chief harm organized religion has done. To drag your past behind you, and look forward to sweet rest in Heaven, is to spread the present very thin ❧ ❧

The man who lives in the present, forgetful of the past and indifferent to the future, is the man of wisdom.

The best preparation for tomorrow's work is to do your work as well as you can today ❧ ❧

The best preparation for a life to come is to live now and here.

Live right up to your highest and best! If you have made mistakes in the past, reparation lies not in regrets, but in thankfulness that you now know better. ❨ It is true that we are punished by our sins and not for them; it is true also that we are blessed and benefited by our sins. Having tasted the bitterness of error, we can avoid it. If we have withheld the kind word and the look of sympathy in the past, we can today give doubly, and thus, in degree, redeem the past. And we best redeem the past by forgetting it and losing ourselves in useful work.

It is a great privilege to live. Thank God! there is one indisputable fact: We are here!

❧ ❧

No man should dogmatize except on the subject of theology. Here he can take his stand, and by throwing the burden of proof on the opposition, he is invincible. We have to die to find out whether he is right.

❧ ❧

Mental dissolution: that condition where you are perfectly satisfied with your religion, education and government.

❧ ❧

To know but one religion is not to know that one ❧ ❧

❧ ❧

What a superb thing it would be if we were all big enough in mind to see no slights, accept no insults, cherish no jealousies, and admit into our heart no hatred!

❧ ❧

To remain on earth you must be useful, otherwise Nature regards you as old metal, and is only watching for a chance to melt you over.

N courts of law, the phrase "I believe" has no standing. Never a witness gives testimony but that he is cautioned thus, "Tell us what you know, not what you believe." ❡ In theology, belief has always been regarded as more important than that which your senses say is so. Almost without exception, "belief" is a legacy, an importation—something borrowed, an echo and often an echo of an echo.

The Creed of the Future will begin, "I know," not "I believe." And this creed will not be forced upon the people.
It will carry with it no coercion, no blackmail, no promise of an eternal life of idleness and ease if you accept it, and no threat of hell if you don't.

It will have no paid, professional priesthood, claiming honors, rebates and exemptions, nor will it hold estates free from taxation. It will not organize itself into a system, marry itself to the State, and call on the police for support.
It will be so reasonable, so in the line of self-preservation, that no sane man or woman will reject it, and when we really begin to live it we will cease to talk about it.
As a suggestion and first rough draft, we submit this.

I KNOW:

HAT I am here. ❡ In a world where nothing is permanent but change, And that in degree I, myself, can change the form of things,
And influence a few people;

And that I am influenced by these and other people;
That I am influenced by the example and by the work of men who are no longer alive,
And that the work I now do will in degree influence people who may live after my life has changed into other forms;

That a certain attitude of mind and habit of action on my part will add to the peace, happiness and well-being of other people, And that a different thought and action on my part will bring pain and discord to others;

That if I would secure a reasonable happiness for myself, I must give out good-will to others;
That to better my own condition I must practise mutuality;
That bodily health is necessary to continued and effective work;

THAT I am ruled largely by habit; That habit is a form of exercise;
That up to a certain point, exercise means increased strength or ease in effort;
That all life is the expression of spirit;
That my spirit influences my body,
And my body influences my spirit;

That the universe to me is very beautiful, and everything and everybody in it good and beautiful when my body and my spirit are in harmonious mood;
That my thoughts are hopeful and helpful unless I am filled with fear,

And that to eliminate fear my life must be dedicated to useful work—work in which I forget myself;
That fresh air in abundance, and moderate, systematic exercise in the open air are the part of wisdom;
That I can not afford, for my own sake, to be resentful nor quick to take offense;

That happiness is a great power for good,
And that happiness is not possible without moderation and equanimity;
And that the reward which life holds out for work is not idleness nor rest, nor immunity from work, but increased capacity,

GREATER DIFFICULTIES, MORE WORK.

BELIEVE in the Motherhood of God. I believe in the blessed Trinity of Father, Mother and Child ❧ ❧

I believe that God is here, and that we are as near Him now as ever we shall be. I do not believe He started this world a-going and went away and left it to run itself.

I believe in the sacredness of the human body, this transient dwelling-place of a living soul, and so I deem it the duty of every man and every woman to keep his or her body beautiful through right thinking and right living ❧ ❧

I believe that the love of man for woman, and the love of woman for man, is holy; and that this love in all its promptings is as much an emanation of the Divine Spirit as man's love for God, or the most daring hazards of the human mind ❧ ❧

I believe in salvation through economic, social and spiritual freedom.

I believe John Ruskin, William Morris, Henry Thoreau, Walt Whitman and Leo Tolstoy to be Prophets of God, who should rank in mental reach and spiritual insight with Elijah, Hosea, Ezekiel and Isaiah ❧ ❧

I believe that men are inspired today as much as ever men were.

I believe we are now living in Eternity as much as ever we shall.

I believe that the best way to prepare for a Future Life is to be kind, live one day at a time, and do the work you can do the best, doing it as well as you can ❧ ❧

I believe we should remember the week-day to keep it holy.

I believe there is no devil but fear.

I believe that no one can harm you but yourself. ❡ I believe in my own divinity—and yours ❧ ❧

I believe that we are all sons of God, and it doth not yet appear what we shall be ❧ ❧

I believe the only way we can reach the Kingdom of Heaven is to have the Kingdom of Heaven in our hearts.

I believe in every man minding his own business.

I believe in freedom—social, economic, domestic, political, mental, spiritual ❧ ❧

I believe in sunshine, fresh air, friendship, calm sleep, beautiful thoughts ❧ ❧

I believe in the paradox of success through failure ❧

I believe in the purifying process of sorrow, and I believe that death is a manifestation of life. ❡ I believe the Universe is planned for good.

I believe it is possible that I shall make other creeds, and change this one, or add to it, from time to time as new light may come to me.

❧ ❧

The pathway to success is in serving humanity. By no other means is it possible, and this truth is so plain and patent that even very simple folk recognize it.

❧ ❧

We need an education which fits a boy to get a living, creates a desire for more education, implants ideals of service, and lastly, teaches him how to spend leisure in a rational manner. Then we can get along with less government.

❧ ❧

If college education were made compulsory by the State, and one-half of the curriculum consisted of actual, useful, manual labor, most of our social ills would be solved and we would be well on the highway toward the Ideal City.

ALITTLE more patience, a little more charity for all, a little more devotion, a little more love; with less bowing down to the past, and a silent ignoring of pretended authority; brave looking forward to the future with more faith in our fellows, and the race will be ripe for a great burst of light and life ❧ ❧

BUSINESSMAN once bought a farm for a diversion, to help balance the day of work ❧ ❧

It was a great joy to him to jump on his saddle-mare and ride through the farm in order to think out a problem that might be puzzling him.

❡ It was a small tract of land and the investment was not great, so how the farm was carried on gave him no serious thought ❧ ❧

However, one day the man who owned the farm adjoining offered the businessman his farm at a price that was reasonable. The farm was worth the money. It was bought.

The land began to be of interest to its owner. Besides there was quite an investment and it must bring some returns. It must be supervised.

Riding across the farm at an unexpected hour one morning, the businessman found several men sitting down by the roadside eating their lunch. He took out his watch. It was eleven o'clock. One of the men sprang to his feet when he saw the " Boss " arriving. The owner thought he would be filled with consternation. But no, the hired man, Bennie, made a gesture which meant, Stop ❧ Then, in a piping voice, he said, " I want to be farm-boss! "

" What 's that you say? " shouted the proprietor ❧ ❧

" I want to be farm-boss," repeated Bennie, all undaunted.

" Who 's hindering you? "

Bennie did not understand.

" Why don't you be farm-boss? Nobody has hindered you. You have every opportunity."

" You just tell the men, now," persisted Bennie, " that I am the farm-boss, won't you? " ❧ ❧

It was foolish to try to explain to this clown the fact that farm-bosses, and any other kind of bosses, evolve.

Shakespeare said, " Some men are born great, some achieve greatness, and some have greatness thrust upon them."

He was wrong. There is only one kind of great men: it is the kind that achieve.

❡ The farm-boss evolves. So does the superintendent. So does the manager. So does the man who is responsible for the business. Bennie's ignorance seems ridiculous, but in every factory, shop and place of industry where many people are employed, the majority of the workers are named Bennie.

Bennie thinks that if the owner would only announce to these " underlings " that he is Boss, all he would have to do would be to sit in the Boss's chair, with his feet on the table, smoking infinite cigarettes; that heaven would be his, and he would be really Boss: that the " underlings " would file past him, doing him honor and glory daily; that all matters of great importance would be brought by some trembling vassal for his sublime judgment, and that he would decide. Then no man, woman or child in the vicinity would do anything but just what the Boss wanted to have them do, and that infinite ease, joy and gladness would be his.

Bennie thinks that a rich man has nothing to do but ride around with a multitude of servants to come and go at his call; that the rich man has a great big cave full of money, some King Midas keeping it perpetually full.

❡ Bennie thinks that all there is to being Boss is to have somebody say he is; if he can only get into the " Front Office " and sit in the manager's chair that he is " It."

You can not explain to Bennie that, " Where MacGregor sits is the head of the table." ❧ ❧

You can never explain to Bennie, had you all the gifts of the gods, that the Boss is he who does the most work, who carries a burden that would crush any man but him. Bennie will never know that with every command that the Boss gives, there goes responsibility that he may be wrong, and that the Boss must have the power within himself of making good every one of his own mistakes and the mistakes of all who work for him. The Boss never resigns, and in the darkest hour that can come has only one thought, and that is to stay with the ship.

The Boss is he who can carry off the

Gates of Gaza. The Boss is he who is big enough to say, " The mistake is mine; I am wrong—I will make this right," and does.

The Boss is he who is big enough to take any criticism, and takes the criticism that he does not deserve with as good grace as he does the criticism which is deserved.

The Boss is he who is willing to start things, stand by them through their entire making, finish and complete them.

❡ The Boss is he who is capable of saying, as did Napoleon, " The finances, I will arrange them."

The Boss is he who is willing to pay the price of success, no matter what it is ๛ ๛

The Boss is he who finds his completest joy in playing the game, seeing the finish, and being ready for a new job.

❡ The Boss is he who demands of himself more than he demands of all the rest of his people.

The Boss is the one who makes good.

๛ ๛

IT is not the attainment of knowledge which marks the superior person—the Master Man—it is the possession of certain qualities.

There are three traits of character, or habits, or personal qualities, which once attained, mean money in the bank, friends at court, honor and peace at home—power, purpose, poise.

These qualities are Industry, Concentration and Self-reliance.

The man who has these three qualities is in possession of the key that unlocks the coffers of the world and the libraries of Christendom. All doors fly open at his touch. " Oh, he's a lucky dog," they say—and he is.

And the strange part of it is, there is no mystery about the acquirement of these three things; no legerdemain; no rites nor ritual; you do not have to memorize this or that, nor ride a goat; the secret of these qualities is not locked up in dead languages; no college can impart them, and the university men who fail, fail for lack of them.

On the other hand, no man succeeded

beyond the average who did not possess them. And it is an indictment of our colleges and universities when we consider the fact that the men who have these qualities plus, usually acquired them at " The University of Hard Knocks "—and in spite of parents, guardians, teachers and next of friends.

❡ Let us take three great Americans and see what made them supremely great: Washington, Jefferson, Franklin.

❡ Let a certain quality stand for each man: Washington (Self-reliance); Jefferson (Concentration); Franklin (Industry) ๛ ๛

But each of these men had all three of these qualities, and without these qualities the world would never have heard of them, and without these three men, America today would not be known as a Nation.

It was only the Self-reliance of Washington at Valley Forge which saved independence from being " a lost hope." Washington was hooted and denounced for preferring starvation to defeat, but the persistence of the man never faltered. It was a losing fight for most of those long, dragging, dread, nine years—a fight against great odds—poverty against wealth, farmers against trained troops, barracks against the wind-swept open. But Washington believed in his cause and best of all he believed in himself.

" It is only a question of which side gets discouraged first. I know we will outlast them. Give in? Never! This fight is mine." ๛ ๛

You can't whip a man who talks like that ๛ ๛

And as time went by, George the Third had brains enough to sense it, Cornwallis felt it, all England began to acknowledge it, and best of all America knew it.

It wasn't fighting that won the independence of the Colonies: it was the generalship and Self-reliance of George Washington ๛ And this Self-reliance shaped his actions, and finally spread over the land. Our political blessings, as a people, come to us through the unrelenting, unrelaxing Self-reliance of Washington ๛ ๛

HE education that aims at mere scholarly acquirement, rather than useful intelligence, will have to step down and out. The world needs competent men; then, if their hearts are right, culture will come as a matter of course. To go in search of culture is to accumulate that which is rotten at the core ✵ ✵

We grow through expression—if you know things there is a strong desire to express them ✵ It is Nature's way of deepening our impressions—this thing of recounting them. And happy, indeed, if you know a soul with whom you can converse at your best.

✵ ✵

IF you have health, you probably will be happy; and if you have health and happiness, you will have all the wealth you need, even if not all you want. ❡ Health is the most natural thing in the world. It is natural to be healthy, because we are a part of Nature—we are Nature. Nature is trying hard to keep us well, because she needs us in her business. Nature needs man so he will be useful to other men. The rewards of life are for service.

And the penalties of life are for selfishness ✵ ✵

Human service is the highest form of self-interest for the person who serves. ❡ We preserve our sanity, only as we forget self in service.

To center on one's self, and forget one's relationship to society, is to summon

misery, and misery means disease. ✵ ✵ Unhappiness is an irritant. It affects the heart-beats of circulation first; then the digestion; and the person is ripe for two hundred nineteen diseases, and six hundred forty-two complications. ❡ The recipe for good health is this: Forget it. ❡ What we call diseases are merely symptoms of mental conditions. Our bodies are automatic, and thinking about our digestion does not aid us. Rather it hinders, since the process of thinking, especially anxious thinking, robs the stomach of its blood and transfers it to the head. ❡ If we are worried enough, digestion will stop absolutely ✵ ✵ The moral is obvious: Don't Worry.

✵ ✵

THERE are persons who are always talking about preparing for life. The best way to prepare for life is to begin to live ✵ ✵ A school should not be a preparation; a school should be life. ❡ Isolation from the world in order to prepare for the world's work is folly. You might as well take a boy out of the blacksmith-shop in order to teach him blacksmithing ✵ ✵ College is a make-believe, and every college student knows it. From the age of fourteen and upward the pupil should feel that he is doing something useful, not merely killing time; and so his work and his instruction should go right along hand in hand.

The truly educated man is the useful man ✵ ✵

WE can gain the Kingdom of Heaven by having the Kingdom of Heaven in our hearts.

It means universality.

We reach God through the love of one.

Love for love's sake — there is nothing better.

It sweetens every act of life.

Love grows by giving.

The love we give away is the only love we keep.

Insight, sympathy, faith, knowledge and love are the results of love—they are the children of parents mentally mated. ❡ Love for love's sake.

N history there are three men who conquered the world ﹏ These men are Alexander, Cæsar, and Napoleon. Their method of conquering was through violence. These men had no desire to give themselves to the world; to make the world a better place because they were here; to merge themselves into the world and be lost in the mass. They were intent on honors, ease, luxury and lust for power.

Alexander began the task when he was twenty years of age and he completed it when he was thirty. He died sighing for more worlds to conquer.

His teacher, Aristotle, twenty years his senior, foretold for him the end. To complete one task and not have another in sight was to die. Aristotle outlived Alexander and saw his prophecy come true. Aristotle refused to have anything to do with the business of destruction, but he told Alexander that when his soldiers died, let them die at the point of the spear. What he meant was this: Let them die fighting, not in the hospital. ❡ Alexander lost more men in battle than he lost by disease, so he surely had a pretty good hold on sanitary science; but his specialty was destruction and dissipation. From one standpoint it was a great feat he performed. With an army of thirty-five thousand men he flung himself against a Persian horde of over a million. He scattered them and destroyed them piecemeal.

﹏ ﹏

ALEXANDER marched Eastward through Persia, through Asia Minor, the Northern part of Africa and a small part of India. This was his world.

We have mapped and plotted the world within our own time. Today we know the geographical world. Yet we will never die from Alexander's disability ﹏ We see a milky way of worlds to conquer. ❡ The worlds for us to conquer are economic, political, pedagogic, philosophic, artistic and scientific. Aristotle told Alexander that the dangers that confronted an army were not in the ranks of the enemy, but were in their own camp—which means all that you can

read into it. ❡ In order that no one may feel there is danger of getting out of a job, I am going to give here a ilst of worlds that we have yet to conquer. We have sighted these worlds, we know their orbit, and there is no excuse now to let them go unconquered.

The University Militant is now engaged in fighting:

1. For the rights of women.
2. For the rights of children.
3. For the rights of criminals.
4. For the rights of dumb animals.
5. To make all work and business beautiful ﹏ ﹏
6. For the elimination of theological fetish—a thing that has caused more misery and bloodshed than all other causes combined ﹏ ﹏
7. For the elimination of medical superstition, to the end that mankind shall be freed from racial fear, one of the most prolific causes of insanity and disease ﹏
8. For the eradication of parasitism, through the reformation of our social ideals and our systems of education, so that every man and woman shall know the joys of earning an honest living —this for the good of the individual and the preservation of the race.
9. Against the tyranny of fashion as applied to clothes, housekeeping and social customs ﹏ ﹏
10. For the disarmament of the nations, and international arbitration, in order that this world shall cease to be a place of the skull ﹏ ﹏

﹏ ﹏

ALEXANDER, Cæsar and Napoleon each lived in a very limited world. They conquered all the world they could reach, and then they erected a shrine to the god Terminus.

Every individual lives in a limited world. And all the world we should attempt to conquer is our own world. Also, it is well to realize the dictum of Aristotle, that the foes of an army are those within its own camp ﹏ That is to say, our enemies are those which lurk in our own hearts—hate, fear, jeslousy, sloth, greed, inertia, appetite. To conquer the foes within is a task indeed. But the recipe for peace at home is a foreign war, and so the person who would be strong and efficient should enlist in the University Militant and help conquer the foreign foe, this as a part of the plan for conquering himself.

Choose your division and enlist in the army that is fighting for Human Rights. Don't be a neutral or a camp-follower.

Get in the fight and stand back to the wall ✒ Be one of a glorious minority. Be a Greek, and never let yourself be swallowed up by a Persian mob. Dare to stand alone, to fight alone, to live alone, to die alone! Otherwise, you will not live at all—you will only exist.

✒ ✒

N educated man is one with a universal sympathy for everything and a certain amount of Knowledge about everything that is known, and who still is on the line of evolution and is learning to the end ✒ ✒

THE very first item in the creed of commonsense is obedience.

Perform your work with a whole heart.

❡ Revolt may be sometimes necessary, but the man who tries to mix revolt and obedience is doomed to disappoint himself and everybody with whom he has dealings.

To flavor work with protest is to fail in the protest and fail in the work.

When you revolt, why, revolt—climb, hike, get out, defy—tell everybody and everything to go to hades! That disposes of the case. You thus separate yourself entirely from those you have served—no one misunderstands you— you have declared yourself. The man who quits in disgust when ordered to perform a task which he considers menial or unjust may be a pretty good fellow; but the malcontent who takes your order with a smile and then secretly disobeys is a dangerous proposition.

To pretend to obey and yet carry in your heart the spirit of revolt is to do half-hearted, slipshod work.

If revolt and obedience are equal in power, your engine will then stop on the center, and you benefit no one, not even yourself ✒ ✒

EVERY day in the year in come pilgrims to Mount Vernon—dozens, hundreds, thousands—and the interest in the place and its memories never fades ✒ ✒

At Monticello we tread softly over the green turf once pressed by the feet of Thomas Jefferson, who said, "That country is governed best that is governed least." ✒

In a quaint little old church at Richmond we are shown the pew where Patrick Henry stood when he exclaimed, " Give me liberty or give me death."

❡ We make quest to Independence Hall, Philadelphia; and at Arch and Third Streets we look through the iron pickets on the grave of Benjamin Franklin.

On Boylston Street in Boston we read the name on a simple slab, " Sam Adams," and our hearts go out in admiration for the pamphleteer.

On Rector Street, in New York, just off busy Broadway, is a marble marked, "Alexander Hamilton," and every day hundreds uncover as they pass.

Then we go to Concord to visit Sleepy Hollow, where rests the dust of Ralph Waldo Emerson. Not long ago I was in Spencer County, Indiana, down near the Ohio River, and visited a little village barely more than a railroad-station, and walked a half-mile up a hillside to a grave at the top of this hill, for here sleeps Nancy Hanks, mother of Abraham Lincoln ✒ ✒

Then we go to Springfield, Illinois, and pay silent tribute to Abraham Lincoln, Liberator of Men.

And then we realize that the name and fame of Lincoln grow brighter as the years go by ✒ ✒

Sometimes the place of pilgrimage is a battleground, at other times a church, or a house, more often a grave.

And the only places that are sacred shrines are where certain men have lived, worked, spoken and died ☙ And the theme of these men has always been one and the same, and that theme is Liberty ☙ ☙

No name lives enshrined in the hearts of humanity save the names of those who have fought Freedom's fight.

On the tombs of a few of these we carve simply the one word—the word *Savior*.

℘ These are the men who died that we might live.

They flung away their lives for a noble cause, and that the only cause worth living for, fighting for, striving for, dying for—the cause of *Freedom*.

And we say with the orator: " I know not what discoveries, what inventions, what thoughts may leap from the brain of the world. I know not what garments of glory may be woven for the years to come. I can not dream of the victories to be won on the fields of thought; but I do know that coming from out the infinite sea of the future there will never touch this bank and shoal of time a richer gift, a rarer blessing, than liberty for man, woman and child."

☙ ☙

A HEART-ACHE is only a huge joke, when it is mine. Yours makes me cry, but mine—goodness! I glory in pain, for all I have endured I now know has been for my lasting benefit ☙ ☙

Yesterday in Buffalo I saw a woman on a street car whose heart was nigh bursting with grief. She was dazed, stunned, bereft. I never saw the woman before, and I am sure she did not know me. Her look of anguish wrung my heart and when at last our eyes met, she gave me such an involuntary look of dumb entreaty that I lifted my hat and tried to smile, as if we were old acquaintances.

℘ She tried to smile back and the lines tightened around her lips, and as she still looked at me, great tears welled to her eyes. Then she turned away and I saw she was shutting her teeth hard so as to master the grief that was gnawing at her heart.

Some much prized thing had gone out of this woman's life—something great and good—some one had ceased to love her, and this woman had such a hunger for love—such capacity for affection!

℘ The car was full of people, but I longed to go right over and hold her hands and whisper to her that I, at least, loved her, that all my being responded to that inward longing her face could not conceal. I wanted to tell her that there is no tragedy except for those who believe in it. What though some loved form was lying cold and rigid in death—will not we, too, some day fold our hands, just so, across our tired breasts and sleep! Or if love had gone to another, why should we desire to compel it, would we not make those free we love? I wanted to say to her, " I know, I know—fate has hammered me, too, hammered my soul into better shape than it was once. Relax, cease the struggle, and you have nothing with which to fight."

The car stopped and the woman got off, turning her face from me as she passed. She turned from me, I knew, because she felt that I was her friend, and she did not wish to burden me with her weight of woe. God fill her with His Love and lend her Peace!

☙ ☙

At last we must admit that the man who towers above his fellows is the one who has the power to make others work for him; a great success is not possible any other way ☙ ☙

☙ ☙

Abnegation: A plan for securing the thing in the easiest and surest way.

☙ ☙

Individuality is a departure from a complete type, and so is never perfect ☙

☙ ☙

The quality of our race turns on the quality of the parents; and especially does the quality of the child turn on the peace, happiness and well-being of the mother. You can not make the mother a disgraced and taunted thing and expect the progeny to prosper.

HEN Grief is great enough it cuts down until it finds the very soul, and this is Agony. And he who has it does not seek to share it with another, for he knows that no other human being can comprehend it — it belongs to him alone, and he is dumb. There is a dignity and sanctity and grace about suffering; it holds a chastening and purifying quality that makes a king or queen of him who has it. Only the silence of night dare look upon it, and no sympathy save God's can mitigate it ✒ ✒

✒ ✒

IF you wish to lessen the worries of the world and scatter sunshine as you go, don't bother to go a-slumming, or lift the fallen, or trouble to reclaim the erring—simply pay your debts cheerfully and promptly. It lubricates the wheels of trade, breaks up party ice, gives tone to the social system and liberates good will.

In the future, the chief duties will consist in so forming one's life as to give the highest possible good, and do the least possible harm to others.

✒ ✒

PUBLIC Opinion is the great natural restraining force. We are ruled by Public Opinion, not by Statute-law. If Statute-law expresses the Zeitgeist it is well, but often law hampers and restrains Public Opinion.

✒ ✒

PEOPLE who belong to one so-called class today are in another tomorrow. Most of our so-called predatory rich wiggled up out of the mass—and they may be poor again.

Many of the poor will be rich. Watch the immigrants landing at Ellis Island. Can you prophesy to what " class "

these boys and girls—curious, quaint, half-frightened—will belong twenty years from now?

Many of them will be contractors, lawyers, bankers, scientists, doctors, teachers—it is all a matter of individual energy, intelligence and desire, modified by the antics of the gods of Chance.

There is no conspiracy in America to hold people down and under.

✒ ✒

LET us be a nation of builders, creators, distributors, not a petulant people whose joy lies in libel and scandal. ❡ As we distrust the person who comes to us with ill news of another, so let us hold aloof from these evil tidings concerning our men of business that Europe so likes to spread ✒ ✒

Shall we cut our *Mona Lisa* from the frame and pawn the smile with a junk dealer? ✒ ✒

Let us be proud of our country, and not bespatter her men of mind with mud ✒ ✒

It is time to build.

It is time to unite.

It is time for faith.

It is time for brotherhood.

Let us be glad we are Americans, and stand together for American institutions.

✒ ✒

LET it not be forgotten that all wages are based primarily on productive power. Anything else would be charity. We want what we earn and we do not want more than we earn, otherwise we are victims of paternalism. And paternalism breeds the beggar ✒

✒ ✒

THE big man at the last is the man who takes an idea and makes of it a genuine success—the man who brings the ship into port ✒

THE world will be redeemed; it is being redeemed ✒ It is being redeemed not by those who shake the red rag of wordy warfare, who threaten and demand, but by its enterprisers, workers, inventors, toilers—the men and women who do the duty that lies nearest them ✒ ✒

BELIEVE in the blessed trinity of Man, Woman and Child. These to me express Divinity. Left alone the woman would be the companion of the man, not his slave, pet, plaything, drudge and scullion ❧ ❧

Happiness lies in equality. The effort you put forth to win the woman, you should be compelled to exercise through life in order to hold her. And you will hold her by so long as Love kisses the lips of Death, and the dimpled hands of the babe encircle the neck of its father ❧ ❧

The house of the harlot exists because love is gyved, fettered, blindfolded and sold in the market places. There is nothing so pulls on the heartstrings of the normal, healthy man as the love for wife and child. Always and forever he wears them in his heart of hearts. To imagine that he would forsake them for the husks of license, unless looked after by Jaggers & Jaggers, is to doubt the Wisdom of the Creator ❧ ❧

In our hearts Divine Wisdom implanted the seeds of loyalty and right. These are a part of the great plan of self-preservation. We do not walk off the cliff, because we realize that to do so would mean death.

Make men and women free, and they will travel by the Eternal Guiding Stars.

❡ That which makes for self-respect in men and women, putting each on his good behavior, increasing the sum of good-will and lessening hate, will have a most potent influence on future generations ❧ ❧

I can not imagine a worse handicap than to be tumbled into life by incompatible parents and be brought up in an atmosphere of strife. "We have bred from the worst in the worst possible way, and the result is a race of scrubs," says Alfred Russel Wallace ❧ ❧

All that tends to tyranny in parents manifests itself in slavish traits in the children. Freedom is a condition of mind, and the best way to secure it is to breed it.

❧ ❧

WHY not be a top-notcher? A top-notcher is simply an individual who works for the institution of which he is a part, not against it.

He does not wear rubber boots and stand on glass when he gets orders from the boss ❧ He is a good conductor, and through him plays the policy of the house. The interests of the house are his — he is the business and he never separates himself from the concern, swabbing the greased shute, by knocking on the place or management ❧ ❧

A top-notcher never says inwardly, or outwardly, "I wasn't hired to do that," nor does he

WHEN an Anarchist gets a job, buys a lot and begins to build a home, the "Cause" has lost him, and can never get him back for a boutonniere, or just for a ribbon to stick on his coat. When a Socialist starts a restaurant and begins to prosper, his Socialistic zeal becomes lukewarm and his comrades go into mourning for him as for one who is dead ❧ ❧

The actual workers have abandoned Marxian Socialism because they know that if the " revolution " should come, the work of rebuilding would fall on them, and the " Yours for the Revolution " folks, who brought it about, would be as helpless as Steve Reynolds at the head of a construction-gang.

❧ ❧

Robbers always give much to charity, for thus do they absolve themselves.

DOCTORS, lawyers and preachers are men, caught in a certain environment, trying to win the world's plaudits and plunder in a certain way ❧ ❧ I may consider the way a mistaken one, but I surely do not hate the man.

¶ And the fact that I have hundreds of close friends among the professions proves that I am not entirely misunderstood in this matter ❧ Doctors are men ❧ ❧ Lawyers are men. Preachers are men. So, also, are judges. Marxian Socialists are men, and all these are very much like the people with whom they mix and associate ❧ ❧ ❧ Rogue clients evolve rogue lawyers to do their work; fool patients evolve fool doctors; and superstitious, silly people in the pew secrete a pretentious, punk party in the pulpit ❧ ¶ For the man, himself, I have only admiration, respect and love— and sometimes pity. ¶ I may despise his business and some of his acts, but how can I hate the man, when I realize that his life is a part of the Great One from which mine is derived?

This man may quit his business and take up something else. The criminal is not wholly a criminal—he is only a criminal at times. Some of his impulses are good, and most of them may be excellent; but one mistaken act will brand him forever as a criminal in the world's assize. Under the same conditions, if I were of the same quality and temper, I would have done the same. ¶ If I criticize lawyers, doctors and preachers, it is simply because there courses through my veins a quality and kind of corpuscle which fits me eminently for success either as a lawyer, doctor or preacher. " A hair, perhaps, divides the false and true," says old Omar ❧ ❧ Yes, and I missed becoming a practicing physician by a hair.

❧ ❧

IF all the world loves a lover, it is equally true that all the world hates a quitter ❧ Stand by the ship! If necessary, go down with it, and go down gloriously, as did Captain Smith on the *Titanic* ❧ ❧ Or, if you leave the ship, leave it as did those survivors on the *Jeannette* in the Arctic Sea ❧ When their gallant little craft was crushed by the overwhelming ice, they took the few effects they could carry out on the ice ❧ ❧ Then they went back and ran up the Stars and Stripes to the highest tip of the mainmast. And as the ship slowly settled in the sea, and the flag disappeared in the crevasse, they lifted three ringing cheers for the Red, White and Blue ❧ ❧ And they were alone on the ice, and unafraid, three thousand miles from civilization ❧ ❧

figure to work exactly eight hours, and wear the face off the clock.

He works until the work is done and does not leave his desk looking like a map of San Francisco after the shake-up. As a general proposition, I would say that a top-notcher prizes his health more than a good time, so he has a good time all the time. Soreheads and belliakers are usually suffering from overeating, lack of oxygen and loss of sleep.

If you want to be a top-notcher beware of the poker proclivity and the pool-room habit — otherwise destiny has you on his list ❧ ❧

What shall we say of the soldier who deserts on the eve of battle; of the sailor who abandons the ship at sea; of the cook who quits on the day of the banquet; of the waiters who walk out when the guests are coming; of the farm-hands who throw up their jobs at harvest-time; of the employee in business, who, having made a bad break and caused a loss to his firm of thousands, thinks to make all good by sitting down and calmly writing: "I hereby tender my resignation," etc., etc.!

When the captain of a ship has put out from Singapore bound for Boston, we have only one question to ask. And this question does not refer to typhoons, hurricanes, pirates, shoals, shallows or icebergs. The one question we ask is, "Did you bring the ship into port?"

If you make a mistake, acknowledge the fact, and show you can make good, even in spite of the blunders you have made

Don't run away from a difficulty. If you do, you'll find the difficulty, like a polar bear, will follow you. Besides, you can't run away from a fault, because you carry the cause of the fault with you.

There is a man who has a farm near mine, at the village of East Aurora

On this farm is a flock of South-Down sheep, quite the finest bunch you ever saw

One day the man and his foreman decided that the sheep should be "dipped."

The next day the foreman ordered one of his helpers to prepare the mixture

The sheep were dipped, twenty of them—and behold the effect! The wool came off in patches. The poor things were scalded, scorched and blistered

The helper had used carbolic acid diluted one-half, when it should have been used as one to one hundred.

Of course, the foreman was to blame—he should have prepared the "dip" himself. But after the damage was done, the average man would have sat down and written a letter to the owner saying "I hereby tender my resignation," etc., etc.

This man did n't He wrote his employer, stating the plain fact, and asked that his pay be cut one-half as punishment

The owner accepted the man's offer to work at the reduced wage and never once after referred to the mishap.

The foreman went to work nursing those injured sheep. He looked after them night and day, as a mother does her children

At the end of the year the owner sent the foreman's check for the difference in wages

The man had made good!

Both men were of the right quality

If faults were met in this straightforward way, instead of trying to run away from them, the mistake would prove a source of strength, rather than a disadvantage.

The employer has a duty to perform, too, when a helper errs.

EMPLOYERS used to "fire" men who had done the wrong thing. I find now that the tendency is to keep the man on and try him out elsewhere, in the hope that he will learn by his mistakes

Says John Ruskin: "It is nothing to give pension and cottage to the widow who has lost her son; it is nothing to give food and medicine to the workman who has broken his arm, or the decrepit woman wasting in sickness. But it is something to use your time and strength to war with the waywardness and thoughtlessness of mankind; to keep the erring workman in your service till you have made him an unerring one, and to direct your fellow-merchant to the opportunity which his judgment would have lost."

One thing sure, that young farm foreman who dipped sheep in a mixture, without knowing exactly what the mixture was, was a better man after that mistake than he ever had been before.

The fool is not the man who merely does foolish things. The fool is the man who does not know enough to cash in on his foolishness.

A person may be very secretive and yet have no secrets.

HIS secret, which I am about to impart, is the most valuable and far-reaching of any known to man.

It is the key to health, happiness, wealth, power, success. It is the open sesame to Paradise, here and now. ¶ A secret is something known only to a few. Often the best way to retain a secret is to let others help you to keep it. ¶ The only way to retain love is to give it away—art and religion the same. ¶ This secret, which I am about to impart, will cause no thrill, save in the hearts of those who already know it ↪ ¶ And all I can do for you, anyway, is to tell you the things you know, but which possibly you do not know you know until I tell you.

↪ ↪

SO here, then, is the secret: Let Motion equal Emotion.

Must I elucidate? Very well, I will: There is only one thing in the world, and that is Energy. This Energy takes a myriad million forms; and its one peculiarity is that it is always in motion. It has three general manifestations: atmosphere, hydrosphere, lithosphere—or, if you prefer, air, water and rock.

From air, water and rock we get fungi and mosses; and then from these spring vegetation ↪ Disintegrating vegetation gives us animal life; and from the animal to the vegetable kingdom, and the vegetable to the animal—with the constant interchange of gas, water and solid—gives us Nature's eternal program.

In Nature there is nothing inanimate. Everything is alive; everything is going somewhere, or else coming back; nothing is static. Fixity is the one impossible thing ↪ ↪

And the fallacy of fixity has been the one fatal error of theology and all philosophies in the past.

Progress consists in getting away from the idea of the static.

Nature's one business is to absorb and to dissipate—to attract and repel—to take in and give out. And everything which Nature makes is engaged in the same business.

Man takes in carbon and gives off nitrogen. ¶ The plant takes in nitrogen and gives off carbon.

All things are in motion, ebb and flow, action and reaction, cause and effect, swirl and whirl.

Centripetal and centrifugal forces make our life on the planet Earth possible ↪ ¶ The heart rests between beats. That which we call static is merely equilibrium. ¶ The tiger crouches for one of two reasons: to spring or to die.

And death is a form of life. Death is a combination where the balance is lost, and gas, water and solids are in wrong proportions. The only thing then is to dissolve the body and use in new masses the substances that composed it.

↪ ↪

MAN is the instrument of Energy ↪ And if you wish to call this energy God, or the First Principle, or The Unknowable, there will be no quarrel. We will only divide when you insist on calling it a Super-Something, or a Superior Being.

If there is any Being superior to man, we have thus far not the slightest evidence of His existence. Man is a part of the Divine Energy.

Also there are no unique men, although men differ in quality, but not so much as we often think. What one man has attained, other men may attain.

To talk about a Superior Being is a dip to superstition, and is just as bad as to let in an Inferior Being or a Devil. ¶ When you once attribute effects to the will of a personal God, you have let in a lot of little gods and devils— then sprites, fairies, dryads, naiads, witches, ghosts and goblins, for your imagination is reeling, riotous, drunk, afloat on the flotsam of superstition ↪ What you know that does n't count. You just believe, and the more you believe the more do you plume yourself that fear and faith are superior to science and seeing.

What I am now telling you is Science, and Science is the classified knowledge of the common people.

↪ ↪

MAN is a transformer of energy. This energy plays through him. In degree he can control it; or at least he can control his condition as a transmitter. ❡ And the secret of being a good transmitter is to allow motion to equal emotion ✺ ✺

To be healthy and sane and well and happy, you must do real work with your hands as well as with your head. The cure for grief is motion ✺ The recipe for strength is action.

To have a body that is free from disease and toxins, you must let motion equal emotion. ❡ Love for love's sake creates a current so hot that it blows out the fuse. But love that finds form in music, sculpture, painting, poetry and work is divine and beneficent beyond words.

That is, love is an inward emotion, and if stifled, thwarted and turned back upon itself, tends to gloom, melancholy, brooding, jealousy, rage and death. But love that is liberated in human efforts attracts love; so a current is created and excess emotion is utilized, for the good not only of the beloved, but also of the race. The love that lasts is a trinity— I love you because you love the things that I love. Static love soon turns to hate, or, to be more exact, try to make love a fixity and it dies.

Safety lies in service. Going the same way, we will go hand in hand.

A lover out of a job is a good man for a girl to avoid.

Religion that takes the form of ecstacy, with no outlet in the way of work, is dangerous. This way horror lies. Emotion without motion tends to madness and despair.

✺ ✺

EXPRESSION must equal impression. If you study you must also create, write, teach, give out. Otherwise, you will become a plaster-of-Paris cat or a brass monkey. If great joy has come to you, pass it along, and thus do you

double it. You are the steward of any gift the gods have given you, and you answer for their use with your life. Do not obstruct the divine current. Use your knowledge and use it quickly, or it will disintegrate and putrefy.

The school where the child learns, and then goes home and tells what he has learned, approaches the ideal.

On the other hand, the college that imparts knowledge but supplies no opportunity for work is faulty in the extreme. A school for adults that does not supply work as well as facts is false in theory and vicious in practise.

MOST of the Socialists I know do not work—they only talk about work ✺ What they want is an orthodox heaven of ease, where the harps are always in tune and the robes are always laundered.

❡ Its pupils do not possess health, happiness or power, except on a fluke.

Emotion balanced by motion eliminates dead tissue and preserves sanity. For lack of motion congestion follows.

Most sickness comes from a failure to make motion balance emotion. Impress and express; inhale and exhale; work and play; study and laugh; love and labor; exercise and rest. Study your own case and decide to get the most out of life. The education of invalids is a terrific waste ✺ ✺

Sickness, unhappiness, ignorance, all tend to inefficiency. And inefficiency is the only sin.

Realize that you are a Divine Transformer ✺ ✺

Make motion equal emotion, and you will eliminate fear, round out the century run, and be efficient to the last. And to live long and well is to accept life in every phase—even death itself— and find it good.—*The Key to Success*

✺ ✺

Good healthy egotism in literature is the red corpuscle that makes the thing live. Cupid, naked and unashamed, is always beautiful; we turn away only when some very proper person perceives he is naked and attempts to better the situation by supplying him a coat of mud.

IVORCE-laws are obsolete in their character, and should die the death.

A marriage that can not be dissolved tends to tyranny.

There is a rudimentary something in man that makes him a tyrant—that divides humanity into master and slave—and to these barbaric instincts we are heir &o &o

The business of civilization is to make men free &o And freedom means responsibility. The curse of marriage is that it makes the parties immune from very much of that gentle consideration which freedom bestows &o&o

Freedom in divorce is the one thing that will transform the marital boor into a gentleman.

Freedom to divorce is the one thing that will abolish the domestic steamroller &o &o

Freedom to divorce is the one thing that will correct the propensity to nag, in both male and female.

We gain freedom by giving it. We hold love by giving it away.

To enslave another is to enslave yourself &o &o

Constancy, unswerving and eternal, is only possible where men and women are free.

&o &o

LIFE is a gradual death. There are animals and insects that die on the instant of the culmination of the act for which they were created. Success is death, and death, if you have bargained wisely with Fate, is victory.

&o &o

I modestly protest that simplicity, truthfulness, mental self-reliance, physical health and the education of the hand, as well as brain, shall not be left out of the accounting when we make our formula for a man &o &o

HE country that sells raw materials will always be poor, just as the farmer who sells corn, and not hogs, will never lift the mortgage. If you have a forest, and can work it up into tables, chairs, bookcases and violins you will make a deal more money than if you sell firewood &o &o

The United States has one-sixteenth the population of the world.

But we have one-third the wealth of the world &o The North American Indians had the raw stock, but they did not know how to use it &o Our wealth comes from the ability to combine coal and iron-ore; lumber and steel bolts; leather and shoe-strings; paint and glue; rubber and steel.

So we have supplied the world automobiles, shoes, farm implements, locomotives, engines, brass castings, machinery and manufactured commodities in a million forms.

We take paper, glue, leather, copper, steel and make a " Kodak." The value of the raw materials that go to make a kodak is, say, twenty cents. The consumer in South Africa, England, Japan or Germany pays five dollars for the machine, and counts it a bargain. It is brain that makes value.

&o &o

NATURE is the best guide of which we know, and the love of simple pleasures is next, if not superior, to religion &o &o

Nature forever strives for a right adjustment, and sends satiety after license.

&o &o

It is foolish to say sharp, hasty things, but 't is a deal more foolish to write 'em. When a man sends you an impudent letter, sit right down and give it back to him with interest ten times compounded—and then throw both letters in the waste-basket &o &o

THE only right
That any man should have &o &o
Is the right to be decent—
That is,
To be agreeable and useful.

WHEN a man ridicules certain traits in other men, he ridicules himself.

How would he know that other men were contemptible did he not look into his heart and there see the hateful things? Thackeray wrote his book on Snobs, because he himself was a Snob, but not all of the time. When you recognize a thing, good or bad, in the outside world, it is because it was yours already. " I carry the world in my heart," said the Prophet of old ❧

❧ All the universe you have is the universe you have within. Old Walt Whitman when he saw a wounded soldier, exclaimed, " I am that man! " and two thousand years before this, Terence said: " I am a man, and nothing that is human is alien to me."

❧ ❧

THE man of genius is everywhere welcome: all doors fly open at his touch. He who has the talent to instruct, amuse or entertain needs no passport. But the person who can neither create nor produce, who can do nothing that the world wants done, and has nothing to say to which the world will listen, requires a certificate.

This social Letter of Credit the college undertakes to supply. It used to give out letters of Marque and Reprisal, but now the college degree is more or less of a pleasantry—valuable only to those who need it. One who is without either character or personality need not feel abashed so long as he has his degree— he can yet join a University Club, proudly wear the pin of his frat and rah-rah-rah! when the mood is on ❧

❧ ❧

It is only life and love that give love and life ❧ ❧

POWER unrestrained is always tragic. The world is held in place by the opposition of forces. The men in power are ballasted by responsibility, as never before in history. ❧ You have your use as an agitator; so go it, Jack, and say your say.

That fly on the wheel of the chariot of Achilles said, " Oh, just see what a dust we do kick up! " ❧ ❧ And this remark of the fly has added to the gayety of nations. But get enough flies on the chariot of Achilles and not a wheel revolves ❧ The Egyptians in Moses' time battled with swarms of flies, when the flies scored home-runs and base-hits.

❧ ❧

EVERY employer is constantly looking for people who can help him; naturally he is on the lookout among his employees for those who do not help, and everything and everybody that is a hindrance has to go. This is the law of trade—do not find fault with it; it is founded on Nature. The reward is only for the man that helps, and in order to help you must have sympathy. ❧ You can not help the Old Man so long as you are explaining in undertone and whisper, by gesture and suggestion, by thought and mental attitude, that he is a curmudgeon and his system dead wrong. You are not necessarily menacing him by stirring up discontent and warming envy into strife, but you are doing this: you are getting yourself upon a well-greased chute that will give you a quick ride down and out.

❧ ❧

How much finer it is to go out in the woods and lift up your voice in song, and be a child, than to fight inclination and waste good energy endeavoring to be proper!

FORCE expends itself and dies; every army is marching to its death; nothing but a skull and a skeleton fills helmet and cuirass; the aggressor is overcome by the poison of his pride; victory is only another name for defeat; but the Spirit of Gentleness and Truth is eternal ❧ ❧

IN this matter of bodily health, just a few plain rules suffice. And these rules fairly followed soon grow into a personal habit. And the habit is a pleasure

Fortunately, we do not have to superintend our digestion, our circulation, the work of the millions of pores that form the skin, or the action of the nerves

Folks who get fussy about their digestion and assume a personal charge of nerves, have " nerves," and are apt to have no digestion

" I have a pain in my side," said the woman to the busy doctor

" Forget it! " was the curt advice

¶ Get the Health Habit, and forget it, is excellent advice. It is the same with your soul as it is with your body.

The man who is always stewing about his soul has a very small and insignificant one

You don't have to trouble about your soul's salvation.

Everything in the universe worth saving will be saved.

Don't worry.

That advice of the busy doctor should be used by the preacher, and when the black-ant breed come around fussing about their souls, the advice should be, " Forget it! "

THERE are three habits which, with but one condition added, will give you everything in the world worth having, and beyond which the imagination of man can not conjure forth a single addition or improvement. These habits are the Work Habit, the Health Habit and the Study Habit. If you are a man

THE man who is anybody and who does anything is surely going to be criticized, vilified and misunderstood. This is a part of the penalty for greatness, and every great man understands it; and understands, too, that it is no proof of greatness. The final proof of greatness lies in being able to endure contumely without resentment

and have these habits, and also have the love of a woman who has the same habits, you are in Paradise now and here, and so is she.

Health, Books and Work, with Love added, are a solace for all the stings and arrows of outrageous fortune—a defense 'gainst all the storms that blow; for through their use you transmute sadness into mirth, trouble into ballast, pain into joy.

¶ Do you say that religion is still needed?

Then I answer that Work, Study, Health and Love constitute religion. Moreover, any religion that leaves any of these out is not religion, but fetish

Yet most formal religions have pronounced the love of man for woman and woman for man an evil thing. They have proclaimed labor a curse.

¶ They have said that sickness was sent from God; and they have whipped and scorned the human body as something despicable, and thus have placed a handicap on health, and made the doctor a necessity.

And they have said that mental attainment was a vain and frivolous thing, and that our reason was a lure to lead us on to the eternal loss of our soul's salvation

Now we deny it all, and again proclaim that these will bring you all the good there is: Health, Work, Study—Love!

¶ Work means safety for yourself and service to mankind. Health means much happiness and potential power. Study means knowledge, equanimity and the evolving mind. Love means all the rest!

¶ But Love must be a matter of reciprocity, not a one-sided affair. ¶ " I love you because you love the things I love."

THAT which does not serve, dies. If the Trusts overcharge they invite competition and dissolution.

Success lies in cooperation and reciprocity, and the hope of the future is in the fact that the world knows it. ❡ We can't go back to chaos ✺ ✺ We must go on. Light lies ahead, not behind.

We won't take off the train-crews, and put on the tramps.

There are accidents occasionally now, but there would be more then. Safety lies in getting rid of the tramps.

One wide-awake, vigilant man at the switch is worth more to society than all the tramps who ride the brake-beams ✺ ✺

Get to work. If you can't find the job you want, take the one you can get! To prove yourself able to rastle a big job, get busy and take care of a little one. ❡ Power does not reveal itself in scolding. And with all your getting, get busy! Yours for the Evolution!

✺ ✺

A man who marries a woman to educate her falls a victim to the same fallacy as the woman who marries a man to reform him. If you marry a woman who is not on your mental wire, you'll either go down to her level or you will live in a water-tight compartment and go to purgatory through mental asphyxiation.

Choose this day the habits you would have rule over you.

IF you work for a man, in heaven's name work for him! ❡ If he pays you wages that supply you your bread and butter, work for him—speak well of him, think well of him, stand by him and stand by the institution he represents ✺ ✺ I think if I worked for a man I would work for him. I would not work for him a part of the time, and the rest of the time work against him ✺ I would give an undivided service or none ✺ ✺ If put to the pinch, an ounce of loyalty is worth a pound of cleverness ✺ ✺

WORDS are tools for the transmission of thoughts. Thoughts are the result of feelings ✺ The recipe for good writing is, write as you feel, but be sure you feel right ✺ ✺ ❡ But before you write you must have an equipment—a literary kit—of mouth-filling, expressive, far-reaching words and phrases.

Sidney Smith said that the man who invented a new dish added to the happiness of the world. Whether this is true or not, the man who invents a new word gives wings to imagination ✺ He links the world into a brotherhood by allowing us to break through the icy silences that surround us.

Through language we touch finger-tips with the noble, the great, the good, the competent, living or dead, and thus are we made brothers to all those who make up the sum-total of civilization.

✺ ✺

DEGENERACY always begins in the cities; and the failure of civilization has come when the cities succeed and the urbanites decline.

✺ ✺

Give me the man, who instead of always telling you what should be done, goes ahead and does it.

✺ ✺

Atlas could never have carried the world had he fixed his thought on the size of it.

✺ ✺

Do not separate yourself from plain people; be one with all—be universal.

HE other day I met a man who was on the ill-fated *Titanic*. When the boilers burst, and the great ship took her final plunge, my friend felt himself going down into the waters.

¶ Being an experienced swimmer, he involuntarily knew enough not to inhale. He held his breath, but he did a deal of thinking. So down he went, but he knew, too, that soon he would be coming to the top, and it was only a question of being able to hold his breath long enough to escape immediate drowning.

When he felt himself coming to the surface a great joy possessed his soul. As his head came above the water, he reached out his arms, flattened himself on the surface of the wave as nearly as possible, and took in a great big breath ❦ ❦

Then he looked up at the stars, and gratitude filled his mind.

He was still alive; his senses were intact; he was able to think, to breathe, to realize, to see the shining stars. He felt as one who had been dead, like Lazarus, and returned to earth. He was alive!

¶ But suddenly there came to him the thought that he could swim for a little while only. The water was icy cold, and he began to look around for deliverance.

¶ About a hundred feet away he saw a floating spar, and it came to him that if he could reach that spar it would indeed be paradise. So he struck out for the spar. It seemed to be floating away from him as he swam, but with great effort he reached it, grasped it with his hands, drew himself up and then sat upon it ❦ ❦

When he felt that it was holding his weight he was relieved. Again he was filled with a great sense of gratitude. And as he sat on that spar, holding on with hands and feet, he looked up at the sky in thankfulness. He was alive; and to know that this spar was holding his weight filled his soul with joy.

But the wind was cold. His frame was chilled, and he knew that it was only a little time that he could hold on.

Just then he saw a boat pulling away at fifty or a hundred yards' distance ❦

¶ He shouted, and called again and again. And slowly the boat turned in his direction. It came nearer and nearer, and he knew that if he could once get in that boat and feel that the boat was under him, it would be paradise, indeed.

In a few minutes the wish came to pass, and he was in the boat ❦ He was exhausted, too weak even to lift his hand. But the joy was exquisite: he was with human beings.

So they floated with the tide, and they pulled the oars. After a long time, a flush of pink came into the East, and they knew that day would soon come.

¶ And then they saw a great gray-like form, with many lights, away off in the distance.

They prayed, they wept, they waited—there was nothing else to do.

The *Carpathia* came nearer, and my friend breathed a great prayer that he might be able to climb the side of the ship and lie on the deck. That was all he would ask—simply the privilege of lying flat on the deck, and knowing that the ship was beneath him.

And his prayer was answered ❦ He climbed up the rope ladder and knelt on the deck in thankfulness.

But soon he realized that strength had gone out of him, and he begged that he be placed in the meanest room in the steerage, just so it was a bed and he was covered with blankets.

Some of the mothers and children in the crowded steerage made room for him, and when he was in the bunk, he said to himself, "Surely, this is paradise!" and he closed his eyes in gratitude.

But after an hour or two the crying of the children, the smell of cooking, the presence of so many people began to pall on him. He felt he must get away from this mob.

So he called to a petty officer and begged that he might have a cabin.

And a bunk was found for him in a cabin. And here in this cabin he was very happy and he said, " This is paradise, indeed! " and he rested and thought, and tried to write out telegrams to send to his friends when he reached shore.

He slept soundly that night, but when he awoke in the morning he realized that the cabin was n't exactly right. And so he asked the steward who came to wait on him if there was not a berth somewhere in a cabin on the upper deck. And the steward said that every bunk was full, except, possibly, one berth in the captain's cabin.

And so my friend took pencil in hand and wrote a letter to the captain of the ship. And this is a copy of the letter:

" Dear Sir:

" This cabin in which I am located is right alongside of the engines. I hear the clank and clash of machinery all the night-time through. I am awakened by the noise and foul air, for this cabin is very small and illy ventilated.

" I understand that you have a vacant bunk in your cabin on the upper deck. Kind sir, please send word by bearer, allowing me to occupy this cabin with you, and I will ever be

         " Your sincere friend."

No answer came from the captain.

But the moral of this true story is this. Nobody is ever satisfied with anything after he gets it.—*Titanic Survivor*

XPORTS of raw materials and foodstuffs mean skimming our milk and giving the cream away. We must use our raw materials and consume our foodstuffs right here. Then let us sell manufactured products. By so doing we siphon into this country the wealth of the world.

Henry Ford sells steel, brass, leather, and wood properly coordinated, at fifty cents a pound. Thereby he is able to pay a minimum wage of five dollars a day to American workmen. He does this with the aid of a manufacturing equipment unequalled in any European country
 Henry Ford first supplies the home market, and then he has facilities to supply the foreign trade. And so today there are Ford agencies in every civilized country. ❡ What America should sell is not raw material—we should sell our genius, our talent, our skill, our efficiency, our organizing ability.

ND when Fate has flung a man into a certain situation, if it is a place of some honor, the man will give himself all the credit for having attained it
 If it is a position that perhaps carries no honor, the party will always blame some one else for putting him there

We credit ourselves for our successes; we blame others for our faults.

Also, we justify ourselves in everything we do. And wise men see plainly that this self-justification is a part of Nature's great plan of self-preservation. The exaggerated Ego is a primal necessity. Good men all and everywhere multiply the value of their work by ten. Success in life consists in convincing yourself that you are the whole cheese, and then getting the world to accept your view.

Rostand's rooster was fully assured in his own mind that the sun would not come up if he did not crow. The hens being told this by the rooster, cackled it back to him, and it became a crystallized part of the orthodox Zeitgeist. And it would have so remained for all time, but for an accident—an accident of love, when a guinea-hen became enamoured of the boss of the barnyard.

So Life is a paradox—and love is not only illusion, but it is also the great enlightener

OMEN are adding greatly to the welfare of society. Woman is a natural economist and a conservator. She does not need patronage, and paternalism is a thing from which she has suffered much

Chivalry is paternalism gone to seed
 ❡ Let women fit themselves for the production of wealth, and wealth will be theirs. Every school now is putting in business courses. There are business colleges everywhere that are doing splendid and helpful work, fitting women for paying positions

Factories, department-stores, are all, in degree, pedagogic institutions.

The world is not moving as fast as we would like, but it is certainly moving, and it is moving in the right direction.

HE people you see waiting in the lobbies of doctors' offices are, in a vast majority of cases, suffering through poisoning caused by an excess of food ᶳᵉ ᶳᵉ

Coupled with this goes the bad results of imperfect breathing, irregular sleep, lack of exercise and improper use of stimulants, or the thought of fear, jealousy and hate.

❡ All these things, or any one of them, will, in very many persons, cause fever, chills, cold feet, congestion and faulty elimination.

❡ To administer drugs to a man suffering from malnutrition caused by a desire to "get even," and a lack of fresh air, is simply to compound his troubles, shuffle his maladies, and get him ripe for the ether cone and the scalpel ᶳᵉ ᶳᵉ

Nature is forever trying to keep people well, and most so-called "disease" (which word means merely lack of ease) is self-limiting, and tends to cure itself.

❡ If you have appetite, do not eat too much ᶳᵉ ᶳᵉ

If you have no appetite, do not eat at all.

❡ Be moderate in the use of all things, save fresh air and sunshine.

The one theme of Ecclesiastes is moderation ᶳᵉ ᶳᵉ

Buddha wrote it down that the greatest word in any language is "equanimity."

❡ William Morris said that the finest blessing of life was systematic, useful work ᶳᵉ ᶳᵉ

Saint Paul declared that the greatest thing in life was love.

Moderation, equanimity, work and love —you need no other physician.

In so stating I lay down a proposition agreed to by all physicians; which was expressed by Hippocrates, the father of all medicine, and then repeated in better phrase by Epictetus, the slave, to his pupil, the great Roman Emperor, Marcus Aurelius, and which has been known to every thinking man and woman since: Moderation, Equanimity, Work and Love! ᶳᵉ

ᶳᵉ ᶳᵉ

A HUNDRED-POINT man is one who is true to every trust; who keeps his word; who is loyal to the firm that employs him; who does not listen for insults nor look for slights; who carries a civil tongue in his head; who is polite to strangers without being "fresh;" who is considerate toward servants; who is moderate in his eating and drinking; who is willing to learn; who is cautious and yet courageous.

IN the Lewis and Clark Expedition there were thirty-four men and one woman ᶳᵉ This woman, Sacajawea, was the guide and chief counselor of Lewis and Clark ᶳᵉ She knew the fords, passes and springs; and when food was scarce she went on alone to the Indian villages where making known her wants to the squaws, she was given food for herself and the men. For two thousand miles she led the way a-foot, her baby on her back. When hope sank in the hearts of the men she cheered them forward.

In Portland, Oregon, the white women of the land have erected a statue of this brave Indian woman. The artist has been singularly happy in his modeling—silent, sober, patient, firmly poised, she looks out wistfully to the western mountains and points the way. On her back is her pappoose, chubby and content, innocent of the thought that he is making history. This noble bronze reveals the honest wife, the loving mother, the faithful friend, the unerring guide. Thousands looking upon this statue have been hushed into silence and tears. There is an earnestness in it that rebukes frivolity and makes one mentally uncover.

HERE is a maxim in law that no good deed shall act as a set-off against bad deeds ✸ This is where life forges ahead of the law. Law always lags and limps behind ✸ Blackstone says, "The business of a good lawyer is to bring the law abreast of the times" ✸ The punishment must fit the criminal, not the crime. Down in our hearts when we hear a man indicted, we all say: "Who is this man? Is this all?" And we usually know it is not. The indictment mentions only the worst, and it repeats this over and over with malice prepense and aforethought. The business of an indictment is to indict. Law is one thing and justice another ✸ All good lawyers and judges now admit this ✸ They do not prate glibly about justice as they once did, any more than doctors talk about "curing" people. We think of how the greatest men in history have been berated, reviled, imprisoned, and their property confiscated; and if they lived long enough, they were executed, and the public was given a holiday ✸ ✸

We think of how Pericles, who built the city of Athens, was destroyed and disgraced, and how he had to go in the Forum and plead for the life of his wife, Aspasia ✸ ✸

We think of how the son of Pericles and Aspasia was executed on order of the Government.

MAN'S only enemy is himself. His ignorance of this world and his superstitious belief in another have blocked his pathway ✸ ✸

Our troubles, like our diseases, come from ignorance and weakness, and through our weakness are we weak and unable to adjust ourselves to better conditions. The more we know of this world, the better we think of it, and the better we are able to use it for our advancement. ❡ So far as we can judge, the unknown cause that rules the world by natural law is a movement forward toward happiness, growth, justice, peace and right. Therefore, the scientist, who perceives that all is good when rightly received and rightly understood, is the priest, the holy man, the mediator and the explainer of the mysterious. As fast as we can understand things they cease to be supernatural. The supernatural is the natural not yet understood.

We think of how Phidias, the right hand of Pericles, and the greatest sculptor the world has ever seen, was executed for blasphemy on account of having put the picture of his patron on a sacred shield; how he was dragged at the cart's tail to the place of execution, and his body thrown to the wild beasts. ❡ We think of how Socrates, the greatest mind, perhaps, the world has ever known, was passed the deadly hemlock on order of a jury of five hundred who sat on his case ✸ Surely, Socrates could not complain that he did not have a fair trial ✸ He had his day in court, and his passing, written by his pupil, Plato, is one of the immortal things in literature. ❡ The glory that was Greece lingers around the life of Socrates, Aspasia, Pericles, Phidias, Herodotus, Hippocrates, Aristotle— all criminals before the law—all disgraced, exiled or executed ✸ Greek history lives but for these, and the men most instrumental in destroying them live in letters, if at all, simply because they linked their names with greatness ✸ ✸

Follow down and see history repeated in the rule of Rome!

And the Middle Ages come with their night of a thousand years, when men forgot how to smile, how to laugh; when enterprise died and originality languished; when the world did not produce a poet, an inventor, a painter, a sculptor, a man of originality ✸ ✸

¶ But the world awakens from sleep in the year, say, Fourteen Hundred Ninety-two, when Columbus sailed, when Martin Luther sang in the streets and held up his cap for pennies, and Michael Angelo and Leonardo da Vinci lived, loved and worked. And for a hundred years thousands on thousands of the best, the greatest, the brightest men who lived were executed, reviled, disgraced, imprisoned —men like Copernicus, Bruno, Galileo and Balboa ✏

¶ Columbus, who had given the world a continent, was thrown into prison, and was only liberated when death filed his chains, and set the captive free.

✏ ✏

¶ You had better be a round peg in a square hole than a square peg in a square hole ✏ The latter is in for life, while the first is only an indeterminate sentence ✏

✏ ✏

EVERY new thing has to fight for its life ✏ Every innovation is opposed. The tug of inertia has us all by the foot, and we would rather fight for the old than take on the new ✏ ✏

Beside that, there is the eternal doubt as to the value of the new invention, and the chances, it must be admitted, are all on the side of failure. In the application of electricity, Edison had not only to discover methods whereby electricity could be utilized, but he had to commercialize the proposition and educate the world to its use. When George Westinghouse invented the airbrake, his real task was to convince the railroad world of its value.

✏ ✏

IT is a wonderful thing to have somebody believe in you. This is the one great benefit of love. Love idealizes its object. It exaggerates little tendencies into great virtues, possibilities into genius. Love is action and reaction ✏ Where much is expected from an individual, he may rise to the level of events and make the dream come true. Mother-love is the great, surging, divine current that plays forever through humanity. We see it manifest in the dumb animals; in the mother bird who dies rather than desert her young; in the tigress who is invincible when she has her babies to Protect. How much men of genius owe to their mothers, will never be told in cold words, because love cannot be analyzed, nor placed under the slide.

GENIUS has always come in groups, because groups produce the friction that generates light. Competition with fools is not bad—fools teach the imbecility of repeating their performances. A man learns from this one, and that; he lops off absurdity, strengthens here and bolsters there, until in his soul there grows up an ideal, which he materializes in stone or bronze, on canvas, by spoken word, or with the twenty-odd symbols of Cadmus. Greece had her group when the wit of Aristophanes sought to overtop the stately lines of Æschylus; Praxiteles outdid Ictinus; while the words of Socrates outlasted them all.

Rome had her group when all the arts sought the silver speech of Cicero. One art never flourishes alone—they go together, each man doing the thing he can do best. All the arts are really one, and this one art is simply Expression—the expression of Mind speaking through its highest instrument, Man.

✏ ✏

The punishment of the liar is that he eventually believes his own lies.

✏ ✏

A man's theories are apt to smile sadly at his practice over the gaping gulf that separates the ideal from the real.

✏ ✏

A seer is the scout of civilization.

✏ ✏

Nothing so fatal to integrity as pretense!

WAS mousing the other day in a book that is somewhat disjointed and disconnected, and yet interesting—*The Standard Dictionary*—when I came across the word " scamp." It is a handy word to fling, and I am not sure but that it has been gently tossed once or twice, in my direction. Condemnation is usually a sort of subtle flattery, so I 'm not sad.

But now I 'll prove that I am not a scamp ✺ ✺

To scamp means to cut short, to be superficial, slip-shod, careless, indifferent. To say, " let 'er go, who cares—this is good enough! " If anybody ever was a stickler for honest work, I am that bucolic party. I often make things so fine that only one man out of ten thousand can buy them, and I have to keep 'em myself ✺ ✺

You know that when you get an idea in your head, most everything you read contains allusions to the same thing ✺ Knowledge is mucilaginous. Well, next day after I was looking up that pleasant word, " scamp," I was reading in the Amusing Works of my old college chum, Erasmus, when I ran across the word again, but spelled in Dutch, then, " schamp." Now Erasmus was a printer and also he became the most learned man of his time. He was a successful author, and he was also the best authority on paper, inks, bindings and general bookmaking in Italy, Holland or Germany. Being a lover of learning, and listening to the lure of words, he never wallowed in wealth. But in his hunt for ideas he had a lot of fun. Kipling says, " There is no hunt equal to a man hunt." But Kip is wrong—to chase a thought is twice the fun. Erasmus chased ideas and very naturally the preachers chased Erasmus—out of England, through France, down to Italy and then he found refuge at Basel with Froben, the great Printer and Publisher.

Up in Frankfort was a writer-printer, who, not being able to answer the arguments of Erasmus, called him bad names. Among the other choice ones he heaved at Erasmus was " bastardicus." Erasmus was used to this, for in his youth he had been taunted with having no name and he said, " Then I 'll make one for myself." And he did.

But this gentle pen-pusher in Frankfort who passed his vocabulary at Froben's proof-reader, Erasmus in time calls a " schamp," because he used cheap paper, cheap ink and close margins. Soon after the word was carried to England and spelled " scamp "—a man who cheats in quality, weight, size and count. But the first use merely meant a printer who scamps his margins and so cheats on paper. I am sorry to see that Erasmus imitated his enemies and was ambidexterous with the literary stinkpot ✺ His vocabulary was equal to that of Muldoon. Erasmus refers to one of his critics as a " scenophylax-stikken," and another he calls a " schnide enchologion-schistosomus." And perhaps they may have been—I really do not know.

But as an authority on books Erasmus can still be read. He it was who fixed the classic page margin—twice as wide at the top as on the inside ; twice as wide at the outside as the top; twice as wide at the bottom as the side. And any printer who varies from this displays his ignorance of proportion.

Erasmus says, " To use poor paper marks the decline of taste both in printer and patron."

After the death of Erasmus, Froben's firm failed because they got to making things cheap. " Compete in quality, not price," was the working motto of Erasmus ✺ ✺

All of the great bookmaking centers languished when they began to scamp. That wordy wordissimus at Frankfort who called Erasmus names, gave up business and then the ghost, and Erasmus wrote his epitaph, and thus supplied Benjamin Franklin an idea—" Here lies an old book, its cover gone, its leaves torn, the worms at work on its vitals." The wisdom of doing good work still applies, just as it did in the days of Erasmus ✺ ✺

A book on cheap paper does not convince. A book should not only be true, it must be beautiful.—*Scamp.*

AITH in your own opinions is a good thing, but—were you ever absolutely certain of the result of an election—prophesying a tidal wave for " our party "—honestly advising your friends to put up all their loose change, and then the next morning awake to know that your basis for belief was built on East Wind?

Did you ever size up a young fellow who wanted work, or who was in your employ, and foretell that there was nothing in him, that he would always be a counter-jumper, and then in a few years have to eat your words?

Did you ever go to a horse-race and lay your money on Sure Thing and never see the hard-earned again?

Were you ever an editor, turned down a Manuscript as rot, rubbish, drivel and diluted idiocy, and then see this same MS. published by your rival and accepted by the public, and the author whom you declared could n't write for shucks, setting you a pace you could not follow?

❧ Have you ever as a businessman had a certain scheme presented and did you reject it as foolish and fanciful, and later behold it make a million dollars for your enemy?

Have you ever fought valiantly for a creed, or a platform, and then in a few years, conclude, of your own accord, that you were on the wrong track, and turn around and denounce the thing you once upheld?

Were you ever a plaintiff in a lawsuit and on the case going to the jury, say with a chuckle, " The opposition has n't a leg upon which to stand," and a little later hear the foreman calmly remark, " We, the jury, find for the defendant? "

❧ Well, if so, and you have thus learned to dilute faith in your own infallibility with a little doubt, you have not lived in vain ❧ ❧

❧ ❧

The author who has not made warm friends and then lost them in an hour by writing things that did not agree with the preconceived ideas of those friends, has either not written well or not been read ❧ ❧

HE world bestows its big prizes, both in money and in honors, for but one thing ❧ And that is Initiative.

What is Initiative?

I 'll tell you: It is doing the right thing without being told.

But next to doing the right thing without being told is to do it when you are told once. That is to say, carry the Message to Garcia!

Next, there are those who never do a thing until they are told twice: such get no honors and small pay.

Next, there are those who do the right thing only when Necessity kicks them from behind, and these get indifference instead of honors and a pittance for pay. This kind spends most of its time polishing a bench with a hard-luck story ❧

❧ Then, still lower down in the scale than this, we find the fellow who will not do the right thing even when some one goes along to show him how, and stays to see that he does it: he is always out of a job, and receives the contempt he deserves, unless he has a rich Pa, in which case Destiny patiently awaits around the corner with a stuffed club. To which class do you belong?

❧ ❧

I THINK it really better, if you have to choose, to drink beer out of an earthen pot—as did the father of John Sebastian Bach—and be kind and gentle, than to have a sharp nose for other folks' faults and be continually trying to pinch and prod the old world into the straight and narrow path of virtue.

❧ ❧

HUMANITY wants help, the help of strong, sensible, unselfish men ❧ ❧ Education is an achievement, not a bequest ❧ ❧

❧ ❧

Light stands for literature. The words have a common root. Literature tokens intelligence, and intelligence mirrors enterprise, thrift, industrialism. Business at the last is largely a matter of sentiment. The light seems to give courage, hope, animation, and binds people together into a common bond.

BUSINESS is a fight—a continual struggle—just as life is. Man has reached his present degree of development through struggle.

Struggle there must be and always will be ∽ ∽

The struggle began as purely physical. As man evolved it shifted ground to the mental, the psychic and the spiritual, with a few dashes of Caveman proclivities still left.

But, depend upon it, the struggle will always be—life is activity. And when it gets to be a struggle in well-doing, it will still be a struggle. When inertia gets the better of you it is time to telephone the undertaker ∽ ∽

❡ The only real neutral in this game of life is a dead one ∽ ∽

Eternal vigilance is not only the price of liberty, but of every other good thing.

❡ A business that is not safeguarded on every side by active, alert, attentive, vigilant men is gone. As oxygen is the disintegrating principle of life, working night and day to dissolve, separate, pull apart and dissipate, so there is something in business that continually tends to scatter, destroy and shift possession from this man to that. A million mice nibble eternally at every business venture ∽ ∽

The mice are not neutrals, and if enough employees in a business house are neutrals, the whole concern will eventually come tumbling about their ears.

I like that order of Field Marshal Oyama, " Give every honorable neutral that you find in our lines the honorable jiu-jitsu hikerino." ∽ ∽

THE spirit of obedience is the controlling impulse that dominates the receptive mind and the hospitable heart. There are boats that mind the helm and there are boats that do not. Those that do not get holes knocked in them sooner or later.

To keep off the rocks, obey the rudder ∽ ∽

Obedience is not slavishly to obey this man or that, but it is that cheerful mental state which responds to the necessity of the case, and does the thing without any back talk—uttered or expressed ∽ ∽

❡ Obedience to the institution —loyalty!

The man who has not learned to obey has trouble ahead of him every step of the way ∽ The world has it in for him continually, because he has it in for the world ∽ ∽

The man who does not know how to receive orders is not fit to issue them to others. But the individual who knows how to execute the orders given him is preparing the way to issue orders, and better still, to have them obeyed.

There is known to me a prominent business house that by the very force of its directness and worth has incurred the enmity of many rivals. In fact, there is a very general conspiracy on hand to put the institution down and out ∽ ∽

In talking with a young man employed by this house he yawned and said, " Oh, in this quarrel I am neutral."

"But you get your bread and butter from this firm, and I do not see how you can be a neutral." ❡ And he changed the subject. ❡ I think that if I enlisted in the Japanese army I would not be a neutral.

BE yourself and think for yourself; and while your conclusions may not be infallible they will be nearer right than the conclusions forced upon you by those who have a personal interest in keeping you in ignorance. You grow through exercise of your faculties, and if you don't reason now you never will advance. We are all sons of God, and it doth not yet appear what we shall be. Claim your heritage!

COMING up from Hot Springs I met a smooth faced, jaunty little man. He was dressed like a youth, and at first sight, I took him for a young man, but another look convinced me he was sixty, at least. Whether he was born sixty years ago or not really makes no difference, he had lived sixty years ✺ Evidently he had made money, but just how, it would have been indelicate to ask. His short, sharp sentences revealed an intimacy with the ringside and the race-track, and the diamond stud in his scarf told of gains I hoped not ill-gotten.

The little man had gone the pace, and he now was paying the penalty. ✺ ✺ This was sure, for sprinkled in his sporty talk were remarks about MacFadden, Rest Cure, No Breakfast, Health Foods and Mental Science. These things were new to him, but in them he had now a direct and personal interest. He asked me what I thought of Mary Baker Eddy; and at another time questioned me as to what the test was for uric acid; and then asked if I wore an Electric Belt. ❐ On the second day of the journey we were in the smoking car together. I was reading and he was sitting looking out of the window in an abstracted way, his neat Fedora slightly tilted over one eye ✺ ✺

The train whizzed through a little village. I was conscious that my friend was looking attentively at something out on the landscape.

He turned to me and said, " There is another one of those graveyards! "

—*Days are as Grass.*

✺ ✺

Preserve a right mental attitude—the attitude of courage, frankness and good-cheer. To think rightly is to create ✺ ✺

MAN, like Deity, creates in his own image.

When a painter paints a portrait he makes two—one of himself and one of the sitter.

If there is a sleazy thread in your character you will weave it into the fabric you are making.

WHENEVER you go out of doors, draw the chin in, carry the crown of the head high, and fill the lungs to the utmost; drink in the sunshine; greet your friends with a smile, and put soul into every hand-clasp ✺ Do not fear being misunderstood; and never waste a minute thinking about your enemies. Try to fix firmly in your mind what you would like to do, and then without violence of direction you will move straight to the goal. ❐ Keep your mind on the great and splendid things you would like to do; and then, as the days go gliding by you will find yourself unconsciously seizing upon the opportunities that are required for the fulfilment of your desire, just as the coral insect takes from the running tide the elements it needs ✺ Picture in your mind the able, earnest, useful person you desire to be, and the thought you hold is hourly transforming you into that particular individual ✺ ✺ ❐ Thought is supreme. Preserve a right mental attitude—the attitude of courage, frankness and good-cheer. To think rightly is to create. ❐ All things come through desire, and every sincere prayer is answered. We become like that on which our hearts are fixed. Carry your chin in and the crown of your head high. We are gods in the chrysalis.

✺ ✺

WHEN you recognize a thing in the outside world, it is because it was yours already.

✺ ✺

Life is a movement outward, an unfolding ✺ ✺

✺ ✺

A pessimist is a man who has been compelled to live with an optimist ✺ ✺

T is just here that a bright woman, who has thoughts as well as feelings, said to me (seated near) that she never ceases to marvel at the miracle of a person making marks on bark, paper or parchment, and when this bark, paper or parchment is looked upon by another person that this second person should weep or laugh or be moved to profoundest thought. A traveler says that once in Africa he sent a written message to his Lieutenant a hundred miles away. After the Lieutenant had looked at the flimsy little piece of paper, behold! he knew just where his chief was and how it fared with him—and this without the messenger saying a word. Then did they who carried the little piece of paper fall down on their faces before the white man and pray him that he would cut off their heads, or do with them whatsoever he would. In Mexico I have been in villages where only one man—the priest—could read and write, and it was not hard to imagine why the people of the place looked upon the priest as the agent of Deity, the mouthpiece of God. Even today, when the rumble of printing-presses never dies from our ears, the anonymous editorial carries a certain specific gravity and is quoted as authority, when the spoken words of the man himself are scarcely listened to, certainly not remembered, even by his barber. And in days agone, when rolls of carefully prepared papyrus were found I wonder not that men looked upon the deathless thought of a man long dead as a message from the gods. Then, forsooth, if the message were so plainly expressed on the surface of the text the Wise Men sought to interpret it and make it plain to those less wise. And as in boyhood's days when I went swimming, the lad who dived the deepest and brought up the most mud was crowned with honor, so the man who found in the words of the papyrus the most portentous meaning was deemed most profound. All people with broad sympathies agree that there is something pathetic in these frantic efforts to wring a message from a Sphinx—

a Sphinx with stony lips. When the inhabitants of that old city in the East were sore beset by enemies, they called upon their god to tell them what to do. They gathered around the statue expecting a reply, but when no answer came and the enemy thundered at their gates, they dragged the speechless Idol from its pedestal and brake it in pieces ⚜ ⚜

⚜ ⚜

WHEN the papyrus-roll seemed to yield no message the Wise Men cast it aside and would fain have destroyed it. The papyrus that gave an answer they called Canonical, and that which answered not at all, or but faintly, they termed Apocryphal. And they determined which was Canonical and which Apocryphal by ballot. That which was declared Canonical was always believed to be Apocryphal by some, and that which was Apocryphal to many was always deemed Canonical by a few ⚜ Canonical books were accepted by the people as the Word of God until certain men called Infidels arose and wished to destroy the Idol because it gave no answer that they could hear: how to bring deliverance from the doubts and fears that besieged their hearts.

And then all the people who accepted the verdict of the Wise Men and believed that the Idol had spoken to others, even though it had not to them, arose, and instead of destroying the Idol they destroyed the Infidels. And this was meet, for the Infidels should have understood that a statue may be beautiful in itself: that it may adorn a niche upon the wall of Time and so speak by silent inference to all who pass. Whether it has ever spoken to others is naught, save to the anthropologist and the historian, and to us—who read their entertaining tales. It was not so very long ago that a Book bound in oaken boards, riveted in bands of iron wrought in curious shapes, locked with ponderous key, born upon a silver salver by a stoled and tonsured priest of God, was carried in solemn processional with silent steps and slow to the Altar ⚜ Then the Book was unlocked, opened and from it the priest chanted in strange, unknown tongue, and the people listened in breathless awe to the words that Deity had dictated in order that men might be surely saved from an impending doom. " In times of old all books were religious oracles. As literature advanced they become venerable preceptors; they then descended to the rank of instructive friends, and as their number increased they sunk, still lower—to that of entertaining companions." There is a certain truth in these ambiguous words of Coleridge, but books have not sunk; rather, men have been raised to a degree where they are the companions of the men who instruct and entertain them. No longer do we crawl with our faces in the dust before a tome.

BUT it is unfortunate that there is no demarcation whatever between Sacred Writ and profane writing: some distinguishing feature that could not be overlooked nor waived aside. Such a mark set on Inspiration would have saved much bitter controversy, for it is mere truism to state that families have been severed, churches divided, cities separated into factions, aye, nations destroyed—all through a difference of opinion as to whether or not certain literary works were directly communicated by God. In one of Mr. Spurgeon's sermons he says, " Holy Writ exists for the purpose of showing man his duty to God," but the poem with which we have to deal is peculiar in that it is one of the two in the Bible that contains no reference to a Supreme Being. A man belonging to the Chosen People is talking with a woman who is a heathen, and if this couple know anything of God they keep the knowledge strictly to themselves. The man makes no effort to convert the woman; indeed, she seems fully as intelligent as he: not a hint of Elohim, or angels, or spirits, or devils, or heaven or hell; of man's duty to God, or man's duty to man; not a single moral injunction, not an ethical precept; not a suggestion of miracle is given, or of things supernatural—nothing but the earth and the beauty that is seen in it. And yet, the canonicity of the Book has

never been challenged save by a few captious critics of no standing in scholarship. The Holy Fathers could be cited at great length to show the high esteem and exalted reverence in which the Song has ever been held.

In the Mishna, Rabbi Akiba says: " Peace and mercy! No man in Israel ever doubted the canonicity of the Song of Songs, for the course of ages can not vie with the day on which the Song of Songs was given to Israel. All the Kethubim are indeed a holy thing, but the Song of Songs is a Holy of Holies." Origin, who is called the Father of Christian Exegesis, enumerates the chief songs of the Bible and then says: " And after thou hast passed through all these, thou must mount higher to sing with the Bridegroom the Song of Songs."

ACCORDING to the statement of Luther, the Book is an allegory representing Solomon's relation to the Commonwealth of Israel; but it is intimated that the author doubtless belonged to the fleshly school of poets ∞ On the other hand, DeWitt Talmage was wont to explain that the Song is a prophetic parable referring to Christ as the bridegroom and the Church as the bride ∞ Indeed, I believe this is the universal Evangelistic belief. But various fanciful interpretations have been given us, some of which are nearly as ingenious as the claim recently made by an English clergyman that the Golden Calf, which was worshiped by the Children of Israel, was prophetic of the British Nation: the gold of the calf signifying the wealth of the Empire on which the sun never sets, and the calf doubtless being a bull calf —for there is no evidence to the contrary —and hence typical of John Bull ∞ Theodoret, long, long ago stated it as his belief that the Song of Songs was simply a love dialogue which passed between Solomon and a certain Shulamite maiden. But to this a clamorous denial has rung down the centuries, and the assertion has repeatedly been put forward that mere love songs chanted back and forth between a young man and a young woman were not lovely things at all, and without there was some deep, hidden and occult meaning in the lines the Song would not have been preserved, either by Divine Providence or by His Instruments, the Wise Men of Old ❧ ❧

WE of today, however, perhaps swinging back to a view which corresponds with that of the author of the lines, do not regard passionate love as an unholy thing. We say, as does Andrew Lang in his preface to *Aucassin and Nicolette*, that a love without conscience admitting that at present it may be bad sociological policy, is delightful to contemplate. And with Herbert Spencer as authority I will add that nothing is " wicked " *per se*. Things are either good or bad as they bring good results or bad results. Even the stern Mosaic Law is merely sanitary in its aim, its design being social good and nothing more. So let us view the statute simply as a statute. We will touch elbows with the theologians as they view it, too, and if they will but allow us to hold that it has no significance to us save the significance that a passionate love without dignity always has, we will allow them to display any result they may bring up from their deep dives after truth. To me the Song of Songs is simply the purring of a healthy young barbaric chief to a sun-kissed shepherdess, and she, tender hearted, innocent and loving, purrs back in turn, as sun-kissed maidens ever have and I suppose ever will. This poem was composed, we have good reason to believe, fully three thousand years ago, yet its impressionistic picture of the ecstacy of youthful love is as charming and fresh as the color of a Titian ❧ ❧
¶ An out-of-door love, under the trees, where " the beams of our house are cedar, and our rafters of fir, and our bed is green," is the dream of all lovers and poets. Thus the story of Adam and Eve in the Garden of Eden, " naked and unashamed," has been told a score of times, and holds its place in all Sacred Writ. Shakespeare, in *As You Like It* and *The Tempest* shows the idea ❧ *Paul and Virginia* gives us a glimpse of the same thought; so does the *Emilius* of Rousseau, and more than once Browning suggests it in his matchless poems. Stevenson has touched deftly on the beautiful dream, and so have several other modern story-tellers ❧
¶ And surely the love of man and woman is not an ungodly thing, else why should God have made it? " God's dice are loaded," says Emerson, and further he adds, "All natural love between boy and girl, man and woman, is a lovely object, for the richness of its mental and spiritual possibilities are to us unguessed."

CHARACTER Is the Result Of Two Things— Mental Attitude and The way we spend Our Time.

SEX holds first place in the thought of God. Its glory pervades and suffuses all Nature. It is sex that gives the bird its song, the peacock his gorgeous plumage, the lion his mane, the buffalo his strength, and the horse his proud arch of neck and flowing tail. Aye, it is sex that causes the flowers to draw from the dull earth those delicate perfumes which delight the sense of smell; it is sex, and sex alone, that secures to them the dazzling galaxy of shapes and colors that reflect the Infinite ❧ The painter knows naught of color, and never could, save as the flowers lead the way. The flowers are at once the inspiration and the hopeless tantalization of the colorist and the perfumer: they can never hope to equal their matchless harmonies. And thus while we see that the sex principle is the animating factor for good in the animal and vegetable kingdoms, man, for the most part, deliberately flings away God's most precious gift. And he is made to answer for his folly with his spiritual life, for man, wise as he is, and pluming himself upon his ability to defeat his fellows, can not with impunity play his tricksy games with God. Savages at heart are boys of twelve or fourteen. Being devoid of pity they often visit on one another and on dumb animals the most shocking cruelties. A few years pass and your young barbarian is transformed into a gentleman—a man of fine feeling and tender sensibilities. The years keep going by and if love is thwarted, perverted or misplaced he passes into savagery again— no matter what his creed may be— controlled by fear and kept in check through awe of society and statute law. After marriage men no longer win their wives; they own them. And women, living in the blighting atmosphere of a continuous personal contact that knows no respite, drift off into apathetic, dull indifference. The wife becomes an animal; the husband a brute. The lively grace, the tender solicitude, the glowing animation, the alert intellect, the sympathetic heart, the aspiring spirit—where are these now? They are gone, gone like time gone—dead as the orange-buds that erstwhile opened their shell-like petals to catch the strains of the Wedding March—dead.

That men and women bring about their spiritual bankruptcy through gross ignorance, I have not the least doubt ᴤ And I am fully convinced that while

> RESPONSIBILITIES
> Gravitate to the Person
> Who can Shoulder them;
> Power flows to
> The Man
> Who Knows How.

woman has a sure and delicate insight into many things, in this particular she is singularly ignorant and wilful. The profound Doctor Charcot says: " I have known many men who endeavored to put their marital relations on a gentle, chivalric basis, but in nearly every case the wife interposed a tearful, beseeching veto, or else she filed a hot accusation of growing coldness that could only be disproved in one way. Virtuous women very seldom know anything of the psychology of love until it is too late to use the knowledge, and young women thinking they know already, can not be taught."

ᴤ ᴤ

THE position of woman as set forth in the Bible is one of slavery. The Pauline doctrine that women should learn in silence with all due subjection runs like a rotten thread through all the fabric of Christianity. The feature is pure Orientalism. And as the Second Commandment was the death of Art for a thousand years, so has the forced servility of woman held our civilization in thrall to a degree that no man can compute ᴤ The flaunting boast that woman owes her freedom to the Christian Religion is only advanced by ignorant and over-zealous people ᴤ ᴤ Honest scholarship knows otherwise The enslaving of women and holding them by law came in only when man was getting a bit " civilized." The pure, happy life of Nature would pale at the thought of abusing one's mate. Among wild animals the females are protected: no tigress is ever abused or imposed upon—in fact, she would not stand it. In a condition of untrammeled Nature, animals are eminently just and moral in their love-affairs. In a state of captivity, however, they will sometimes do very unbecoming things. The wild duck is monogamous; the proud and showy greenhead lives with his pretty, Quaker-gray partner in happy comradeship ❧ They are as true and sacred to each other as though they were married by a Methodist preacher and lived in Syracuse, New York, watched over by the police and looked after by the neighbors. But domesticate your ducks and at once a life of promiscuity begins ❧ ❧

Man, in a state of Nature, is true to his mate, but civilize him and perhaps he may be. " Civilized man is imperfectly monogamous," says Mr. Howells. From this we see that civilization for man acts like captivity on an animal. Is it the law of " Thou Shalt Not " that breeds immorality?

❧ ❧

IN the *Germania,* Tactus says that among the ancient Teutons the women were looked up to with a sort of sanctity ❧ They were the mothers of men yet to be, and were treated with delicacy and deference; and in the state councils their advice was always listened to. Between the man and his wife there existed a noble comradeship. Paganism in Scandinavia evolved a sturdier type of womanhood than Christianity has since ❧ In pagan Iceland women were treated better than we treat them today. The Icelanders recognized their intelligence and were in full possession of the truth that the children

CIVILIZATION is a way of doing things. Civilization turns on organization, and every man's success is a matter of rendering service for other people.

The savage succeeds by looking after Number One.

He grabs, appropriates and fights for the particular thing that he wants. If he succeeds in getting away without being killed, he calls it "success."

No man is ever fired from a factory. He fires himself when he no longer serves the institution.

So, in one sense, every man is an instrument of civilization. He is one of the tools with which the Deity works.

of a man and a woman who live on mental equality and who mutually respect and love each other, are far better than chance children born of slaves ❧ To this end, where love had died, they freely granted divorce when both parties desired it, and in all ways they sought to strengthen and encourage marriages prompted by love ❧ All this as opposed to the Oriental method of marrying for place and power, "unsight and unseen," which is even to this day carried on by the crowned heads, that lie uneasy. Christianity accepted the Semitic idea of woman's inferiority as a matter of course, emphasizing a strange delusion born of a sated appetite, that " through woman's fault man fell." ❧ Thus woman was blamed for the evil of the world, and we have even been guilty of speaking of the little souls fresh from God being born in sin ❧

❧ ❧

THE Jewish law required a woman to do penance and make sacrifice for her fault of bearing a child; all of which monstrous perversion of truth seems pitiable when compared with pagan Greece, where men uncovered their heads on meeting a woman with child, solemnly made way, feeling that they were in the sacred presence of the mystery of the Secret of Life. Birds are blessed with no such things as "rights." The male wins and holds his mate by the beauty that is manifest in his life, and by this alone.

But man vaunts the proud boast that he has found a better way. He calls his scheme "the crown of Christian civilization." As a matter of expediency I admit the plan has many advantages, but to say it is perfect is to reveal a dullard's mind. A higher civilization will build on the ruins of this, and a universal sublime attainment will yet come ❦ When it does arrive it must come as every sublime attainment now comes, and has ever come, through the conservation of an energy that the respectable mob millions now degrade. But as yet we are like the people of the Eastern plains who consider the chetah, that often devours them, a sacred thing.

❦ ❦

I HAVE no perfect panacea for human ills. And even if I had I would not attempt to present a system of philosophy between the soup and fish, but this much I will say: The distinctively modern custom of marital bundling is the doom of chivalry and death of passion. It wears all tender sentiment to a napless warp, and no wonder is it that the novelist, without he has a seared and bitter heart, hesitates to follow the couple beyond the church door. There is no greater reproach to our civilization than the sight of men joking the boy whose heart is pierced by the first rays of a life-giving sun, or of our expecting a girl to blush because she is twice God's child today she was yesterday.

GOD operates through man, and man's business is to be a good conductor of the divine current which we call Life.

Civilization is the efficient way of doing things.

Art is a beautiful way of doing things.

Economy is the cheapest way of doing things; and in order to do things rightly we must combine efficiency, industry, art, and economy, and cement all with love.

All modern efforts of commerce are in the line of making life pleasant, safe, agreeable and beautiful.

TO me the love of man for woman is as sacred a thing as Christ's love for the Church, and all of its attributes are as divine as any of the fantastic hazards of mind. Indeed, we would know nothing of love did we not see it manifest in man, and the only reason we believe in the love of God is because we find love on earth. The thought of the love of God can not be grasped in the slightest degree ❦ even as a working hypothesis, by a man who does not know human love. And fully believing that the mysterious desires of the body are as much emanations of the Eternal Spirit as the most altruistic of moral promptings, I feel that we are fully justified in waiving all explanations of the theologians, testing the poem before us with the emotions that we ourselves have felt.

❦ ❦

AND after all, have not those Wise Men of Old builded better than they knew? How else can we reach Heaven save through love? Who ever had a glimpse of the glories that lie beyond the golden portals save in loving moments? For disobedience the man and woman were put out of the Garden —they wandered far—and they can only return hand in hand! Yes, this we know: all of man's handiwork that finds form in beauty has its rise in the loves of men and women. Love is vital, love is creative, love is creation. It is love that shapes the plastic clay into forms divinely fair; love carves all statues, writes all poems, paints all the canvases that glorify the walls where color revels, sings all the songs that enchant our ears. Without love the world would only echo cries of pain, the sun would only shine to show us grief, each rustle of the wind among the leaves would be a sigh, and all the flowers fit only to garland graves. Love —that curious life-stuff—which holds within itself the spore of all mystic possibilities: that makes alive all dull wits, gives the coward heart and warms into being the sodden senses: that gives joy, and gratitude, and rest and peace: shall we not call thee God?

ALTHOUGH the two characters in this poem go back to times when the earth was young, we see that love had bestowed upon them a wonderful alertness, a clearness of insight and a closeness in observation such as love alone can give. The scene of the poem is laid in the wooded district of Northern Palestine, near the bride's home, where the bridegroom, after the manner of Oriental princes, is spending the Summer. According to all writers the lovers have been living together long enough so that all embarrassment has entirely disappeared. The bride has no coyness, affected or otherwise; they are thoroughly well acquainted. Their love is complete, and consequently their joy in all created things is supreme. This is shown in the fact that, although the poem is short, the constant reference to flowers, herbs, trees and landscape tells of walks and talks by light of moon, and of days when summer winds sang gentle love-ditties through the soughing branches. And as for flowers, they are essentially lovers' property. Many a good man and true can allow his thoughts to go back to a time when love made earth a vast garden of posies. Who but lovers ever botanize? Many is the troth that is plighted over the collector's drum, and indeed, I verily believe that God made flowers only that lovers might give suitable gifts. " Send me flowers, only flowers, a bouquet each morning that shall never cost more than a shilling," wrote the charming Peg Woffington to Sir Henry Vane. And when Mohammed said, " If I had but two loaves of bread, I would sell one of them and buy white hyacinths to feed my soul," the sentiment was expressed only for a woman's ear.

The inconsequential quality of the text and the charming inadvertence of the questions and answers are all very lover-like

TO lovers all things are of equal importance, and this is the highest sanity. In fact, Kant takes a long chapter to prove that nothing is trivial, nothing unimportant. Neither is there anything so vital that it should have an exclusive attention   Schleiermacher sums up the case by saying: " Nothing really matters, for all things are of equal value. So far as man is concerned, nothing is worthless, nothing important   Death is as good as life; sleep as activity; silence as speech."

On their walks hand in hand, by field and grove, over hill and dale, across moor and mountain, our lovers see to the north the towering heights of Lebanon and Amana with the opposing peaks of Senir and Hermon, the dens of lions there and the haunts of leopards; the branching cedars and the spreading cypresses; the bright, green, flower-enameled sward. They hear the gentle gurgle of running streams, and breathe deeply of the incense-laden breeze that fans their cheeks. Moving southward on the east of Jordan, they behold Gilead with its trees of healing balm, its flocks and herds feeding in rich valleys; the heights of Bithron, the district of Mahanaim, and toward the west, Carmel with its olive-groves, fish-pools and cultivated fields. Just beyond is Sharon, where roses clamber over old stone walls, its lowland rich with nodding blossoms, troops of gazelles feeding among the lilies, milk-white doves cooing and sporting by the water-side or hiding in the clefts of the rocks and in the turtle-haunted groves.

Then, turning to the south, our lovers tell of En-gedi with its palaces, gardens, and well-placed towers of the Royal City, henna plantations, and of Heshbon with its reservoirs; of the beautiful for situation; but the thought of the city does not satisfy, and they hasten back to the simple pleasures of country life, to the vineyard, the orchard, the open field, and the spreading forest, where all is so free and beautiful, yes, even if the foxes, the little foxes, do come and spoil the tender vines ✍ ✍

OUR lovers keep their feet on earth, even though their heads were sometimes in the clouds: they were not indifferent to good things eatable and drinkable, for they tell of going into the garden and tasting of pleasant fruits, of mandrakes, apples, grapes and palm-nuts, and reference is made to the juice of the pomegranate and the wine, the well-spiced wine. Yet they are not true children of Nature, for when the Summer is gone they intend to go to the city, and they anticipate it by references to the Tower of Lebanon that overlooked Damascus, and David's Tower in Jerusalem with its hanging shields, battlements and courtways. They tell of rings and jewels, signets and precious stones, crowns and necklaces, studs of silver and gold, palanquins and chariots, of rich furniture, palaces with pillars of marble, towers of ivory and of various kinds of spice and costly perfume ✍ ✍

❡ And because these luxurious things are mentioned, the Wise Men have never for a moment doubted that the lover was a king. Yet when we think of the lavish richness that love lends the imagination, there is no good reason why a pair of rustics having talked a bit with travelers and listened to the tales told by those who yearly went

---

ALL Good Men
And Women
Crave Comradeship;
But to have Any One
Accept your Word
As Holy Writ,
Is a Dire Calamity

---

to market, could not have reared the whole fabric right out of their hearts. I do not say positively that this was so, but like the preacher already referred to who has told of the Golden Calf, I say there is no proof that it was not. And now behold that while love is the mainspring of all animate Nature, and without it the earth would be shrouded in hopeless night; and while under its benign influence the human lover is transformed, and for him, for the first time the splendors of the earth are manifest and the wonders of the stars revealed— finding good in everything—possessing a key to the mysteries of the Universe that before he wist not of, right here Man halts and hesitates. He does not go on. Either his capacities limit, or else Society thrusts him back and our so-called Enlightened Age grins at him and says in hoarse guttural, "You are a fool!" and he, being one, believes it.

OF course, I do not pretend to fathom the meaning of all the inferences in this poem: doubtless much of it is just simple love-prattle that the lovers alone understood, for lovers dote on curious ways to communicate. Forsooth, I doubt not that it was lovers who first formed an alphabet! Lovers are hopelessly given over to mysteries and secrecy, to signs and omens and portents; they carry meanings further and spin out the thread of suggestion to a fineness that scowling philosophers can never follow.

AND thus I think that I am safe in saying the remarks in the poem addressed to third persons are merely monologue and interjectory exclamations, daydreams and love-musings, in which young men and maidens ever revel. No man can tell exactly what the twittering of the bluebirds means, nor can he logically interpret the chirping of the chickadees, and I am very sure that I can not explain the significance of the song the robin sings to his lost mate from the top of a tall poplar-tree when the sun goes down. But these things are very beautiful, and even when you think of them, perhaps when you are alone at the twilight-hour, the holy, unbidden tears will start ❧ ❧ ❧ It is pitiful, wondrous pitiful, that the Magic Wand of Nature suddenly breaks, and that doubt, conflict and division enter where unconscious harmony erstwhile prevailed! Today death stares and devils dance where but yesternoon white hyacinths bloomed to feed the lovers' souls. And the note of warning and last word of counsel that the priest gives is often summed up in the barren formula, " Bear and forbear." Do you say that I place too much importance on the Divine Passion? I say to you that man has not sufficient imagination to exaggerate the importance of Love. It is as high as the heavens, as deep as hell, as sublime as the stars and great as the

galaxy of worlds that fade on our feeble vision into mere Milky Ways. Love holds within her ample space all wrecks, all ruins, all grief, all tears; and all the smiles, and sunshine and beauty that mortals know are each and all her priceless gifts, and hers alone ❧ ❧ ❧ ❧

A LETTER from a friend — why it is a window flung open to the azure! What's that? — Oh, I see, you haven't any glad tidings and you owe a letter! Well, don't you remember that immortal letter written by Dr. Johnson to Mrs. Thrale? It seems the Doctor had made an engagement to breakfast with the Thrales. He could not go—was unavoidably detained. In truth, he was struck by paralysis the night before. His tongue was dumb and his body helpless ❧ But in the morning he could move the fingers of his right hand a little, and his head could think, so he wrote the lady a letter— a cheery letter of goodwill and explanation, tinted with soul, like a sea-shell.

GOD of Mercy, whose name is Love! Look Thou upon us and in pity pluck from our hearts that deep-rooted unbelief, and that miring uncleanliness of thought that causes us yet as a people to learn from the lips of vice and stupid ignorance our knowledge of the most vital and profound and potential of all human faculties! Through love—for there is no other way—lead us back to life and light, so that like the flowers, the tendrils of our hearts may draw from Thee those delicate perfumes of inspiration and those rich harmonies of color that alone can give beauty and proportion to our thoughts and acts ❧ ❧ We have wandered far, and know not the path, but hearken Thou unto us, for we thirst and are never quenched, our hearts hunger and are never satisfied, we cry and the heavens are but brass! God of Mercy, we beseech Thee to hear us, and in pity bring us back, through love, to Thee!

—From *The Song of Songs*.

HERE is the outline of a New Party. The truths it expresses are the oldest known to man ✤ ✤

It is to be called the Commonsense Party.

It is at once political, social, economical, ethical, commercial and religious ✤ ✤

Women and children are eligible and vote the same as men. No one is too old, and none too young to join. Your past record will not count against you, unless you are too boastful of it.

There are no rites of initiation! no goats to ride—and you can never be put out of the Commonsense Party unless you hand in your resignation to your cosmic self. Here is the basis of the Commonsense Party: Cheerfulness, Courtesy, Kindness, Industry, Health, Patience, Economy.

There are two ways to live—just two— one right way and one wrong. If your life benefits humanity you are on the right track; but if you are a bother, a worry, a menace and a burden to the world you are on the wrong route and will soon be " up against it."

Everybody and everything will have it in for you, because you will have it in for yourself. Then when you begin to repine, your bodily health will wane, and inertia and weakness will seize you hand and foot.

Weakness is the only slavery. Freedom is the supreme good—freedom from self-imposed limitation.

It is the law of nature that the world helps every person who is trying to help himself. If you want to be well and strong work with nature not against her, and she will make you well and strong and keep you so, barring collision with a benzine buggy. Nature is on your side,

THE great Big Black Things that have loomed against the horizon of my life, threatening to devour me, simply loomed and nothing more. The things that have really made me miss my train have always been sweet, soft, pretty, pleasant things of which I was not in the least afraid.

if you prove that you are on hers. We should all be in partnership with Nature.

❡ If you are sincerely trying to do your share of the necessary work of the world, Nature will reward you in honors, money and power.

Keep good-natured. Do not look for slights or insults. If you can't get the job you want, then take the one you can get. The only way to get a big place is to show that you are not ashamed to fill a little one.

The world needs more Commonsense Men and Women—just plain everyday folks who belong to the Commonsense Party ✤ The motto of the New Party is this: Do unto others as if you were the others ✤ ✤

Commonsense Culters, when in doubt, mind their own business and if they do not know what to say, do not say it. When they speak of their neighbors, they mention only the best concerning them, for Commonsense Culters know that none of us are so very good—certainly not good enough to be put in a glass case.

The Commonsense Man knows that he must get eight hours sleep; that he must not overeat; that he must give out good will if he is to get it back; that he must exercise in the open air every day if he is to keep well; and he realizes that if he does not keep well he will be more or less of a nuisance to everybody in his vicinity and that he will fail utterly in getting his share of Health, Wealth and Happiness.

❡ Commonsense Folks do not borrow trouble—or small sums of money, anticipating pay-day. They live within their means, pay their debts, accept what comes and are thankful that things are not worse ✤ ✤

N Lunnon, where live all sorts and conditions of men, once lived one Sir Walter Besant. Sir Walter often took a walk out through Hyde Park. At the entrance to the Park there used to crouch an old beggar woman, who held out a grimy hand and mumbled a woeful tale of a dead soldier husband and hungry mouths at home. Sir Walter always gave the woman a big copper penny as he passed. ❡ It grew into a habit.

After a few months Sir Walter and the old woman were on friendly terms: he nodded to her and spoke of the weather as he gave her the penny, and she showered on him blessings with a tongue needlessly glib.

One day as he gave her the penny he stopped to talk a moment, as he occasionally did, and the old woman handed him back the penny. "Guv me siller or nawthink," said the woman, "the idea of a gent like you guvin a poor old woman like me a dirty penny—guv me siller!"

The woman came close and stuck her face up close to his and waved her arms in threat.

Sir Walter started to go.

Her voice shot up into a cracked and vicious falsetto, she grabbed the lapel of his coat and screamed, "Guv me siller, you rascally rogue! Guv me what you owe me!"

Other beggars began to crowd around. Cabmen came running from across the road, pedestrians stopped. There was a mob gathering.

The woman made her appeal to the crowd. "Look at him now! Just look at him—he's the man that did it! He ruined me self-respeck—he ruined me self-respeck!"

The cabbies gathered close and began to mutter threats—they were clearly in sympathy with the old woman. "He ruined me self-respeck! He guv me dole—he guv me dole!"

Sir Walter reached into his pocket, and taking out a handful of small coin, scattered it among the crowd.

During the scrimmage he made his escape ❧ ❧

The next day Sir Walter took his walk in another direction.

Once after that in Whitechapel he was startled by a shrill voice, calling, "There he goes, there he goes,—the man wot ruined me self-respeck! Look at him, the fine rascal—he guv me dole—he guv me dole!"

Sir Walter saw a bus approaching, and barely reached the ladder and climbed to the top, when there was a gang of urchins and old women behind, pointing him out, thus—"That's 'im—the fine rogue wi' the long wiskers—the bloke in the 'igh 'at!"

Sir Walter's experience is not unique among philanthropists. Everybody who is anybody has gotten the hatred of people by trying to help them. Your enemies are those you have helped most. ❡ This sort of thing is what so often turns the milk of human kindness to bonny-clabber. But if we were strong enough we would never resent it; and Sir Walter, big, generous soul that he was, did not complain of his treatment—it was all a queer little comedy, with a touch of pathos in it, as all true comedy has, just as tragedy itself is flavored by comedy. The world is not made up of beggars, ingrates and fools—it is the patient workers and the active, kindly sympathetic men and women who hold the balance of things secure.

No man who does a good deed should expect gratitude. The reward for a good deed is in having done it. And possibly Sir Walter made a mistake ever to give that first penny to the old woman. His heart was right, but perhaps his act was wrong—who knows!

Anyway, keep sweet—in the main humanity wishes to do what is right. For a few days that old beggar assumed a place in Sir Walter's horizon quite out of keeping with her importance. But in this transaction you should pity the woman, not the man.

She forfeited the friendship of Sir Walter Besant.

God help all those, who through ignorance or folly, push from them the generous hearts that might benefit and bless!—*A Question of Charity.*

THE success of every great man hinges on one thing—to pick his men to do the work. The efforts of any one man count for so very little! It all depends on the selection and management of men to carry out his plans. In every successful concern, whether it be bank, school, factory, steamship company or railroad, the spirit of one man runs through and animates the entire institution ๑ The success or failure of the enterprise turns on the mental, moral and spiritual qualities of this one man. And the leader who can imbue an army of workers with a spirit of earnest fidelity to duty, an unswerving desire to do the thing that should be done, and always with animation, kindness and good-cheer, should be ranked with the great of the earth.

LIFE, now, is human service ๑ ๑ To deceive is to beckon for the Commissioner in Bankruptcy ๑ ๑ Nothing goes but truth ๑ ๑ We know this — because for over two thousand years we have been trying everything else. Academic education is the act of memorizing things read in books, and things told by college professors who got their education mostly by memorizing things

read in books and told by college professors ๑ ๑ It is easier to be taught than to attain. ¶ It is easier to accept than to investigate. It is easier to follow than to lead —usually ๑ ๑ Yet we are all heirs to peculiar, unique and individual talents, and a few men are not content to follow. These have usually been killed, and suddenly ๑ ๑ Now, our cry is, " Make room for individuality! "

๑ ๑

USUALLY the English language contains all of the words necessary to express an idea; but for the French phrase, " esprit de corps," we have no equivalent ๑ ๑ Get busy you word-mongers—here is your chance! The success of a business turns on its esprit de corps. There is an animating spirit or soul in every concern, otherwise it is a dead one ๑ Neither a commercial enterprise or an army can succeed as long as it is filled with strife, jealousy, doubt, fear and uncertainty ๑ ๑

I TRY to fix my thought on the good that is in every soul, and make my appeal to that. And the plan is a wise one, judged by results. It secures for you loyal helpers, worthy friends, gets the work done, aids digestion and tends to sleep o' nights. And I say to you that if you have never known the love, loyalty and integrity of a proscribed person, you have never known what love, loyalty and integrity are. I do not believe in governing by force, or threat, or any other form of coercion. I would not arouse in the heart of any of God's creatures a thought of fear, or discord, or hate, or revenge. I will influence men, if I can, but only by aiding them.

This esprit de corps is largely supplied by the leader. And a leader who can not inspire his corps with a spirit of victory has on his hands a force to feed, not one with which to fight. The Tenth Legion of Cæsar was invincible on account of its esprit de corps.

RUTH," says Doctor Charles W. Eliot, " is the new virtue." Let the truth be known about your business.

The only man who should not advertise is the one who has nothing to offer in way of service, or one who can not make good. ❡ All such should seek the friendly shelter of oblivion, where dwell those who, shrouded in Stygian shades, foregather gloom, and are out of the game ✧ ✧

Not to advertise is to be nominated for membership in the Down-and-Out Club ✧ ✧

About the best we can say of the days that are gone is that they are gone.

The Adscripts and the Adcrafts look to the East. They worship the rising sun. The oleo of authority does not much interest them. They want the Cosmic Kerosene that supplies the caloric.

A good Adcraftscripter is never either a philophraster or a theologaster—he is a pragmatist. He seeks the good for himself, for his clients, and for the whole human race.

The science of advertising is the science of psychology. And psychology is the science of the human heart.

The advertiser works to supply a human want; and often he has to arouse the desire for his goods. He educates the public as to what it needs, and what it wants, and shows where and how to get it ✧ ✧

The idea of the " ethical dentist " who refrains from advertising was originally founded on the proposition derived from the medicos that advertising was fakery. This view once had a certain basis in fact, when the only people who advertised were transients. The merchant who lived in a town assumed that every one knew where he was and what he had to offer. The doctor the same.

This no longer applies. We are living so fast, and inventing so fast, and changing so fast, and there are so many of us, that he who does not advertise is left to the spiders, the cockroaches and the microbes.

The fact that you have all the business you can well manage is no excuse now for not advertising ✧ ✧

TO supply a thought is mental massage; but to evolve a thought of your own is an achievement. Thinking is a brain exercise—and no faculty grows save as it is exercised.

✧ ✧

TO stand still is to retreat. To worship the god Terminus is to have the Goths and Vandals that skirt the borders of every successful venture pick up your Termini and carry them inland, long miles, between the setting of the sun and his rising. ❡ To hold the old customers, you must get out after the new. When you think you are big enough, there is lime in the bones of the boss, and a noise like a buccaneer is heard in the offing.

The reputation that endures, or the institution that lasts, is the one that is properly advertised.

The only names in Greek History that we know are those which Herodotus and Thucydides graved with deathless styli ✧ ✧

The men of Rome who lived and trod the boardwalk are those Plutarch took up and writ their names large on human hearts. All that Plutarch knew of Greek heroes was what he read in Herodotus. ❡ All that Shakespeare knew of Classic Greece and Rome and the heroes of that far-off time is what he dug out of Plutarch's *Lives*. And about all that most people now know of Greece and Rome they got from Shakespeare.

Plutarch boomed his Roman friends and matched each favorite with some Greek, written of by Herodotus. Plutarch wrote of the men he liked, some of whom we know put up good mazuma to cover expenses ✧ ✧

✧ ✧

Our greatest deeds we do unknowingly.

UT of all the Plenipotentiaries of Publicity, Ambassadors of Advertising, and Bosses of Press Bureaus, none equals Moses, who lived fifteen centuries before Christ. Moses appointed himself ad-writer for Deity, and gave us an account of Creation, from the personal interviews. And although some say these interviews were faked, this account has been accepted for thirty-five centuries ॐ ॐ

Moses wrote the first five books of the Bible, and this account includes a record of the author's romantic birth and of his serene and dignified death. Moses is the central figure, after Yahweh, in the whole write-up ॐ ॐ

Egyptian history makes not a single mention of Moses or the Exodus, and no record is found of the flight from Egypt save what Moses wrote ॐ ॐ

At best it was only a few hundred people who hiked, but the account makes the whole thing seem colossal and magnificent. And best of all, the high standard set has been an inspiration to millions to live up to the dope.

The phrase, " The Chosen People of God," was a catch-phrase unrivaled ॐ Slogans abound in Moses that have been taken up by millions on millions.

When Moses took over the Judaic account, Jehovah was only a tutelary or tribal god. He was simply one of the many. He had at least forty strong competitors, The Egyptians had various gods; the Midianites, Hittites, Philistines, Amorites, Ammonites had at least one god each.

Moses made his god supreme, and all other gods were driven from the skies. What turned the trick?

I 'll tell you—the writings of Moses, and nothing else. So able, convincing, direct and inclusive were the claims of Moses that the world was absolutely won by them.

In the Mosaic Code was enough of the saving salt of commonsense to keep it alive. It was a religion for the now and here. The Mosaic laws are sanitary laws, and work for the positive, present good of those who abide by them.

℄ It is not deeds or acts that last— it is the written record of those deeds and acts ॐ It was not the life and death of Jesus that fixed His place as the central figure of His time— and perhaps of all time—it was what Paul and certain unknown writers who never even saw Him claimed and had to say in written words ॐ ॐ

VERY life is its own excuse for being, and to deny or refute the untrue things that are said of you is an error of judgment. All wrong recoils upon the doer, and the man who makes wrong statements about others is himself to be pitied, not the man he vilifies. It is better to be lied about than to lie. At the last no one can harm us but ourselves.

ॐ ॐ

ORATIUS still stands at the bridge, because a poet placed him there ॐ ℄ And Paul Revere still rides a-down the night giving his warning cry, because Longfellow set the meters in a gallop ॐ ℄ Across the waste of waters the enemy calls upon Paul Jones to surrender, and the voice of Paul Jones echoes back, " Goddam, your souls to Hell—we have not yet begun to fight! " And the sound of the fearless voice has given courage to countless thousands to snatch victory from the jaws of defeat.

In Brussels there is yet to be heard a sound of revelry by night, only because Byron told of it.

Commodore Perry, that rash and inpulsive youth of twenty-six, never sent that message, " We have met the enemy and they are ours," but a good reporter did, and the reporter's words live, while

Perry's died on the empty air   Lord Douglas never said,

" The hand of Douglas is his own,
  And never shall in friendship grasp,
  The hand of such as Marmion clasp."

Sir Walter Scott made that remark on white paper with an eagle's quill, and schoolboys' hearts will beat high as they scorn the offered hand on Friday afternoons, for centuries to come.

¶ Virginius lives in heroic mold, not for what he said or did but for the words put into his mouth by a man who pushed what you call a virile pen and wrote such an ad for Virginius as he could never have written for himself.

Andrew J. Rowan carried the Message to Garcia, all right, but the deed would have been lost in the dustbin of Time, and quickly, too, were it not for George H. Daniels, who etched the act into the memory of the race, and fixed the deed in history, sending it down the corridors of Time with the rumble of the Empire State Express, so that today it is a part of the current coin of the mental realm, a legal tender wherever English she is spoke.

      ⋙ ⋙

ALL literature is advertising. And all genuine advertisements are literature   The author advertises men, times, places, deeds, events and things. His appeal is to the universal human soul. If he does not know the heart-throbs of men and women, their hopes, joys, ambitions, tastes, needs and desires, his work will interest no one but himself and his admiring friends.

Advertising is fast becoming a fine art. Its theme is Human Wants, and where, when and how they may be gratified. It interests, inspires, educates—sometimes amuses—informs and thereby uplifts and benefits, lubricating existence and helping the old world on its way to the Celestial City of Fine Minds.

      ⋙ ⋙

We are moved only by the souls that have suffered and the hearts that know; and so all art that endures is a living, quivering cross-section of life.

ONLY character counts   And what is character?

Well, first, character is a matter of habits. The young man or woman who, working all day in a shop or factory, will get a certain amount of outdoor exercise and then buckle down to some course of intellectual improvement for one hour out of the twenty-four, is going to become a distinguished person.

But to slide, glide, drift, loll, dawdle, with no definite objective point in mind, is to arrive at the point of Nowhere and to have your craft lie hopelessly becalmed on Mud Flats. Then is your name Mudsocks

Walk in the open air, dig in the garden, play ball, then buckle down to half an hour at the lessons, and you are bound to be a winner

Continually comes the tramp of marching feet

" What is this army? " you say.

It is the youth of the land. They are arriving, arriving!

Babies grow into children, children into youth, youth into men and women

¶ The mass of humanity is a marching mass—steady, irresistible, onward and upward they come!

There are more of us on this old earth than ever before.

Life is complex, difficult. The struggle exists as it never has before.

We need all the equipment we can get.

¶ But in spite of numbers, opportunities were never so great as they are today

There is no such thing as complete success. After every achievement comes the voice, " Arise, and get thee hence, for this is not thy rest! "

So we never arrive, but always we work, we struggle, we strive, and this continual endeavor is all there is of life.

But when life is methodized, when we work, study, play and laugh, flavoring all with love, we have found the key to the situation.

      ⋙ ⋙

Respectability is the dickey on the bosom of civilization.

HE laws of health are very simple, and for the most part are understood by all people of average intelligence ᕲ ᕲ ᕲ

One reason why we do not all have good health is not because we are ignorant, but because inertia has us by the foot. The trouble is in our heads—we lack will ᕲ ᕲ

If a high degree of health were the rule, instead of the exception, we would cease to talk about it. We discuss health, because pallor, langor, and breaths that almost derail trolley-cars ride, Godiva-like, adown the times, and put us on the binkereens.

In one respect at least we have made head. It is no longer necessary to order people to keep personally clean—humanity's hide is now daily soaped, soaked and scrubbed. Whereas, in the days of Good Queen Bess, who they say was not so very good, the courtier who took a bath in his altogether between November and May was unknown.

Even fifty years ago, the man who ordered a bath at a tavern was regarded as reckless of both health and money. It was an event! The water had to be heated in the kitchen and carried in buckets to his room, and a porter stood by to see that the carpets and plaster did not suffer. The danger of catching cold through bathing, except in hot weather, was considered very great ᕲ Scientific plumbing is less than forty years old. The famous Fifth Avenue Hotel did not have a single room with bath attached when it was built ᕲ Now everybody bathes, and we have ceased to talk about it. Will the time come when we will cease to advocate outdoor exercise, deep breathing and kind thoughts? I hope so.

ᕲ ᕲ

Caste is a Chinese Wall that shuts people in as well as out ᕲ ᕲ

AY it please the Court, I arise to present certain reasons why judgment should not be passed upon humanity. The time has not yet arrived when it is fair, reasonable, proper or right to judge my kind. Man is not yet created—he is only in process. I have a few excuses to make for him.

Emerson says, "I have not yet seen a man." That is to say, he had never seen a man as excellent as the man he could imagine. And he thought the man that one man could create in imagination would some day become an actual, living reality. Before the act comes the thought; before the building is completed, we draw the plans. This is true in all our activities—we have the feeling, the desire, the idea, the thought, and after this comes the deed. So Deity has the desire for a perfect man, and the universe is working toward that achievement ᕲ ᕲ

All the men we now see are fractional men—parts of men. To get a really great man we have to take the virtues of a score of men and omit the faults.

The great man now is only supremely great after he is well dead, or to people who see him from a distance. To those who have to live with him he is at times more or less of a trial—a tax upon the patience and good nature of his friends.

ᕲ ᕲ

CONDUCT, culture and character are graces that go through life hand in hand, never separate or alone. Happy is he who has more than a speaking acquaintanceship with each.

FOR the individual, Nature has little thought—her care is for the race. What her intentions are we think we, in part, know. She desires to incarnate herself in the form of perfect men and women. The reason we know this is because it is the chief instinct in the minds of the best and strongest men and women to grow, to evolve, to become. After every achievement comes discontent. After every mountain scaled there are heights beyond. Always and forever we are lured and urged on. Hope, prayer, desire, aspiration are yearnings for perfection. For many this hope of perfection is centered in their children; and with all, in moments of calm, the needle points toward the North. Deity creates through man—we are the Divine Will ᔈ ᔈ ᔈ ᔈ

THE old idea, now happily discarded by all thoughtful people, that man loves darkness rather than light is a libel on the race and a denial of the wisdom and goodness of the Supreme Intelligence ᔈ Men have sought to enslave other men, and these slaves struggling with their gyves and fetters have done many things so strange, erratic and violent that it looked like self-destruction, but so far as we know the life of the present race, there has ever been progress and a movement forward. The normal man hungers and yearns after righteousness ᔈ It is, of course, admitted that progress has often taken a zigzag course, as ships tack and beat up against the wind at sea, and at times humanity's craft has been becalmed, and we seemingly had lost our reckoning; but such periods of drifting have been followed by a lifting of the fog. At such times the forward movement of civilization has been true and rapid ᔈ ᔈ

GOD is good, there is no devil but fear, nothing can harm us, the Universe is planned for our good! Ah! a new thought — all life is one, and we are brothers to the birds and trees. Our life is a necessary and integral part of the Energy that turns the wheeling planets, and holds the world in space.

All life is one—God is on our side. We are freed from fear, emancipated from apprehension, and filled with kindness toward every living thing because all is ours, and we are a part of all we hear and feel and see.

Circulation is increased, secretions flow, eyes brighten, beautiful thoughts animate us — saved by an idea. New thoughts are hygienic. Love is a tonic.

HE other day I wrote to a banker-friend inquiring as to the responsibility of a certain person. The answer came back, thus: "He is a Hundred-Point man in everything and anything he undertakes." I read the telegram and then pinned it up over my desk where I could see it. That night it sort of stuck in my memory. I dreamed of it. The next day I showed the message to a fellow I know pretty well, and said, "I'd rather have that said of me than to be called a great this or that."
Oliver Wendell Holmes has left on record the statement that you could not throw a stone on Boston Common without caroming on three poets, two essayists, and a playwright ᔈ ᔈ
Hundred-Point men are not so plentiful ᔈ ᔈ
A Hundred-Point man is one who is true to every trust; who keeps his word; who is loyal to the firm that employs him; who does not listen for insults nor look for slights; who carries a civil tongue in his head; who is polite to strangers, without being "fresh;" who is considerate towards servants; who is moderate in his eating and drinking; who is willing to learn; is cautious and yet courageous ᔈ ᔈ
Hundred-Point men may vary much in

ability, but this is always true—they are safe men to deal with, whether drivers of drays, motormen, clerks, cashiers, engineers or presidents of railroads so
¶ Paranoiacs are people who are suffering from fatty enlargement of the ego. They want the best seats in the synagogue, they demand bouquets, compliments, obeisance, and in order to see what the papers will say next morning, they sometimes obligingly commit suicide.

so so

THE paranoiac is the antithesis of the Hundred-Point man. The paranoiac imagines he is being wronged, and that some one has it in for him, and that the world is down on him. He is given to that which is strange, peculiar, uncertain, eccentric and erratic.
The Hundred-Point man may not look just like all other men, or dress like them, or talk like them, but what he does is true to his own nature so He is himself.
¶ He is more interested in doing his work than in what people will say about it. He does not consider the gallery. He acts his thought, and thinks little of the act so so
I never knew a Hundred-Point man who was not brought up from early youth to make himself useful and to economize in the matter of time and money.
Necessity is ballast.
The paranoiac, almost without exception, is one who has been made exempt from work. He has been petted, waited upon, coddled, cared for, laughed at and chuckled to so so
The excellence of the old-fashioned big family was that no child got an undue amount of attention. The antique idea that the child must work for his parents until the day he was twenty-one was a deal better for the youth than to let him get it into his head that his parents must work for him so so
Nature intended that we should all be poor—that we should earn our bread every day before we eat it.

so so

WHEN you find the Hundred-Point man you will find one who lives like a person in moderate circumstances, no matter what his finances are. Every

man who thinks he has the world by the tail and is about to snap its demnition head off for the delectation of mankind, is unsafe, no matter how great his genius in the line of specialties so
¶ The Hundred-Point man looks after just one individual, and that is the man under his own hat; he is one who does not spend money until he earns it; who pays his way; who knows that nothing is ever given for nothing; who keeps his digits off other people's property. When he does not know what to say, why, he says nothing, and when he does not know what to do, does not do it. We should mark on moral qualities, not merely mental attainment or proficiency, because in the race of life only moral qualities count. We should rate on judgment, application and intent. Men who, by habit and nature, are untrue to a trust are dangerous just in proportion as they are clever. I would like to see a university devoted to turning out safe men instead of merely clever ones so so
How would it do for a college to give one degree, and one only, to those who are found to be worthy—the degree of H. P.?
Would it not be worth striving for, to have a college president say to you, over his own signature: " He is a Hundred-Point man? "

so so

God, too, is only in process. He is getting an education out of His work, at His work.

so so

THE Reverend Sydney Smith once made up a list of things that we could do without. It will be remembered that he finally ended by saying we could eliminate everything but cooks.
Yet Charles Lamb used to go without food in order to save money to buy books. And Andrew Lang said that if there were no good books in Heaven he would not want to go there.
Also, we find several modern cults founded on the idea of eliminating cooks by eating raw food.
I know a man who consumes only nuts, raisins, prunes and milk, and he seems to thrive on the diet.

Our ancestors only a few hundred years ago ate their meat raw and worshiped fire ♠ ♠

Nevertheless, in spite of these quillets and quibbles, the fact remains that Sydney Smith is right—the person who prepares food for the people is a necessity ♠ ♠

Let us define a bit: The cook is the individual who prepares our food for us. ❧ But before food is prepared it must be secured, and so we must have the farmer who evolves the food out of the ground ♠ ♠

In the preparation of hare-soup, the first move, we are told, is to "catch your hare," to which the would-be joker has written an advertisement for a certain firm that supplies hair-dye and explains, "The first requisite in dyeing your hair is to secure your hair."

♠ ♠

HIS country is suffering from over-legislation. Our reformers seem to have small faith in natural law. They have an eczema for regulating things. When they realize on their little thousand-dollar policies, and they reach another world, they will want to seize the pitchfork and run the place to suit themselves ♠ ♠

What this country really will have to do is to reform its reformers. We live in a marvelous country, and in a marvelous time. Let the age unfold—let the times blossom—let humanity grow and expand. ❧ The Dark Ages were a time when by over-government human evolution was absolutely blocked. Let us cease being brakemen, and give conductors and engineers a chance. The country is all right —or will be as soon as we repeal a few silly laws and give God's law of gravitation a chance ♠ ♠

Cease setting your brake against the power! ♠ ♠

♠ ♠

YES, yes, I am a Zionist. I long to be a citizen of the Eternal City of Fine Minds. I would belong to that brotherhood which cultivates the receptive heart and the generous mind. My neighbors are often hundreds of miles apart. They are the men and women of earth who think and feel and dream, and ask themselves each morning, "What is Truth?" We think better of Pilate for his question. To meet a god face to face and not ask would have betokened complete imbecility. But Jesus did not answer. He could not. All truth is relative, and that message which comes out of the great Silence to you can only be interpreted to another who, too, has listened and heard. Yes, let us all be Zionists and dwell in the New Jerusalem of Celestial Truth ♠ ♠

♠ ♠

If calamity, disgrace or poverty come to your friends—then is the time they need you.

♠ ♠

Reformers are those who educate people to appreciate the things they need ♠ ♠

♠ ♠

OLSTOY somewhere tells of a priest who saw a peasant plowing and asked him this question, "If you knew you were going to die this night, how would you spend the rest of the day?" The peasant thought a moment and answered, "I would plow." A man of the true type, if he had but a day to live, would not change his occupation. Every day he is preparing to live; and men who are prepared to live are prepared to die ♠ ♠

In family life the average man is apt to treat every other woman with more courtesy than he does his wife, and other people's children with more consideration than his own. A man in his home may be an absolute tyrant, and at the same time be known to the world as a "good fellow." Communism has no more use for the tyrant than it has for the good fellow. In family life, usually, a man sees too much of his family and they see too much of him; and society does not see enough of the good fellow with his antique brass, if he would be well squelched.

The good fellow is one who bothers the busy; deals in pretense and hypocrisy; encourages the idle—assuming both virtues and vices. He has not the courage to live his life, and so has neither friends nor foes. His praise and blame are alike futile, and his lavish spending and "treating" are at the expense of some one else —he lives to impress the waiters. Such a one may deceive a society made up of individuals, but he can not deceive a community ❧ There his measure is quickly taken. He does not have to be sent away—he goes. In a community, an ounce of loyalty is worth a pound of cleverness ❧ ❧

No coin of conduct is current in a community but sterling honesty— truthfulness alone is legal tender and passes at par ❧ Apologies and explanations are never in order; your life must proclaim itself and must be its own excuse for being. And while all faults are forgiven in the man of perfect candor, the smile that does not spring from the soul will transform itself into a grimace ❧ A community can not be deceived. Only those who deal in deception can be duped. William Penn once asked a man who was much given to drawing the long bow, " Why do you not lie to me?" And the liar answered, " What 's the use ? "

In Athens of old the criterion or standard of art sprang from the most competent; so in a community the criterion of conduct is formed by the best. The highest minds fix the standard, and the lesser ones try to adapt themselves to it; but there is an unseen mark which, if they drop below, eliminates them absolutely from the community.

❧ ❧

Let this be a world of friends! ❧ ❧

O not go out of your way to do good whenever it comes your way. Men who make a business of doing good to others are apt to hate others in the same occupation. Simply be filled with the thought of good, and it will radiate—you do not have to bother about it, any more than you need trouble about your digestion.

Do not be disturbed about saving your soul—it will be saved if you make it worth saving. Do your work. Think the good. And evil, which is a negative condition, shall be swallowed up by good.

Think no evil; and if you think only good, you will think no evil.

Life is a search for power. To have power you must have life, and life in abundance. And life in abundance comes only through great love.

❧HE question may here be asked, " Why may not a special community be formed where the standard of conduct is low, and so make the good fellows, idlers and rogues feel at home? "

❧ And the answer is this: A community is only possible where truth and loyalty abide. Weakness never formed a community and never can. And if it could the institution would not hold together a day ❧ In weak and vicious people there is no attractive force, no coalescing principle ❧ The weak pull apart—they thwart, retard and impede one another ❧ They are like drowning people—they clutch and strangle one another. A goodly degree of integrity disinterestedness and unselfishness are demanded even to start a community, and the more of these qualities you can get the more enduring the institution. A partnership of weak men does not give strength. Weakness multiplied by weakness equals naught. Two weak people will not make a strong team. Strength multiplied by strength gives strength. Weak men need a monarch, and defectives need a priest. They want some one to direct—to think for them ❧ But the enlightened cooperate, and in pooling their best in thought and effort they reach a degree of power and excellence that can be obtained in no other way.—*The Good Fellow.*

❧ ❧

It requires a Pharaoh to develop a Moses, just as it took a George the Third to evolve George Washington. Blessed be stupidity!

HERE is an honest farmer in East Aurora who has over ten thousand dollars in the bank. All farmers in East Aurora are honest, but not all farmers in East Aurora have ten thousand dollars in the bank. In fact, this is the only farmer in New York State, of whom I know, who has ten thousand dollars in the bank. This man placed the money there thirty years ago, the funds being secured, mostly, from the sale of logs and lumber that he sold off his broad acres.

This farmer, and his father before him, owned a very large tract of pine forest, and they cut the timber off all of it, except ten acres that covered the shores of a beautiful little lake, near the village.

❡ This pine grove was the only bit of primeval pine forest left in this part of the country. It was as charming a piece of the handiwork of God as one ever saw.

❡ To walk out there on a summer's day, recline on the soft pine needles, watch the gently swaying branches overhead, breathe the aromatic flavor of the pines, and listen to the lullaby of the breeze, was a blessing and a benediction ❧ ❧ You felt glad you were alive, and your heart was lifted in a prayer of thankfulness ❧ ❧

One day a man came along and said to the honest farmer who owned the grove, "Them 'ere pine trees is about right to cut, and I'll give you two hundred dollars cash for 'em just as they stand— it's now or never, take it or leave it."

❡ Now, the farmer had ten thousand dollars in the bank, he was owing no money, he owned six hundred acres of land that brought him all the income he needed, but the offer of two hundred cash was more than he could stand ❧ He sold the beautiful pine-trees, the last of their race.

The man who bought them moved in his portable sawmill, and cut them down.

❡ The logs were sawed up and the lumber placed in piles ready to ship.

It was in the Autumn and everything was dry. And God caused the winds to blow, and tumble-weeds rolled in big piles up against the lumber, and in some mysterious way fire came and in a single night all that lumber was reduced to ashes—that is to say, was burned. Now, the party who owned the portable sawmill had not paid the honest farmer, claiming he could not pay him until he got his money for the lumber.

And the lumber being burned the sawmill man vamoosed, and the farmer got no money ❧ ❧

And, behold, one Ali Baba, a blasphemous man with chin whiskers who lives in East Aurora, when he heard that the lumber was burned, said, "I'm damn glad of it."

As for myself, I never swear, but when Ali Baba made that remark I simply added, "So am I."

Today there quivers and quavers about the streets of this village the honest old farmer, yammering because he lost his two hundred dollars. He never says a word about the grove. But the beautiful pine-trees are gone—gone forever ❧ ❧

❧ ❧

E take an interest in the lives of others, because when we think of another we always imagine our relation to him. Then, too, other lives are to a degree repetitions of our own life. There are certain things that come to every one, and the rest we think might have happened to us, and may yet. So, as we read, we unconsciously slip into the life of the other man and confuse our identity with his. To put ourselves in his place is the only way to understand and appreciate him and so enrich our own lives. It is imagination that gives us this faculty of transmigration of souls; and to have imagination is to be universal; not to have it is to be provincial. ❧ ❧

❧ ❧

THE habit of borrowing small sums of money—anticipating pay-day— is a pernicious practice and breaks many a friendship. It is no kindness to loan money to a professional borrower ❧ ❧

❧ ❧

There are six requisites in every happy marriage. The first is Faith and the remaining five are Confidence.

HEN I speak well, as I occasionally do, I know a dozen words ahead just exactly how these words are to be expressed. Last week at Pittsburgh I reached a point in my lecture where I usually give a certain quotation, and this quotation was so familiar to me that I neglected to formulate it in my mind before voicing it. In other words I ran right up on it a-tilt, without taking a good look at it, and when I got to it I was looking down in the auditorium at a big hat all covered with nodding roses, the whole as big as a bushel basket so And for the life of me the quotation would not come at my bidding so I grasped for it in mid-air, gasped, coughed— it was no use. The circuit between me and the listeners was broken. The audience was away off there, a goggle-eyed, staring monster, spread out over a hundred feet—just staring at me, little me dressed in black, standing all alone on a big platform.

The room seemed to be teetering up and down, and then it began to swirl. ❧ I dived for my quotation, but brought up the wrong one, when from the back of the room came a stentorian voice, thus: " Two Strikes! "

There was a grim silence, just as you see a gun fired from a mile away and then hear the report. Then came a wild burst of applause, and laughter from the audience, and in it I, too, joined. The self-appointed umpire had saved the day. I seized the quotation firmly by the collar, and all the rest of my speech as well. And the lesson taught me was this: Don't be too sure so so

NATURALLY, every man thinks well of himself. If no one ever told us that we were worms of the dust, we would never come to the conclusion ourselves. If no one ever told us that we were "lost," we would never have guessed it. We naturally carry our chins in and the crowns of our heads high. Fear is fostered by those who would control us.

GREAT men are not so great as we think them, and dull people are not quite so dense as they seem. It is really a question in my mind whether the Great Man ever existed. Seen at an angle across the distance, so the light strikes on a certain facet of his being, we say the man is brilliant so In his own household he is probably considered something else so so He is great to us only because we do not know him. He does a few things well, but special talent in any direction is purchased with a price. If you have much skill in certain lines, you are lacking in other directions. Like a chain, a man's real strength is no greater than his weakest part.

so so

THE average man believes a thing first, and then searches for proof to bolster his opinion. Every observer must have noticed the tenuous, cobweb quality of reasons that are deemed sufficient to the person who thinks he knows or whose interests lie in a certain direction. The limitations of men seem to make it necessary that pure truth should come to us through men who are stripped for eternity. Kant, the villager who never traveled more than a day's walk from his birthplace, and Coleridge, the homeless and houseless aristocrat, with no selfish interests in the material world, viewed things without prejudice so so

so so

THE Brotherhood of Consecrated Lives admits all who are worthy; and all who are excluded, exclude themselves. If your life is to be a genuine consecration, you must be free. Only the free man is truthful.

EDUCATION up to the time of Friedrich Froebel was the evolution of intellect so so Froebel held that education for character was the only education worth striving for.

Now comes Stanley Hall, who not only endorses Froebel's dictum, but declares that the first aim in the education of both boys and girls should be in the line of enabling the pupil to earn his own living so so

And to earn your own living you must be able to serve humanity.

Society is a vast interchange of service through labor, ideas and commodities.

❡ Now before you can wait on others you must be able to wait on yourself.

❡ And before you can wait on yourself, you have to decide upon what should be done, and what you want to do.

"The ability to make a decision—to think—then decide—is the very first element in pedagogy," said Froebel.

❡ Again he says to mothers, "Do not decide everything for your children. You can not live their lives for them; and life consists in making decisions—clinging to the good and rejecting the wrong." so so

So if life consists, as Froebel says—and it seems to me that he is right—in making decisions, women should be encouraged to express their preferences.

so so

THE Suffrage for woman means freedom—freedom from her own limitations. It means a better education of women. And woman needs education for three reasons:

First, for her own happiness and satisfaction so so

Second, so she may be a better mother, and add her influence to racial education so so

Third, so that she may be a better companion for man, for all strong men are educated by women.

so so

Woman's inaptitude for reasoning has not prevented her from arriving at truth; nor has man's ability to reason prevented him from floundering in absurdity. Logic is one thing and commonsense another.

OPINIONS are much divided in East Aurora whether Ali Baba is a genius or a fool. It has always been so. Socrates did not stand very well, according to all reports, in Athens. But Baba excels Socrates in that he does something beside dream and talk philosophy. Baba, like Socrates, can converse with you on any subject, and has an opinion ready on any theme you care to mention. Usually he takes the contrary side, and is " agin it," no matter what you bring up.

This habit of " argufying " is one that he acquired full half a century ago. I think it was forced upon him by the determined efforts on the part of his parents and elders in early life to "convert him." so so

so so

WHEN going to the Grocery or Postoffice, if Baba does not hitch up the pony to the wagon, he pushes the wheelbarrow. There may be something to bring back, you know so Then the wheelbarrow is the symbol of industry and civilization. Baba hates a shiftless man. He believes in doing something: he is always busy so The wheelbarrow takes the curse off—and if he wishes to rest, and the Baba, being human, has to rest occasionally, the wheelbarrow is handy so so

The matter is too personally poignant to discuss directly, so in all the twenty-seven years of our intimate acquaintanceship I have never brought the matter squarely up. Still, when you are in perfect rapport with your friend there really is no need of discussing everything—you know his mind.

And so on this wheelbarrow question I must admit that Ali Baba is self-deceived, and a hypocrite if you will have it so. It is the one weak point in his character, and my affection for the man is so great that I never have gone into the psychology of the wheelbarrow in any of our very many logical lucubrations so so

If Ali Baba wants very much to go down to Hamlin's barn in the middle of the forenoon and " see a feller," he throws a shovel or gunny sack into the trusty wheelbarrow and starts down the middle of the street. To deliberately leave his work, to shirk duty, and go to Hamlin's barn merely to tell some horse-driver a story that has come into his head—no sir! Baba would never do it. But through a self-imposed hypnotism he is led into the belief that he has to go down that way after some sand for the baby to play in, or for some particularly well rotted compost that he has located, for the plants, and of course as he has to go by Hamlin's barn, there's no harm in stopping in a minute ❧ ❧

❡ As the Baba goes trundling his wheelbarrow down the road, he bestows civilities on all he meets—men, women and children.

❡ Usually he goes scarcely a block before he sees some wee toddler that wants to ride, and so he tenderly lifts the little one into the wheelbarrow and goes on his way, scattering jokes and lively repartee on all sides. I have many a time seen him take a baby out of a fond mother's arms to give it a ride in the wheelbarrow; and other village women seeing him go by, often explain, "Oh, how lucky! here comes Ali Baba—he'll give us a lift!"

And so the Baba is called over and delivers a bag of meal, a trunk, a rocking chair, or anything up to a piano, to some particular place, and is rewarded with smiles, kind words, a piece of pie (his weakness for pie being an open secret), or a quarter of a dollar, as the case may be. On these little hatched-up wheelbarrow excursions Ali Baba is often called upon to beat a carpet, put up a stove or give a lift on getting a trunk upstairs. He is ever obliging, and the task is always lightened by many little

pleasantries, thus: ❡ "Hello! Baba, give us a lift on the cook-stove, please!"

"I can't," says Baba wearily, as he stops and sits down in the wheelbarrow —"I'm not feelin' well, myself!" ❧ ❧

"What's the matter—no appetite?"

"That's it, my appesy is all upset—still I s'pose I got to help you tho'—how's the old woman?"

"Oh, she's all right." ❧ ❧

"Jerush with you yet?"

"Yes." ❧ ❧

"Well, Jerush is the kind for me!" All the time Jerusha is watching out of an upstairs window, and now calls down threats in a shrill voice at old Ali Baba ❧ ❧ Baba affects surprise, and says something about not being as young

O undertake to supply people with a thing you think they need, but which they do not want, is to have your head elevated on a pike, and your bones buried in the Potter's Field. But wait, and the world will yet want the thing it needs, and your bones may then become sacred relics.

as he once was, or all the beauty in this town wouldn't be going to seed, etc. ❧ After the task of lifting the stove is done, Ali Baba usually emerges from the door suddenly, chased by Jerusha with a soapy dishcloth or a broom, amid loud laughter from others of the household. What the particular offense is that he has committed can only be guessed—let us hope it is nothing worse than purloining a piece of pie, or grabbing into a pan of Jerusha's cookies.

"Well, so long, Jerushy," calls Baba as he starts off with the wheelbarrow, "I'd really like to stay, but can't do it you know—I'm a married man!" This last in a voice that can be heard by all the neighbors. All laugh loudly and Baba joins in the chorus.

And so he continues his triumphant march down the street to Hamlin's stock-farm ❧ ❧

A carping quibbler might say that if we hire this man by the day, and he leaves his duties to go off and gossip, he is inflicting on his employer a wrong.

Such an argument has no basis in truth. The fact is, Ali Baba never leaves urgent work to go off and visit. He is always around at half-past five in the morning, winter or summer, and he works until nine at night. He knows neither Sunday nor legal holiday, and if a horse or cow is sick, he 'll stay all night. And often, when thunderstorms come up in the night, he will come over to Roycroft House and go through every room, shutting down windows. He may go around and tuck the children in, see that the visitors are comfortable, or turn down the lights a little, and always there is this earnest, loyal desire to help lubricate the wheels of existence.

Such cheerful service surely deserves an hour's holiday now and then, and if Ali Baba trundles his wheelbarrow over to the Grocery when he has nothing to go for, I 'm not the one to say him nay. ¶ Ali Baba being a Corner Grocery Infidel, may not go to Heaven, but if he does I hope that Gabriel, instead of giving him a crown and harp, will supply him a nice old hat and a wheelbarrow; and I am sure that his presence there will make the environment more endurable, and help to dissipate the monotony which probably pervades the place ❧

❧ ❧

HERBERT SPENCER deals at length with what he is pleased to term the " Messianic Idea." It seems that all nations have ever held the hope of the coming of a Strong Man, who would deliver them from the ills that beset their lives. This hope never dies, although it assumes different forms, varying according to conditions. No doubt that the hope that springs eternal in the United States, when each four years roll round, is a rudimentary survival of the Messianic Idea. As yet, however, the President who is to take the bitterness out of this cup of life has not been elected ❧ ❧

❧ ❧

A vast number of men and women see the fact that immunity and exemption are not desirable, that nothing can ever be given away, and that something for nothing is very dear.

 AMONG the world's great workers—and in the front rank there have been only a scant half-dozen — stands Fra Junipero Serra. This is the man who made the California Missions possible. In artistic genius, as a teacher of handicrafts, and as an industrial leader, he performed a feat unprecedented, and which probably will never again be equaled. In a few short years he caused a great burst of beauty to bloom and blossom, where before was only a desert waste.

The personality of a man who could not only convert to Christianity three thousand Indians, but who could set them to work, must surely be sublimely great. Not only did they labor, but they produced art of a high order. These missions which lined the Coast from San Francisco to San Diego, every forty miles, were Manual Training Schools, founded on a religious concept.

Junipero taught that, unless you backed up your prayer with work, God would never answer your petitions. And the wonderful transformations which this man worked in characters turned on the fact that he made them acceptable and beautiful. Here is a lesson for us! He ranks with Saint Benedict, who rescued classic art from the dust of time and gave it to the world. Junipero is one with Albrecht Durer, Lorenzo the Magnificent, Michelangelo, Leonardo da Vinci, Friedrich Froebel, John Ruskin and William Morris. These men all taught the Gospel of Work, and the sacredness of Beauty and Use.

Junipero was without question the greatest teacher of Manual Training which this continent has so far seen. Without tools, apparatus or books, save as he created them, he evolved an architecture and an art, utilizing the services of savages, and transforming these savages in the process, for the time at least, into men of taste, industry and economy. ¶ This miracle of human energy and love could not endure, and after Fra Junipero had passed out, there being none to take his place, the Indians relapsed into their racial ways.—*Fra Junipero Serra.*

ENJAMIN FRANKLIN was the strongest all-round man that America has produced He was laborer, printer, businessman, inventor, scientist, publisher, financier, diplomat, philosopher. ❦ Everything Franklin touched he flavored with love and enthusiasm. Courage in his heart never died. He had wit and humor: and humor is the sense of values He knew a big thing from a little thing. He was able to laugh at all of the little misfits of life; and he sympathized with those who had failed or stumbled, or who had been mired and gone down to defeat and " the tongueless silence of a dreamless dust."

If ever a man saw the future illumined by the flambeaux of a great and living imagination, it was Benjamin Franklin

Three countries honored him. He borrowed money from France when America had no credit, and with this money Washington fought the battles of the Revolution. If any man can be named who gave us freedom, it is Benjamin Franklin. He gave us freedom from superstition, from fear and doubt, woe and want. His plea was always and forever for industry, for economy. He prized the fleeting hours, and life to him was a precious privilege.

All things work together for good, whether you love the Lord or not

Whoever you are! claim your own at any hazard!

CULTURE is the cream of conduct. It is the sure result of the Study Habit, linked to Self-Reliance and blessed by concentration.
Fortunate are we if we evolve from our hearts these great gifts with which the Creator, in His goodness and wisdom, has endowed us.
Culture, like all of life's blessings, can not be hoarded—it is for service.
Those who are wise give their culture away, and thus do they retain it.

HATE has bumped me a few, but I believe in every case I invited the punishment
For instance, I can think back to a time when my mother used to sing at her work. She eliminated the servant problem and thereby cut out one topic of conversation. ❦ She used to cook, sew, scrub, wash, make garden, and when she washed dishes I can remember that she would prop a book up against the castor —now an obsolete thing—and let a table-fork hold the pages open And as she worked she read
She would knit us stockings and mittens—warm woolen mittens for Winter—and this knitting she would do after supper while some one read aloud
When she was doing her ironing she would sing, loud and clear, some good old Baptist hymn

I admired her voice, even if at times I provoked a discord. She could lift a high C that you could hear a quarter of a mile. And certainly she did make that iron sizz! I can hear it hit the table now, and closing my eyes, I can see her test the heat of the iron with a moistened finger
And so she ironed and sang, and I, perhaps three or four years of age, would occasionally creep softly into the room, navigate under the table and suddenly clutch the soloist by the feet.
This would stop the song and cause a good spitball Baptist expletive to spin through the air, and I was apt to get a good kick at the same time. And certainly it was coming to me.

I HAVE a profound respect for boys ✤ ✤

Grimy, ragged, tousled boys in the street often attract me strangely ✤ ✤

A boy is a man in the cocoon—you do not know what it is going to become—his life is big with many possibilities.

❧ He may make or unmake kings, change boundary-lines between States, write books that will mold characters, or invent machines that will revolutionize the commerce of the world.

Every man was once boy: I trust I shall not be contradicted: it is really so.

❧ Would n't you like to turn Time backward, and see Abraham Lincoln at twelve, when he had never worn a pair of boots? The lank, lean, yellow, hungry boy—hungry for love, hungry for learning, tramping off through the woods for twenty miles to borrow a book, and spelling it out, crouched before the glare of the burning logs!

Then there was that Corsican boy, one of a goodly brood, who weighed only fifty pounds when ten years old; who was thin and pale and perverse, and had tantrums, and had to be sent supperless to bed, or locked in a dark closet because he would n't "mind!" Who would have thought that he would have mastered every phase of warfare at twenty-six; and when told that the exchequer of France was in dire confusion, would say, "The finances? I will arrange them!"

Very distinctly and vividly I remember a slim, freckled boy, who was born in the "Patch," and used to pick up coal along the railroad tracks in Buffalo. A few months ago I had a motion to make before the Supreme Court, and that boy from the "Patch" was the Judge who wrote the opinion granting my petition. Yesterday I rode horseback past a field where a boy was plowing. The lad's hair stuck out through the top of his hat; his form was bony and awkward; one suspender held his trousers in place; his bare legs and arms were brown and sunburned and briar-scarred. He swung his horses around just as I passed by, and from under the flapping brim of his hat he cast a quick glance out of dark, half-bashful eyes and modestly returned my salute ✤ ✤

His back turned, I took off my hat and sent a God-bless-you down the furrow after him ✤ ✤

Who knows?—I may go to that boy to borrow money yet, or to hear him preach, or to beg him to defend me in a lawsuit; or he may stand with pulse unhastened, bare of arm, in white apron, ready to do his duty, while the cone is placed over my face, and Night and Death come creeping into my veins.

Be patient with the boys—you are dealing with soul-stuff. Destiny awaits just around the corner.

Be patient with the boys!

The Boy: A Potentiality.

✤ ✤

MOST social reformers indict the times in which we live. This is their substitute for argument. They picture for us the ideal, and paint the present black.

❧ These things are right and well, but not final. We live in a world of cause and effect, sequence and consequence, and only a calm, commonsense view brings a solution ✤ ✤

Pascal says, "In viewing the march of the race, we should not view humanity in the mass; we should regard humanity as one man who has come marching down the centuries."

Look back two, three, four thousand years! Aye, look back two hundred years; look back a hundred years; look back thirty years, and see the distance we have traveled!

Woman, as a factor in business life, arrived in the year Eighteen Hundred Seventy-six, discovered, if you please, at the Centennial Exposition by a man by the name of Remington.

With the typewriter, woman's advent into the business world was assured ✤

Before the Civil War, women were not employed even as schoolteachers. The scarcity of men in the years Eighteen Hundred Sixty-six, Sixty-seven and Sixty-eight brought the woman schoolteacher into view, and Normal Schools sprang up all over the United States to fit country girls for the office of teaching.

NO greater shock ever comes to a young man from the country, who makes his way up to the city, than the discovery that rich people are, for the most part, wofully ignorant. He has always imagined that material splendor and spiritual gifts go hand in hand; and now, if he is wise, he discovers that millionaires are too busy making money, and too anxious about what they have made, and their families are too intent on spending it, to ever acquire a calm, judicial, mental attitude ✒ ❡ The rich need education really more than the poor. " Lord, enlighten Thou the rich ! " should be the prayer of every man who works for progress ✒ " Give clearness to their mental perceptions, awaken in them the receptive spirit, soften their callous hearts, and arouse their powers of reason. ❡ Danger lies in their folly, not in their wisdom; their weakness is to be feared, not their strength.

That the wealthy and influential class should fear change, and cling stubbornly to conservatism, is certainly to be expected. To convince this class that spiritual and temporal good can be improved upon by a more generous policy has been a task a thousand times greater than the inciting of the poor to riot.

It is easy to fire the discontented, but to arouse the rich, and carry truth home to the blindly prejudiced, is a different matter. Too often the reformer has been one who caused the rich to band themselves against the poor.

✒ ✒

Life without absorbing occupation is hell —joy consists in forgetting life.

OF all examples of blind imbecility on the part of men, none is so preposterous as the opinions men hold of other men. Genius does not recognize genius; worth is blind to worth ✤ Men often taunt women with treating other women unjustly, but the records of great men who have scorned other great men leave the injustice of women towards women quite out of the race.

ONLY the heart suffers. The brain is the peaceful, undisturbed, eternal spectator of the monstrous paradox called Life ✒ ✒

The mind never worries, is never perturbed, is never in pain. The heart— that great lupanar of desires—may seduce the brain to participate in its earth-itches; but in itself the mind is a detached, impersonal observer of the great tangled web of passion and error that is spun by the heart of man. ❡ Mind as mind has the placidity of a mirror ✒ ✒

All things are reflected in it, but for the image of Lady Macbeth it cares no more than for the image of Falstaff. The unconscious universe struggled and fought until it evolved a brain ✒ In mind, the star and planet rise to thought. The World-Spirit contemplates itself through the brain of man. It is the light born out of darkness. Through the brain, nature passes from actor to observer, from blind, eyeless combat to wide-eyed intelligence, from an immemorial pain to the beginnings of an immemorial mirth.

✒ ✒

IMPERSONAL contemplation—that is the secret of laughter. Mirth is as old as the first mind that detached itself—even for a single hour—from the service of emotions and the lower nature generally. The first man who said, " I will retire from the combat a little while to yonder hill to watch the fray," was the first man who laughed with his brain. Distance, aloofness, height, strike out by a magic psychic friction the spark that bears in its center the germ of philosophy. Only cosmic comedians become as the gods.

A PRAYER OF GRATITUDE

AM thankful for the blessed light of this day, and I am thankful for all the days that have gone before.

I thank the thinkers, the poets, the painters, the sculptors, the singers, the publishers, the inventors—the businessmen —who have lived and are now living.

I thank Pericles and Phidias, who made the most beautiful city the world has ever seen, and were repaid by persecution and death. I thank Aristotle, the mountain-guide and schoolteacher, who knew how to set bad boys to work.

I thank Emerson for brooking the displeasure of his Alma Mater ๑๑ I thank James Watt, the Scotch boy who watched his mother's tea-kettle to a purpose.

I thank Volta and Galvani, who fixed their names, as did Watt, in the science that lightens labor and carries the burdens that once bowed human backs.

I thank Benjamin Franklin for his spirit of mirth, his persistency, his patience, his commonsense.

I thank Alexander Humboldt and his brother, William Humboldt— those great brothers twain, who knew that life is opportunity ๑๑ ๑๑ I thank Shakespeare for running away from Stratford and holding horses at a theater-entrance—but not forever.

I thank Arkwright, Hargreaves, Crompton, from whose brains leaped the looms that weave with tireless hands the weft and warp that human bodies wear.

I thank Thomas Jefferson for his writing the Declaration of Independence, for founding a public-school system, for dreaming of a college where girls and boys would study, learn and work in joy.

I thank Baruch Spinoza, gardener, lens-maker, scientist, humanist, for being true to the dictates of the tides of divinity that played through his soul.

I thank Charles Darwin and Herbert Spencer, Englishmen, for liberating theology from superstition. I thank Tyndall the Irishman, Draper the American, Herschel the German, Bjornson the Scandinavian, and Adam Smith the Scotchman, for inspiration and help untold.

These men and others like them, their names less known ,have made the world a fit dwelling-place for liberty. Their graves are mounds from which flares Freedom's torch.

And I thank and praise, too, the simple, honest, unpretentious millions who have worked, struggled, toiled, carrying heavy burdens, often paid in ingratitude, spurned, misunderstood—who still worked on and succeeded, or failed, robbed of recognition and the results of their toil. To all these who sleep in forgotten graves, my heart goes out in gratitude over the years and the centuries and the ages that have passed. Amen, and Amen!

HE daily newspaper the educator of the people!

God help us, it may be so! It educates into inattention, folly, sin, vacuity and foolishness. It saps concentration, dissipates aspiration, scrambles gray matter and irons out convolutions. Watch the genus commuter rush for his Dope when he reaches the station in the morning ✺ He may be a Sunday School Superintendent, a college graduate, a man of social standing, but he must have his mat-in-mess of rottenness or he would die of fidgets. He reads of how a man in Manitoba elopes with another man's wife, with consuming interest ✺ He scans the advertising pages with their columns of fakery and filth, and it never occurs to him that a certain ✺ amount of the slime that slides into his brain must stay there and line the vacuum.

At night when he goes home he buys the last edition, reads the whole thing over again written 't other end to. He does this for ten years, twenty—does it not make him what he is? Would you like to go to Heaven with him?

I knew one commuter, ten years ago, who refused to read the daily papers, but instead carried with him in his side pocket a volume of Emerson. That man is now a marked personality, wielding a large and healthful influence in a rational way. His old-time fellow passengers are still feverishly guzzling their last edition. Every city in the land has periodic perturbations about " Jack the Stabber," " Jack the Snipper " and " Jack the Peeper " fanned into flame by the molders of public opinion, these beneficent educators of the people. Even staid old Boston had a week of fits a short time ago, when every paper in the city combined to terrorize women and children by conjuring forth an awful " Jack," who finally was run to cover and found to be a mischievous cigarettist boy who should have been left, from the beginning, to the police and alienists ✺ ✺ But not so! The newspapers saw their chance and they grabbed it in gladsome glee ✺ The pernicious effects of such an epidemic of fear, to say nothing ✺ about a million people devoting an hour a day to reading and talking ✺ about it, can not be computed ✺ ✺ If the men who prepare the copy for the daily papers were allowed to write out of their hearts and state their beliefs, what they would say might be worth reading; although the printed words of a commonplace person exert an influence far beyond the speech of the same person, for we still worship the fetish and miracle of a printed book. But what shall we say of the writing of mediocre men who write on order! What the world needs is a great temperance revival where men will swear off and quit reading the newspapers ✺ Quit and you 'll be the gainer.

✺ ✺

The man at his work! There is nothing finer. I have seen men homely, uncouth and awkward when " dressed up " who were superb when at work.

✺ ✺

Expose not thyself by four-footed manners ✺ ✺

LIFE is a paradox. Every truth has its counterpart which contradicts it; and every philosopher supplies the logic for his own undoing.

I plead for mercy, unselfishness, service and the love that suffereth long and is kind, and yet I know that over against this, enthroned on his pedestal of old, sits the Great God Might, and smiles at our mushy talk about altruism, abnegation and self-sacrifice. ❡ It is all a paradox.

E were watching a litter of little pigs up at the farm. They were busily intent on getting a square meal ๑ They were only about a week old.

Suddenly two of the pigs left the lunch-counter and began to fight.

"What do you suppose they are quarreling about?" asked Terese.

"I think one of them must have referred to the other as a pig," was the answer. "But," said Terese, "if he did, and did not use any adjective, the remark was certainly true."

"This, however, had nothing to do with the case. Truth is seldom pleasing, especially when it refers to ourselves."

❡ The fact is, however, those pigs were fighting just about nothing—and that is just what men fight about.

Quarrels are built on a misunderstanding. Friendships are founded on an understanding.—*The Quarrel.*

๑ ๑

ALI BABA came over to the Shop the other day, followed by a fugacious fice. "I am going to kill that dog," said Ali to me, "and make a pair of gloves out of his hide."

"What's the matter with the dog?" I said. "He looks like a good one."

"Why!" said Ali, "He is what you call a gravedigger dog."

"Go on," I said; "I don't exactly understand." ๑ ๑

"Well, it is this way," he says; "that dog is like some folks: he is always digging up things that have been buried; and I believe that when things have been buried properly they ought to be left buried. Let 'em rest in their graves. Don't you think so?" And I thought so. —*The Grave Digger.*

๑ ๑

WHAT is a Business Man? ❡ Listen, Terese: A Business Man is one who gets the business and completes the transaction ๑ ๑

Bookkeepers, correspondents, system men, janitors, scrubladies, stenographers, electricians, elevator-boys, cash-girls, are all good people and necessary and worthy of sincere respect, but they are not Business Men, because they are on the side of expense and not income ๑ When H. H. Rogers coupled the coalmines of West Virginia with tide-water, he proved himself a Business Man. ❡ When James J. Hill created an Empire in the Northwest, he proved his right to the title. The Business Man is a Salesman. And no matter how great your invention, how sweet your song, how sublime your picture, how perfect your card-system, until you are able to convince the world that it needs the thing which you have to offer, and you get the money for it, you are not a Business Man. —*What is a Business Man?*

๑ ๑

AND so we say that happiness hinges on habits; because habits rule our lives.

Our habits put us to bed and they get us up in the morning. They seat us at the table, and they set us to work. And the quality of our work turns on the kind we are in the habit of doing. Slipshod, lazy, indifferent, careless, reckless habits do not produce good results; they do not secure the respect of good people, the confidence of society, nor the approval of one's own conscience. And happiness to such a one is far afield.

There are three habits which seem essential to the well-rounded life. These are the Health Habit, the Work Habit, and the Study Habit.

Herbert Spencer said, "The first requisite is to be a good animal."

Without dissenting from this dictum, we say, "The first essential is that the individual shall earn his own living." No man can be called educated who is a parasite on the community.

Sobriety, sanity, health, good cheer, and positive usefulness to humanity are all primal requisites in education. Any system of education which tends to reduce human efficiency neutralizes and destroys human happiness and is to that extent vicious and objectionable. Moreover, any system of education that is not a positive moving force for good is bad. ❡ The "happy habit" is the possession of those alone who have habits of industry and wise economy.

XPANSION without system spells failure. Organization means that a man shall grow with his business.

I used to work in a country store where a ten-year-old boy stole eggs from us at the back door and brought them around in front and sold us our own property. He kept this up for a year, and he might have kept it up indefinitely had he not taken in a partner and tried to do wholesale business. ❡ Success did much for him, too! ❡ Dead stock, bad accounts, pilfering clerks, pinching setters, and lime in the bones of the boss work the certain ruin of every country store.

If the business is so small that the proprietor and his wife can remember everything they have in stock, and then sell for cash, and can not get or will not accept credit, then the business is safe until the sons grow up and take the management. A thousand mice nibble at every business concern.

In order to avoid leaks there must be a system that will locate them. The department store, where there is a system that tells every day, every week, or every month just what every department pays is the safest business that exists. If any one department does not pay it is reformed and made to pay or else is eliminated.

ᴥ ᴥ

NO big business can possibly pay unless it is divided up into departments *ᴥ ᴥ*
A non-paying department is never allowed to continue and drag the whole concern down to bankruptcy as in the good old general store, where jumble and guess work audit the accounts. ❡ The successful country store is an easy mark for every petty thief and little poker-player in town. The village Smart Aleck hires out as clerk and supplies his friends the things they need, just as a sneakerino reads the postal cards and hands out the news, if he or she clerks in the post-office.

❡ Success in business nowadays turns on your ability to systematize.

ᴥ ᴥ

NO business long remains greater than the man who runs it *ᴥ* And the size of the business is limited only by the size of the man. Our limitations say to our business, "Thus far and no farther." *ᴥ* We ourselves fix the limit. Without system the most solid commercial structure will dissipate into thin air. ❡ The Gould System, the Vanderbilt System, the Hill System, the Harriman System, the Pennsylvania System —they are all rightly named. It is system that makes a great business possible *ᴥ* When Jay Gould gathered up a dozen warring, struggling streaks of rust and rights of way and organized them into a railroad system, he revealed the master mind. The measure of your success is your ability to organize, and if you can not bring system to bear, your very success will work your ruin. The average life of a successful general store is twenty years—then it fails. And it fails through its lack of system—the man does not grow with his business. An army unorganized is a mob. Napoleon's power lay in his genius for system, and he whipped the Austrians, one against three but only because he had the ability to systematize. "But the finances?" asked his secretary. "I will arrange them,"

WOULD you have your name smell sweet with the myrrh of remembrance and chime melodiously in the ear of future days, then cultivate faith, not doubt, and give every man credit for the good he does, never seeking to attribute base motives to beautiful acts. Acts count.

was the reply. ❡ The character of the man at the head mirrors itself in every department of every enterprise. A certain kind of landlord can care for a certain number of " guests "—and the quality of the guests attracted is according to the quality of the landlord. Increase the number of people to be fed and housed, and usually your hotel-keeper quickly gets into very hot water. Fifty extra people upset his system, and either his guests leave or his " help " steal him to a standstill. A new and better manager must then come in, or the referee in bankruptcy awaits around the corner with a stuffed club.

THE measure of a man's success in business is his ability to organize. ❡ The measure of a man's success in literature is his ability to organize his ideas and reduce the use of the twenty-six letters of the alphabet to a system so as to express the most in the least space. The writer does not necessarily know more than the reader, but he must organize his facts and march truth in a phalanx

In painting, your success hinges on your ability to organize colors and place them in the right relation to give a picture of the scene that is in your mind.

Oratory demands an orderly procession of words, phrases and sentences to present an argument that can be understood by an average person.

Music is the selection and systematization of the sounds of Nature.

Science is the organization of the common knowledge of the common people. ❡ In life everything lies in the mass— materials are a mob—a man's measure is his ability to select, reject, organize.
—*System and Success*

Young women with ambitions should be very crafty and cautious, lest mayhap they be caught in the soft, silken mesh of a happy marriage, and go down to oblivion, dead to the world.

Do your work with your whole heart and you will succeed—there is so little competition!

HERE was a Jail-Bird, once upon a time, in a small town in the state of Iowa. This J. B. had had all that he wanted, and it was his firm intention if he ever got another chance, he would show what he was made of. Many other J. B.'s have made similar resolves. After he got out almost everybody gave him the Icy Mitt, but finally he Accepted a Position (or as some might say, Found a Job) in a Factory. He started in at four dollars a week, working with the boys, for jail-birds can not afford to be either fastidious or finicky. They have to take whatever offers.

Responsibilities gravitate to the person who can shoulder them, and power flows to the man who knows how.

And so it happened that before the J. B. was in that factory a month the boys were going to him asking him where things were. When they ran out of one kind of work they would ask him what they should do next; and he, knowing the sequence of the work, would advise them. Now, there be employers who are Proud and Overbearing, but others there be who have Common-Sense. And it so happened that the man who owned the factory where the J. B. worked had a modicum of Common-Sense. Seeing that the J. B. knew where things were and what should be done next, and that the J. B. put the work away at night and got it out in the morning, and planned things at home, and picked things up instead of walking over them or kicking them aside, why, the Boss encouraged the J. B. and Raised his Wages.

SO the J. B. evolved into a Right Hand Man, and in time came to know a deal more about the details of the business than the Boss, and I believe eventually married the daughter of the Boss, inherited his money and became sole owner of the Factory, but of these things I am not certain, so I do not record them. But the little incident I am about to record really happened. One day the Boss saw two girls who worked in the factory coming in with a basket of wild clematis. These girls proceeded to festoon the pillars of the big room with the beautiful plant. " Who told you to do that? " demanded the Boss.

" Why, Mr. So-and-so," said the girls, referring to the J. B.

" Did you send those girls away during working hours after weeds? " asked the Boss shortly after of the J. B. ❡ " Certainly," was the answer. " You see, I noticed those particular girls seemed very white, and not very strong and sort of nervous and worn—they say they have things tough at home— and I just thought I would try to improve their complexions and spirits by giving them a run out in the sunshine."

" Oho, you thought they were getting Prison Pallor, did you? " ✎ ✎

" Yes, you guessed it—I was thinking of Prison Pallor."

" And so contrived an excuse to send the girls on a two-mile walk out across the fields? "

" Yes."

" Had Prison Pallor yourself, eh? "

" Yes."

" Used to look into a pocket mirror and thought it was a Ghost? "

" Possibly."

" Never saw the blue sky except through a grating, or when walking lock-step across a stone-paved courtway? " ✎ ✎

" You have it."

" Well, look here, J. B., don't stand around here keeping me from work— I wish t' Lord I could find a few more J. B.'s to help me run this shebang ✎ And say, make a little list of the pale, nervous, yellow and scared girls and send them out by turns for clematis whenever the sun shines—don't stand around keeping me from work—don't you think I have anything to do myself? "

" Go on with you! "

—*J. B. Runs Things.*

I F all Christians were like Christ, there would be no necessity for Christianity; for when once we have achieved absolutely and in every particular our object, our passion, our dream, the motives that urged us on to that consummation disappear, and we are left in exactly the same predicament from which we wiggled.

There is no Utopia that would be worth living in for a single month.

Unless you are prepared for pain, prepared to kill, skirt precipices and be killed, you will always remain a decadent, that is, an idealist, a sick man.

A NDREW Lang had drunk deep from the Pierian spring. His was true culture, if there is such a thing, and we believe there is. By some he has been accused of arrant dilettanteism, a charge implying what Lamb was pleased to call "superficial omniscience." ✎ ✎

To others Lang represented a " syndicate " and the implication is a genuine compliment to the man's versatility ✎ ✎ Andrew Lang was thoroughly at home in a wide multiplicity of literary fields ✎ ✎ As an all-round litterateur he had, perhaps, no peer among modern writers ✎ ✎

He was a poet of marked ability, a first-class critic and book-reviewer, a graceful essayist, a faithful and charming translator, and an enthusiastic Classicist.

Not essentially and primarily a stylist, in the sense in which Walter Pater and Edgar Saltus, for instance, are stylists, he yet possessed an easy, fluent style which radiates through all his works and renders them eminently readable and entertaining. He commanded the Midas literary touch, and transmuted into purest gold whatever he committed to paper. ❡ Despite the fact that he was a prodigally prolific penman, his works were endued with unfailing freshness and novelty of treatment, and were never tinctured with the odor of midnight oil ❧

S a rule, the man who can do all things equally well is a very mediocre individual. ❡ Those who stand out before a groping world as beacon-lights were men of great faults and unequal performances.

It is quite needless to add that they do not live on account of their faults or imperfections, but in spite of them.

Henry David Thoreau's place in the common heart of humanity grows firmer and more secure as the seasons pass, and his life proves for us again the paradoxical fact, that the only men who really succeed are those who fail.

Thoreau's obscurity, his poverty, his lack of public recognition in life, either as a writer or as a lecturer, his rejection as a lover, his failure in business, and his early death form a combination of calamities that make him as immortal as a martyr.

Especially does an early death sanctify all and make the record complete, but the death of a naturalist while right at the height of his ability to see and enjoy —death from tuberculosis of a man who lived most of the time in the open air— these things array us on the side of the man 'gainst unkind Fate, and cement our sympathy and love. Nature's care forever is for the species, and the individual is sacrificed without ruth that the race may live and progress.

This dumb indifference of Nature to the individual—this apparent contempt for the man—seems to prove that the individual is only a phenomenon.

Man is merely a manifestation, a symptom, a symbol, and his quick passing proves that he is n't the thing.

Nature does not care for him—she produces a million beings in order to get one who has thoughts—all are swept into the dustpan of oblivion but the one who

thinks; he alone lives, embalmed in the memories of generations unborn.

The Thoreau race is dead.

In Sleepy Hollow Cemetery at Concord there is a monument marking a row of mounds where half a dozen Thoreaus rest. The inscriptions are all of one size, but the name of one Thoreau alone lives, and he lives because he had thoughts and expressed them for the people.

One of the most insistent errors ever put out was that statement of Rousseau, paraphrased in part by Thomas Jefferson, that all men are born free and equal. No man was ever born free, and no two are equal, and would not remain so an hour, even if Jove, through caprice, should make them so.

If any of the tribe of Thoreau get into Elysium, it will be by tagging close to the only man among them who glorified his Maker by using his reason.

Nothing should be claimed as truth that can not be demonstrated, but as a hypothesis (borrowed from Henry Thoreau), I give you this: Man is only the tool or vehicle—Mind alone is immortal —THOUGHT IS THE THING.

❧ ❧

HEN there is a question of success, do not look to this man or that newspaper for help—look to your work, and make it of such a quality that the market must come to you.

❧ ❧

Keep your ray of reason! It is your only guiding star. He who says you would see better if you would blow it out is a preacher ❧ ❧

❧ ❧

HRIFT is a habit. ❡ A habit is a thing you do unconsciously or automatically, without thought. We are ruled by our habits.

When habits are young they are like lion-cubs, soft, fluffy, funny, frolicsome little animals. They grow day by day. Eventually they rule you.

Choose ye this day the habit ye would have to rule over you. The habit of thrift is simply the habit which dictates that you shall earn more than you spend. In other words, thrift is the habit that provides that you shall spend less than you earn. Take your choice.

If you are a thrifty person you are happy. When you are earning more than you spend, when you produce more than you consume, your life is a success, and you are filled with courage, animation, ambition, good-will. Then the world is beautiful, for the world is your view of the world, and when you are right with yourself, all's right with the world. ❡ The habit of thrift proves your power to rule your own psychic self. You are captain of your soul. You are able to take care of yourself, and then out of the excess of your strength you produce a surplus ॐ ॐ

Thus you are not only able to take care of yourself, but you are able to take care of some one else—of wife, child, father and mother, to lend a hand to sick people, old people, unfortunate people. This is to live.

The man who can not earn a living for himself is something less than a man. The man who can barely get a living and no more is little better than a barbarian or a savage.

Loving labor and thrift go hand in hand. He who is not thrifty is a slave to circumstance. Fate says, "Do this or starve," and if you have no surplus saved up you are the plaything of chance, the pawn of circumstance, the slave of some one's caprice, a leaf in a storm. ❡ The surplus gives you the power to dictate terms, but most of all it gives you an inward consciousness that you are sufficient unto yourself.

Therefore, cultivate the habit of thrift, and the earlier you begin, the better. And no matter how old you are, or how long you have lived, begin this day to save something, no matter how little, out of your earnings.—*Let Thrift Be Your Ruling Habit.*

HE corporation had its rise in the fertile brain of Julius Cæsar, and was founded on the idea of the Tenth Legion that never died. The soldiers in the Tenth Legion may have been killed in battle, but the ranks closed and the column advanced over their dead bodies. That night, when the Legion camped, new men were put in place of those who were lost, and so, although individuals might die, the Tenth Legion lived on forever.

The Romans were builders and engineers. Cæsar set apart a hundred men to build an aqueduct. Knowing that it would take probably longer than the lifetime of these men to complete the task, Cæsar ordered that whenever one of the hundred died the rest should elect his successor, and thus, though the entire original hundred men would pass away, yet the corporation would live on ॐ ॐ

ॐ ॐ

❛HE modern joint-stock company is built on the Roman idea, and had its evolution in England about two hundred years ago. A hundred men would go out and start an English trading colony. Each man would represent one share of interest ॐ He had the privilege of selling this share of stock to any one else, and when he died it would descend to his oldest son.

It was an easy step for men to put money into a stock company and receive two shares instead of one through paying twice as much as the rest did. ❡ Then we got companies chartered by the Crown, say like the East India company, and behold, the joint-stock company then was fully organized. ❡ With the discovery of the expansive power of steam and the ability of a steam-engine to turn a vast number of wheels and run a great many machines, manufacturing in factories took the place of the handicrafts in the homes. Instead of whittling out commodities by the fireside, or the wife weaving by the hand-loom, things were done in a big way in the factories.

At first all the shares in joint-stock companies were owned by the workers, but gradually it was discovered that the investments in factories were good ones, and we find royalty embarking in business on a joint-stock basis. A trust is a partnership among corporatons.

T is well to cultivate a mild, gentle and sympathetic voice, and the one way to secure a mild, gentle and sympathetic voice is to be mild, gentle and sympathetic. The voice is the index of the soul. Children do not pay much attention to your words—they judge of your intent by your voice. Your voice reassures ❧ " My sheep know my voice." We judge each other more by voice than by language, for voice colors speech, and if your voice does not corroborate your words, doubt will follow. We are won or repelled by a voice ❧ Your dog does not obey your words—he does, however, read your intents in your voice. ❡ The best way to cultivate the voice is not to think about it. Actions become regal only when they are unconscious; and the voice that convinces, that holds us captive, that leads and lures us on, is used by its owner unconsciously. Fix your mind on the thought, and the voice will follow. If you fear you will not be understood, you are losing the thought—it is slipping away from you—and you are thinking of the voice. Then your voice rises to a screech, subsides into a purr, or bellows like the vagrant winds. Anxiety and intent are shown, and your case is lost. If you fear you will not be understood, you probably will not. If the voice is allowed to come naturally, easily and gently, it will take on every tint and emotion of the mind. So, to get back to the place of beginning, my advice is this: The way to cultivate the voice is not to cultivate it ❧ ❧ The voice is the sounding-board of the soul. God made it right. If your soul is filled with truth, your voice will vibrate with love, echo with sympathy, and fill your hearers with the desire to do, to be and to become. Your desire will be theirs. By their voices ye shall know them.

❧ ❧

WHO is the great man? Listen, and I will tell you; He is great who feeds other minds. He is great who inspires others to think for themselves. He is great who tells you the things you already know, but which you did not know you knew until he told you. He is great who shocks you, irritates you, affronts you, so that you are jostled out of your wonted ways, pulled out of your mental ruts, lifted out of the mire of the commonplace ❧ ❧ That writer is great whom you alternately love and hate. That writer is great whom you can not forget. Certainly, yes, the man in his private life may be proud, irritable, rude, crude, coarse, faulty, absurd, ignorant, immoral—grant it all, and yet be great. He is not great on account of these things, but in spite of them. The seeming inconsistencies and inequalities of his nature may contribute to his strength, as the mountains and valleys, the rocks and woods, make up the picturesqueness of the landscape. ❡ He is great to whom writers, poets, painters, philosophers, preachers and scientists go, each to fill his own little tin cup, dipper, calabash, vase, stein, pitcher, amphora, bucket, tub, barrel or cask. These men may hate him, refute him, despise him, reject him, insult him, as they probably will if they are much indebted to him; yet if he stirs the molecules in their minds to a point where they create caloric, he has benefited them and therefore he is a great man ❧ ❧ His very faultiness brings him near. His blunders make him to us akin.

MAN, like Deity, creates in his own image. And if you grind all the personality out of a man, and make him but part of a machine, you are hastening the death of Art, for Art is born of Individuality. Love, we say, is life; but love without hope and faith is agonizing death.

HOULD the Angel Gabriel come to me and in a confidential undertone declare that a certain man, any man or any angel, was a vlifier of tr uth, a snare to the innocent, a pilferer, a sneak, a robber of grave-yards, I would say: " Gabriel, you are troubled with incipient paranoia— I do not believe a word of what you say. The man you mention may not be a saint, but he is probably just as good as you or I. In fact, I think he must be very much like you, for we are never interested in either a person or a thing that does not bear some direct relationship to ourselves. Then, Gabriel, do you not remember the words of Bishop Begum, who said that no man applies an epithet to another that can not with equal truth be applied to himself? " ❧ ❧

❧ ❧

WHEN we remember that hoarse, guttural cry of "Away with him— away with him!" and when we recall that some of the best and noblest men who have ever lived have been reviled and traduced, indicted and executed, by so-called good men—certainly men who were sincere—how can we open our hearts to the tales of discredit told of any man? The Billingsgate Calendar has been exhausted in attempts to describe Walt Whitman, and the lexicon of abuse has been used to hammer the heads of such men as Richard Wagner, Victor Hugo, Count Tolstoy and William Morris. Knowing these things, as every one does, shall we imitate folly, accept concrete absurdity for our counsel and guide.

❧ ❧

When you grow suspicious of a person and begin a system of espionage upon him, your punishment will be that you will find your suspicions true.

ET a man once see himself as others see him, and all enthusiasm vanishes from his heart; and when that is gone he might as well die at once, for enthusiasm is the one necessary ingredient in the receipt for doing good work.

AN is a migratory animal. We learn by keeping in motion; by travel; by transplantation; in moments of joy and times of grief. Only running water is pure, and Sir Oliver Lodge says that a planet not in motion would dissolve into a gas and be lost. Young men and women should be allowed to try their wings. The desire to "go somewhere" has its proper and natural use. Do not oppose it. Also, do not insist on the chaperon ❧ ❧ The chaperon habit is a bad one, since it may become chronic and make the chaperon a necessity. The chaperon is n't so bad, but the need of one is simply fierce.

❧ ❧

THE youth of fifteen or sixteen who is allowed to go away a hundred miles or so on a visit, or on a business errand, will often get more good out of the trip than he would get in a year at a boarding-school under the fussy care of a man with his collar buttoned behind, or one with brass buttons all up and down his martial front. We grow through making decisions.

If you travel with some one who looks up the route, keeps tab on the train and buys the tickets, you lose, in great degree, the benefits of travel.

That young man of meager means who could not afford a wedding-trip for two, and so sent his bride away on a tour alone, was no fool ❧ ❧

The girl who can not go single in safety is not fit to work in double harness ❧

❧ ❧

The actual benefit of college does not come so much from curriculum as from the change of environment. New people, new scenes new conditions with which to cope—these are the things that work for growth.

The simple act of going into a dining-car or restaurant and selecting from the bill of fare a dinner is a lesson in life which many a well-bred girl, full-grown, has never been allowed to gain.

ം ം

O the plea is this: Give your children liberty; let them develop their self-reliance through the exercise of choice, and of all methods or plans of education, travel, without head-cheese chaperonage, is the best.

Alexander and William Humboldt are the two greatest brothers in history, judged by achievements. They attended six universities and never remained more than a year in any one. They thus secured points of comparison, and evolved a self-reliant habit of thought which seldom comes to a man who has gone to but one college.

To the Humboldts, the university was never a finality.

The fact that they never graduated was an advantage. They never "got through."

¶ They never banked on a degree, because they never had one. They got all of the advantages of college with none of its petty plaster-of-Paris, dwarfing, caste influences.

The reason that the special-student plan has never become popular is because the special student never gets the social prestige that a pupil does who goes through or graduates and thus becomes a member of an order.

Cast the bantling on the rocks. Let him acquire an education, instead of being presented with one. And that's a part of the process that goes into the making of a man.—*Youth and Freedom.*

ം ം

The age is crying for men; civilization wants men who can save it from dissolution; and those who can benefit it most are those who are freest from prejudice, hate, revenge, whim and fear.

ം ം

There is no moment that comes to mortals so charged with peace and precious joy as the moment of reconciliation. The ineffable joy of forgiving and being forgiven forms an ecstacy that might well arouse the envy of the gods.

F all the writers that lived in Rome in that wonderful time which we call the Age of Agustus, none now is so widely read as Plutarch. Plutarch was a farmer, a lecturer, and a Priest of Apollo. On investigation, I find that the office of Priest of Apollo corresponded about with that of an American Justice of the Peace.

Between pasture and palaver, Plutarch became rich, and owned an estate on the Isle of Malta. And there he lived when Paul was shipwrecked on his way to Rome ം ം

Plutarch never mentions Paul, and Paul never quotes Plutarch. What a pity they did not meet!

Plutarch wrote the lives of twenty-three Romans, and compared each with some noted Greek, usually to the slight advantage of the Greek; for although Plutarch lived under the rule of Rome he was born in a province of Greece, and his heart was true to his own.

It is quite probable that no sure-enough literary man—who knew he was one, and acknowledged it—would mention all of the many trifles which Plutarch brings to bear, shedding light on the subject. Whether Plutarch gathered some of these airy, fairy, pleasing tales of persiflage from his imagination or from the populace, is a question that is not worth while discussing. Practically all we know of the great men of Greece and Rome is what Plutarch tells us.

It is Plutarch's men who live and tread the boardwalk with us. The rest are dead ones, all.

The only men who endure are those whose lives are well launched on the inky wave. Heave ho!

Such trifles as Cæsar's remark that he was deaf in one ear; that Pericles had a head like an onion; that Cleopatra employed a diver to attach a salt codfish to the hook and line of Mark Antony; that Socrates made pastoral calls on Aspasia; that Aspasia was very well acquainted with Cyrus, King of Persia, and from him gained her knowledge of statecraft —these are the things that endear

Plutarch to us. ❡ The things that shouldn't be told are the ones we want to hear ✺ ✺

And these Plutarch discreetly gives us. Shakespeare evidently knew Plutarch by heart. He was inspired more by Plutarch than by any other man who put pen to paper. It was the one book in which he dived and swam, in the days of his budding and impressionable youth and most of his plots are those of Plutarch. Lives of great men all remind us — of a great many things that we would do if we were able. Plutarch's writings have passed into the current coin of language ✺ His works are literary legal tender, wherever thinkers meet. Whoever writes, and writes well, is debtor to Plutarch for much wit, wisdom and gentle philosophy.

Academic writing dies and is forgotten. Information about men, women and events, and that which relates to practical life, lives on and on.

Biography broadens the vision and allows us to live a thousand lives in one; for when we read the life of a great man we unconsciously put ourselves in his place, and we ourselves live his life over again ✺ ✺:

We get the profit without the risk, the experience without the danger.

✺ ✺

MOST of the frightful cruelties inflicted on men during the past have arisen simply out of a difference of opinion arising through a difference in temperament. The question is as live today as it was two thousand years ago: what expression is best? That is, what shall we do to be saved? And concrete absurdity consists in saying we must all do the same thing.

✺ ✺

THE delight of creative work lies in self-discovery — you are mining nuggets of power out of your own cosmos, and the find comes as a great and glad surprise.

✺ ✺

I LOVE the diamond for its own sake—it symbols infinity, eternity.

The diamond is pure carbon; at least, we can resolve it back into carbon, but this done we can not make it over into a diamond.

It is like life, we can take it away, but we can not give it. The secret of the diamond is not ours—it took an eternity to produce it.

I am as old as the diamond and I shall never die.

JOHN BURROUGHS has no use for tobacco or stimulants; and so you find him turning into the last lap of the three score-and-ten with breath sweet as a baby's, muscles that do the bidding of his brain, and nerves that never go on a strike ✺ ❡ Yet he has been a man of strong passions and appetites. In stature he is rather small, but the way he carries the crown of his head and his chin, reveals the wellsexed man. He is a natural lover ✺

❡ How do I know? Well, any man is a lover who writes well. Literature is a matter of passion ✺ All Art is a secondary sexual manifestation, just as the song of birds, their gay and gaudy plumage, the color and perfume of flowers ✺ It is love writes all true poems, paints all pictures, sings all songs.

This man is a lover. Yet I know nothing of his private history, neither do I want to. He never told me " the sad story of his life "—only weaklings have the confessional habit—neither does he explain or apologize. His life is his own excuse for being. The man himself is explanation enough; every man is to a great degree the product of what has gone before—he is a sequence. More than that—man is a tablet upon which is written his every word, and thought, and deed. He is the Record of himself. The Record is the Man, and the Man is the Record. It will be easy to reckon accounts at the Last Great Day. The Judge will only have to unfold the heart and look—all is graven there—nothing was ever hidden nor can it be. God is not mocked ໑ ໑ This man will say to his Maker, "See, thus was I — my claim is only this!" And the chief gem in his diadem shall be a great, sublime and all-enfolding love.

Why do I say this? I say it because the truth is this:—No man ever reached the spiritual heights that this man has attained save through the love of One. From this love of One, his love radiates to all—he becomes Universal.

Men who have not tasted the Divine Passion belong to a sect, a society, a city, a country. They work for their own little church, hurrah for their own society, canvass for their pee-wee party, fight for their own country. They can not love virtue without hating vice. If they regard America, they detest England. They are like Orange John of Harvard, whose loyalty to Cambridge found vent in the cry, "T' 'ell wi' Yale!"—a sentiment to which even yet most Harvard men inwardly respond.

໑ ໑

JOHN BURROUGHS is the most Universal man I can name at the present moment. He is a piece of Elemental Nature. He has no hate, no whim, no prejudice. He believes in the rich, the poor, the learned, the ignorant. He believes in the wrong-doer, the fallen, the sick, the weak and the defenceless. He loves children, animals, birds, insects, trees and flowers. He is one who is afraid of no man, and of whom no man is afraid. He puts you at your ease—you could not be abashed before him. In his presence there is no temptation to deceive, to overstate, to understate—to be anything different from what you are. You could confess to this man—reveal your soul and tell the worst; and his only answer would be, "I know! I know!" and tears of sympathy and love would dim those heavenly blue eyes.

❧ Yet when I alighted from a West Shore train, I got off alone, and he was the only man at the railroad station. No faces peered from the windows as he stood there leaning against the building; no one came out upon the platform to see him; the trainmen did not call out, "This is the home of John Burroughs!" Neither conductor, brakeman, baggageman, nor mail agent glanced toward the simple old farmer standing there, meditatively chewing a straw. The fireman, however, knew him, for he dropped his shovel and leaning out of the cab waved a salute which was returned as comrade greets comrade.

John Burroughs was in no hurry to rush forward and greet me—the only man that I ever knew who is never in a hurry about anything. He has all the time there is. We met as if we had parted yesterday ໑ ໑

໑ ໑

JOHN BURROUGHS has written delightfully of boys and told how they could live in a world of their own, oblivious absolutely of the interests of grown-ups. He is a good deal of a boy himself: he has the eager receptive mental attitude. He is full of hope and is ever expecting to see something beautiful— something curious. Each day for him is a New Day, and he goes out in the morning and looks up at the clouds and scans the distant hills; and as he walks he watches for new things, or old things that may appear in a new light. This habit of expectancy always marks the strong man. It is a form of attraction—our own comes to us because we desire it; we find what we expect to find, and we receive what we ask for. All life is a prayer— strong natures pray most—and every earnest, sincere prayer is answered. Old John Burroughs' life is a prayer for beauty. He looks for beauty and goodness, and lo! these things are added unto him.—*John Burroughs—A Man.*

໑ ໑

Forms change but nothing dies. Everything is in circulation. Men as well as planets, have their orbits. Some have a wider swing than others, but just wait and they will come back.

A horse! A horse! My kingdom for a horse!—Richard III.

I RIDE horseback because I prize my sleep, my digestion and my think-trap.

That is to say, I ride in order that I may work.

I wish to be a good transformer of divine energy. I want to add to the wealth and happiness of the world, and to make two grins grow where there was only a grouch before.

To take care of myself, and then produce a surplus for the benefit of the world, is my ambition.

"We are strong," says Emerson, "only as we ally ourselves with Nature."

¶ I find that when I go in partnership with a good horse, I keep my nerves from getting outside of my clothes. I am better able to act sanely, serenely, and happily, dispose of difficulties and surmount obstacles.

A horse helps you to "forget it."

A horse has no troubles of his own.

¶ He does not pour into your ear a sad tale of woe.

I have ridden horseback almost daily for the last forty years.

And I enjoy horseback riding today more than ever before.

❧ ❧

I HAVE never been sick a day in my life; and I have never lost a meal except through inability of access.

¶ I have made fortunes for myself—and for other people. Also, I have lost fortunes; but, thank Heaven, I have always had all the mazuma I needed, even if not all I wanted. The man who keeps his strength and goodcheer in this country will never be out of a job. And of work I have always had a plenty.

❧ ❧

GOD has certainly been good to me. I think I have had as much fun and as many laughs as any man in the wide world ❧ ❧

"I know what pleasure is, for I have done good work," said Robert Louis Stevenson, the well-beloved.

One of the principal reasons why I have been able to do good work is because I have always kept on close, chummy terms with at least one good horse.

¶ Alfred Russel Wallace says that civilization had its rise in the domestication of animals; that where men domesticated the horse, the ox, the camel, the elephant, civilization thrived and man evolved; but that in countries where man had nothing in the way of domestic animals, except a tame wolf—that is, the dog—there was no evolution.

A man on horseback was pretty nearly invincible until the invention of gunpowder; and the first use of gunpowder was to scare horses. The idea of the explosion heaving a rock or an iron ball was a later idea.

My opinion now is that if we are going to preserve our vigor, our courage, our enjoyment, we will have to be on good terms with Mother Earth and close up to Equus Caballus.

❧ ❧

THE two greatest men the world has ever seen were both horsemen. Aristotle was the world's first schoolmaster and the world's first scientist. He taught school out-of-doors, and all of his pupils were taught to ride horseback ❧ ❧

Aristotle was the tutor of Alexander the Great. He taught Alexander to ride the wild horse, Bucephalus, and Aristotle sat on the top rail of the corral and watched his pupil turn the trick.

Aristotle wrote a book of a thousand pages on the horse. He said all there was to say on the subject, and no man can ever write at length about the horse without quoting Aristotle.

❧ ❧

THE next man to write a book on the horse was Leonardo da Vinci. Leonardo was the most accomplished, graceful, gracious, efficient and versatile personality that the world has ever seen.

¶ Leonardo was a horseman. And one of the big things that Leonardo did was to write a book on the horse. Aristotle wrote the first book, Leonardo the nest, and nearly two thousand years separate these men. No one has ever tackled the job of writing on the horse exhaustively since the days of Leonardo.

Leonardo attributed much of his bubbling, perennial joy in life to his close association with the horse. He was a horseback rider from childhood until his eighty-fourth year, when death, through accident, claimed him, and he went out with a smile and a wave of the hand, first intimating with broken breath that if there were no horses in Paradise he did not care to go there.

THE other day a man came along here from New York City and asked Ali Baba this question; "Is Mr. Hubbard giving many lectures this year?" And the old man replied: "Good Lord! How can he go off giving lectures? Don't you know that his mare has a colt?" And it is so.

Garnet, my best saddle-animal, has the greatest little baby horse that ever came jogging down the cosmic pike.

Garnet and Miriam were on very good terms from the first.

Garnet is the genuine saddle-horse told of by Leonardo, for she knows how to mix psychologically with the rider. She anticipates where you want to go and the speed at which you want to travel. You guide her by the motion of your body, and by merely "holding the thought."

Any man with horse instinct soon comes to a perfect understanding with one of these highbred horses.

Garnet is eighteen years old, and I have ridden her almost daily for fifteen years. Night or day, Winter or Summer, storm, sleet, wind, hail, snow, or glorious sunshine, it makes no difference. Garnet enjoys stormy weather, and so do I.

It is a great thing to feel that you are bigger than the elements. And a horse of the right kind helps you to hypnotize yourself into the belief that you are a part of all you see, and hear and feel.

No man can have melancholia who loves a horse and is understood by one.

You shake off your troubles and send your cares flying into the wanton winds when you ride horseback.

—*On Horseback*

There is a touch of pathos in the thought that while lovers live to make themselves necessary to each other, the mother is working to make herself unnecessary to her children.

To be gentle, generous, lenient, forgiving, and yet never relinquish the vital thing—this is to be great

This working for a common cause dilutes the sectarian ego, dissolves village caste, makes neighbor acquainted with neighbor, and liberates a vast amount of human love, which otherwise would remain hermetically sealed.

WE are lost children, and when alone and the darkness begins to gather, we long for the close relationship of the brothers and sisters we knew in our childhood, and cry for the gentle arms that once rocked us to sleep. We are homesick amid this sad, mad rush for wealth and place and power. The calm of the country invites, and we fain would do with fewer things, and go back to simplicity and rest.

When sympathy finds vent in vengeance and love takes the form of strife, who can say where it will end?

THIS habit of expectancy always marks the strong man. It is a form of attraction: our own comes to us because we desire it.

We find what we expect to find, and we receive what we ask for

All life is a prayer—strong natures pray most—and every earnest sincere prayer is answered.

HE intent of all art is to communicate your feelings and emotions to another. Art has its rise in the need of human companionship. You feel certain thoughts and you strive to express them. You may express by music, by chiseled shapes, by painted canvas or by written words. At the last all art is one. And as you work, over against you sits another who says "Yes, yes, I understand!" The person I write for is a Woman. At times she sits and looks at me, leaning forward, resting her chin on her hand.

She smiles indulgently, and sometimes a little sadly, as my pen runs on. She knows me so perfectly that she often anticipates what I would say and thus saves me the trouble of writing. She guesses my every mood. This woman has suffered and known and felt, and that is why she understands. Her heart has been purified in the white fires of experience. She knows more than I, for she sees all around me, and any little effort to palm off a white lie, or the smallest attempt at insincerity or affectation brings only a wondering look, that stings me for a week and a day. I can say anything to her I choose: no topic is forbidden—she only asks that I be honest and frank.

I always know when I have pleased this woman with the wistful eyes, for then she holds out her arms in a slow, sweeping gesture. She is the sister of my soul, and for her I write — because she understands.

❧ ❧

A RELIGIOUS concept has always been supreme in every community that has succeeded. For the lack of it, communities without number have failed. It is the Something that binds people together and holds human hearts in leash ❧ ❧

The things that influence civilization are not its warriors, preachers or reformers—progress comes through the struggle for bread and the effort to make a home ❧ ❧

INVENTION in language should no more be discouraged than should invention in mechanics.

Grammar is the grave of letters. ❡ Spirit is supreme. He who can express most in fewest terms will be crowned with laurel, and pilgrims will make little journeys to his grave ❧ ❧

We are changed through our activities, and when you give a man a pleasurable job, put upon him responsibility, set him to work, he then, for the first time, gives bonds for his good behavior and evolves the virtue that make for length of days ❧ ❧

❡ All creeds, held simply as intellectual beliefs, have small effect on the man, save as he works his belief up into his daily toil ❧

❧ ❧

IT is the belief now, among all thinking men, that Moses, when he led the Children of Isræl out of captivity, was not a religious fanatic, but a pragmatist, and a pragmatist is simply an opportunist. Moses did the thing he could do. He managed his people in the only way he could manage them. He did for them what was best; and the Mosaic Code is a sanitary code. It is a code for the Here and Now. It is a mode of living, and it is the sensible mode.

The Judaic Religion was a commonsense religion. It has passed through periods of fanaticism, but again, at this writing, for the most part, it has emerged out into the clear sunlight of reason. Rational Judaism is universal religion, and its cornerstone is commonsense.

❧ ❧

A retentive memory may be a good thing, but the ability to forget is the true token of greatness.

HEN you reach the Ozarks, you are in a land of glorious sunshine, where the air everywhere is flavored with the healing odor of the pines, kissed by the soft winds of the South, where the mocking bird sings you a welcome, and the robins, the blackbirds and the brown thrush have preceded you.

These things come as a great and glad relief—a delightful change. Here the water comes hot out of Nature's laboratory, bubbling cheerily up right out of the heart of the earth.

No wonder that the Indians used to say that this is the dwelling place of the Great Spirit.

And here they came for hundreds and thousands of years before the whites discovered the Ozarks, before a bath-house was built, before a building was erected ❧ ❧

They bathed in the waters of the bubbling pools, and they were relieved of their disorders and diseases, and went away refreshed, rejuvenated, healed, breathing prayers of gratitude to the Great Spirit. And then the white man came, and seeing the results obtained by the red brothers, he too utilized the healing waters ❧ ❧

❧ ❧

ADAM SMITH'S dictum that all wealth comes from labor applied to land is true, but it is not true that labor applied to land will necessarily produce wealth. Another factor is needed —the factor of intelligence, which implies purpose, system, order, intent— enterprise ❧ ❧

The result of labor turns on the quality of superintendence.

In the raising of fruits and flowers love is just as necessary as labor.

No drunkard ever had success with flowers, and for him fruits will not ripen. ❧ You can not fertilize land with whiskey, nor can you successfully irrigate with strong drink and woman's tears ❧ ❧

Fruits and flowers are primal sex products, and are best raised by men and women in partnership.

Something for nothing is always paid for. ❧ The cure for hoodlumism is manual training, and an industrial condition that will give the boy or girl work—congenial work—a fair wage, and a share in the honors of making things. Salvation lies in the Froebel methods carried into manhood ❧ ❧

❧ ❧

IVE miles up the creek from East Aurora is the village of South Wales. Society there centers around a schoolhouse where the Presbyterians hold service each Sunday morning and the Methodists in the afternoon. South Wales has two stores, a blacksmith shop and a town-pump where you always water your horse and get a drink for luck. The first turning to the left after the four corners, where the pump stands, up on the hillside, second house on the right, lives a fine Philistine, beloved by all who can appreciate plain, hard, common sense, honesty of purpose, and a dash of wit.

This man was a forty-niner, but some way things with him never panned. His motto once was, "Pike's Peak or bust." He reached Pike's Peak, and managed to get back to East Aurora, busted. ❧ But some one loaned him money to buy a team and a few implements, and he bought a farm where boulders grew lush and lusty. There was no market then for boulders. When crops were good, things didn't bring any price, and when prices were high there was nothing to sell.

However, the man and his wife managed to get a living, and send their boy and girl down to East Aurora to school—the boy going in the winter and the girl attending the spring and fall terms. And so the years passed, as years will.

❧ ❧

BUT there came an evil day when Deacon P. closed in on his mortgage, and the occupants of the old farm found themselves just exactly where they were when they took the place twenty years before.

Then it was that the Philistine and his family moved down to South Wales, first turning after you leave the town-pump, second house on the right.

They raised bees, and as the mother was now the business man, they got along first-rate — their income one year was three hundred and eighty dollars!

❧ ❧

YESTERDAY I watered my saddle mare, "Garnet," at the South Wales town-pump, and then took the first turning to the left. At the second house to the right an old man with white hair and a long white beard sat in a chair on the veranda. By his side, just below him, seated in the doorway, her hand in his, was an auburn-haired young woman, say thirty years of age.

"Don't speak—don't speak!" called the old man in a loud voice, as I reined in. "Don't speak! I've bet Maud fifty cents that it is Colonel Littlejourneys; I know the one-two-three-four step of that horse—Oh! you can't fool me!" laughed the old man.

The man and his daughter are both blind ❧ ❧

I tied my horse, and went in. There were merry greetings, much asking after the folks, and urgent demands that I should put my horse in the barn and remain to dinner ❧ ❧

"Oh, but that Mozart was bad!" said Maud. "Why didn't you give the colored man a dollar and let him throw it after the first one?"

"What's the Ashtabula Disaster got to do with Mozart?" demanded the old man in pretended wrath.

"What business have you to know anything about literature, music or art?" I demanded in turn. "Why, you are nothing but a farmer!"

"I used to be a farmer, but now I am a literary critic. I'm what you call a dilettante, for I even have some one read for me!"

"Surely, Colonel, Papa is right—we are not only dilettantes, but aristocrats—why, we have a bank account!" said Maud. "Indeed," I answered.

"Why, yes, you know Jack is getting along famously at his work. He is supervising architect at San Francisco for a government building that will cost a million dollars. And then he built the Crocker Hotel, and when the Crocker Estate gave him a check for nine thousand dollars for his services, what do you think he did?"

"Never could guess!"

"Why, he sent us a New York draft for a thousand dollars—that's the way we got our bank account."

The old man got up and I followed him into the house, where he groped his way to a bureau drawer and brought forth the book which he insisted I examine. ❡ "How much is it to our credit?" he demanded ❧ ❧

"A thousand dollars," I answered.

"What did I tell you!" was his proud answer ❧ ❧

❧ ❧

IT wasn't the money so much, either; it was the consciousness that Jack was succeeding—Jack who had plowed and sowed and reaped and cultivated stone bruises! Jack who had gone to the East Aurora "Academy" in winter and then taught school, and gone to the Boston Tech, and won a Foreign Travel Scholarship, and worked in McKim, Mead & White's (because they wanted a first-class man) and then had gone to San Francisco and was making a fortune —that is what made Jack's sister and Jack's father so proud and happy. Only one thing blurred their joy—Mother didn't live to know of Jack's success. Of course, she knew he would succeed, but she grew tired, so tired, and fell asleep and didn't awake, and that was four years ago.

"Let us show you some photographs of Jack's buildings," said the old man. He arose and started for a little side bedroom, the spare room. Maud was going after the photographs, too, and they met in the doorjamb and stuck there like humpty dumpty and Pantaloon. There were mutual apologies and finally the photographs were brought forth, the father leading the daughter and the daughter leading the father, and each cautioning the other to look out for the big rocking-chair.

I took the photographs in my hand, and sightless eyes gazed into vacancy over my head. I tried to look at the pictures, but could n't see them for the tears were running down my nose. Luckily no one saw me mopping.

Why did I cry? Really I do not know—perhaps I cried because I am a fool, and think sometimes I have troubles, when there is no trouble and no calamity excepting to those who think trouble and recognize calamity ✒ ✒

I bade my dear friends good-bye out there on the little veranda. The summer breeze stole through the wistaria and kissed the flowing white locks of the old man, and caressed the golden hair of the young woman, as they stood there hand in hand ✒ ✒

I mounted my horse and rode away down the dusty road. I took the first turning to the right, and looked back as I passed the corner.

❡ The father and daughter were still standing ⸢there, motionless. Their faces were raised, and they were looking out over me, completely over me, looking clear to San Francisco, where Jack is ✒ ✒

I thought of a little book that was in my sidepocket. I had been reading it that very morning. I took the volume out and read the title: WHERE LOVE IS, THERE IS GOD.—*Where Love Is.*

✒ ✒

There was one who thought himself above me, and he was above me until he had that thought.

CULTIVATE the intellect, and you shall have a mind that produces beautiful thoughts, worthy images, helpful ideas; that will serve as a solace in times of stress, and be to you a refuge 'gainst all the storms that blow. The cultured mind, as compared with the uncultured, is the difference between a beautiful garden which produces vegetables, fruits or flowers, and a tract of land that is overgrown with weeds and brambles.

❡ To be a person of culture is to be at home under all conditions. Your mind is stored with mental images, and memory comes to keep you company, and guide you from nostalgia and the sense of separateness to universality or oneness with the Divine. The country will be beautiful to you in any season, and society and solitude each will be welcomed by you in turn. You are to reject nothing, despise nothing, knowing that everything belongs somewhere, and that it is needed to make up the great mosaic of life.

JOAQUIN MILLER is dead. His body was burned on the funeral-pyre that he had made ready, and his ashes were scattered to the four winds. But the good in him abides. For him I had a great affection. For twenty-five years I wrote him every little while, anything that happened to be in my mind—foolish little nothings, stories about children, dogs, bears, cats—things I imagined, things that might have been so; and he in turn responded in kind.

Some of his letters I was able to read.

❡ He sent me presents of books; bits for bridles; spurs; and if anybody gave him anything he did not want or had not the time to care for, he sent it to me by express collect. I joyed in the society of the man, perhaps for the reason that he was not on my hands, and that I did not have to endure his society for long ✒ ✒

When he came to East Aurora, everybody took a holiday, and we laughed and played and picnicked the livelong day.

Then we built a bonfire and told ghost-stories until midnight.

Whenever I was in San Francisco, which has been about once a year for the last two decades, I made a pious pilgrimage to " The Hights."

And usually I waited to see the sun go down and sink a golden ball through the Golden Gate—with the permission of

Joaquin. His estate of several hundred acres at the top of the mountain was purchased about thirty years ago, out of the royalty received on *The Danites*. The site overlooked the city of Oakland, San Francisco, the Bay, and gave a panoramic view of the Golden Gate and the blue Pacific beyond. He spelled it " Hights " because a visitor once called it " The Heights," and anyway Joaquin didn't do anything as others did.

⟪ It was a tumbled mass of rocks, trees, vines, wild flowers, with here and there a great giant redwood. For agricultural purposes it would have bankrupted anybody who owned it. Joaquin Miller bought the land for purposes picturesque and poetic. No one else wanted it. To reach it you had to climb up a winding road, a distance of about four miles from the turnpike below, where eventually the street-car came and stopped. Civilization has gradually moved that way, until now the land has a tangible value, and if sold, it will certainly clear off the debts of the dead poet and leave a snug little sum for his heirs.

⟨◦⟩ ◦

MILLER got tired of the world at fifty. Perhaps the world was a little tired of him. And here he fled for sanctuary. He had a little money, a few hundred dollars; but he made raids down into the lowlands, and gave lectures and readings for which he received from fifty to a hundred dollars per evening. Like Thoreau, he loved solitude—when he was able to escape it, any time.

⟪ He occasionally got twenty-five dollars for a poem. And all the money he made he invested in lumber, which was hauled up the hill by a weary route. He constructed a dozen little houses about as big as drygoods-boxes some with cupolas, curious little verandahs, strange observatories ◦ ◦

Any visitor who came this way was given a house to live in, and told to remain as long as he wished and go away when he wanted. His conversation was entertaining, illuminating, surprising, witty, profound, contradictory. He had a way of abusing his friends when they called. Before you could formulate a word of greeting, he unlimbered his vocabulary ◦ He told of your sins, your crimes, your misdemeanors, your faults, your foibles, your limitations. He knew where you had been, what you had done, and his frankness might have been positively shocking were it not for the fact that he carried it over the ridge until you laughed and everybody screamed for joy.

On the gateway where you entered " The Hights" there was a sign: " No admittance; keep agoing. Better view higher up." This did not mean, however, that you were not welcome. Miller expressed things by contraries. His heart was friendly, tender, sympathetic. He was a poseur, but he posed so long that the pose was natural.

He wore long hair that fell to his shoulders. His beard came to his waist. His dress-trousers were buckskin, and he wore high-top boots with flapping ears. When he went down town he often wore jangling spurs. He wore a leather vest, with solid-gold nuggets for buttons, brought from the Klondike. His necktie was red, the symbol of anarchy, and in it nestled a thousand-dollar diamond-pin.

YOU are not to draw close about you the skirts of intolerance, nor look with disdain on those less fortunate; but always, and at all times, be able to place yourself, thru the gift of imagination, in the position of others.

Thus do you evolve sympathy and pity, two sentiments without which a man is indeed but a mental mendicant.

JOAQUIN had no respect for law or for society—that is, if you believed his conversation. But the fact is that he was not a criminal in any sense. He only played in his mind at being a lawbreaker.

¶ He got his name through his defense of an outlaw by the name of Joaquin. In merry jest his mining companions gave him the name of the man that he had so vigorously defended and whom they had helped to hang. And finally the name stuck. He accepted it as his own; and instead of Cincinnatus Heine Miller, he chose to be called plain Joaquin Miller. He was born in a moving wagon, somewhere between Indiana and Oregon, in the year Eighteen Hundred Forty-one. He claimed Indiana as his birthplace, however, because that is where his parents started from.

He was the first, save the Hoosier Schoolmaster, to locate Indiana "literary zone."

His name, Cincinnatus Heine, reveals the literary bias of his parents. Any one who loves Heinrich Heine and enjoys the wonderful lilt and lure of the Heine lines, and who knows the one fact about Cincinnatus, that he left his plow in the field and went to fight his own country's battles, is an educated person. Joaquin Miller would leave a plow in the field, any time, and he always maintained that Cincinnatus was only looking for an excuse to forsake the stump-lot.

JOAQUIN MILLER was a poet by prenatal tendency. He was brought up among the Indians, and a deal of their poetic splendor and love of color splashed his soul. At times he was just as dignified, just as impassive, as any Sioux Chief

Alas and alack! Here in America there were many to say that he was an Egotist, a Poseur Plus; and, of course, he was. But his pose was as natural as the pose of a peacock, and his song much sweeter. He was at home everywhere and anywhere. Children loved him. Boys worshiped him. Women said, "Ah," and "Oh!" when he entered the room. If a man thought he was sure-enough-easy, Joaquin could call him, just as

Jack Crawford used to land on the beak of the party who got fresh on the subject of hair. Joaquin Miller loved his friends and hated his enemies. He had positive ideas, as long as he held them; and he could change them with lightning-like rapidity. He was writer, actor, speaker, editor, poet, gentleman. In him there was something specially childlike and innocent. Anything he had, he was willing to divide with any one who wanted it

During the Nineties he had so many visitors, hoboes, tramps, criminals, poets, preachers, reformers, who called on him, that they nearly ate up his substance. But as long as he could get food for them, they were welcome. And he himself, at times, wrapped himself in a blanket, and slept out-of-doors, in order that visitors might have his cottage.

¶ He was Utopian, and was always picturing a society where friendship would be supreme, and where everything would belong to anybody who wanted it; where none would have too much, but everybody would have enough.

¶ Poetlike, Joaquin spent most of the money he made. It would have made no difference how much he made; he would have given it away. Yet he was never in want. There were always a few friends to whom he turned by divine right, and asked for his own; and he never asked for anything he did not need; and when he could, he paid it back. He was honest, sincere, affectionate, talented. Needless to say, he lacked synthesis. He added to the world's stock of harmless pleasure. He made smiles to grow where there was none before.

One man of this kind was enough. He died uncomplaining. He was a beautiful Pantheist, a wit, a dreamer, an idealist, who had tasted life and found it good. He was as frank as Omar Khayyam, and as intellectually intrepid.

The average man plays to the gallery of his own self-esteem.

The average woman sees only the weak points in a strong man, and the good points in a weak one.

IN Grecian History the time between the years Four Hundred Sixty-one and Four Hundred Twenty-nine Before Christ is known as the Age of Pericles. ❡ It is known as the Age of Pericles because in twenty years of that time he adorned the city of Athens, and so beautified it that it has been the despair of builders of cities to this day. This present age resembles the Age of Pericles, in that it is a time of great unrest, a time of great activity, a time when people are working, a time of great enlightenment. Pericles had for his supervisor of public works, Phidias, a sculptor to whom the ages have not given a rival. Phidias was a great teacher. The people of Athens appreciated art. He taught by example; his work was ever before the people. He set thousands of men to work with mallet and chisel, carving out wonderful marble ideals which their minds created. ❡ One of the men who worked for Phidias was Sophroniscus. He married Phaenarete, a woman who had much skill in taking care of the sick, who knew something of the laws of life. Phaenarete's son was Socrates. Socrates learned the trade of Sophroniscus and became a sculptor of some renown. He worked with hand, heart and brain until he had made a statue that fulfilled his ideal, when he said, " I have learned what I can from sculpture." ❡ Then he set himself to another task. He made his brain think to a purpose. Everything that Socrates did had a purpose. Even his marriage with Xantippe seems to have served him even better perhaps than it served Xantippe. She could not understand his logic, and clever as was Socrates, he never understood the needs of his wife. ❡ Socrates lived more than two thousand and three hundred years ago. We have not yet caught up with the teachings of Socrates. Our word "school" comes from a Greek word, the meaning of which we have changed. Originally the word meant leisure, spare time. It is the spare time that every one has, when walking, after supper in the evening, on the way to the theater, a concert ❧ Such occasions to Socrates were leisure.

And Socrates thought, and always came to a conclusion in his thinking ❧ ❧ " What is its use?" was the Socratic question ❧ ❧ Socrates had many pupils who have been world teachers ❧ Plato and Aristotle are the two whom we know best.

NO, it is not for the rude breath of man to blow out the lamp of hope.
Instead, let us hold it high, a guide by day, a pillar of fire by night, to cheer each pilgrim on his way.
For have there not been times, O God, when we peered into the gloom, and the heavens were hung with black, and then when life was well-nigh gone, we saw a light.
It was the Star of Hope!

There came to Socrates one day a rich man's son named Alcibiades. He asked the way to eternal life. For, to the mind of Socrates, a searcher after knowledge was a searcher after virtue. Said Alcibiades, " Socrates, how shall I become educated?" Socrates said: " What can you do? Can you drive a mule to the top of the Acropolis, carrying one of those shining blocks of marble to be put in the top of the Parthenon?"
" Oh, no, the muleteer does that."
" Can you drive a chariot?"
" Oh, no, the charioteer does that."
" Alcibiades, can you carve a statue?"
" Oh, no, we hire our statues carved."
" Can you cook your dinner?"
" Oh, no, we have cooks to do this."
" Is it not strange, Alcibiades, that your father should give to his humblest servant a better education than he does to his son ?" And Alcibiades went away sorrowful, for he loved ease and was slothful.—*Socrates.*

IT is a night of a thousand stars. The date, Sunday April 14, 1912. The time, 11:20 p. m.

The place, off Cape Race—that Cemetery of the sea.

Suddenly a silence comes—the engines have stopped—the great iron heart of of the ship has ceased to beat.

Such a silence is always ominous to those who go down to the sea in ships. "The engines have stopped!"

Eyes peer; ears listen; startled minds wait!

A half-minute goes by ᴐᴏ ᴐᴏ

Then the great ship groans, as her keel grates and grinds. She reels, rocks, struggles as if to free herself from a titanic grasp, and as she rights herself, people standing lose their center of gravity ᴐᴏ ᴐᴏ

Not a shock—only about the same sensation that one feels when the ferryboat slides into her landing-slip, with a somewhat hasty hand at the wheel.

On board the ferry we know what has happened—here we do not.

" An iceberg!" some one cries. The word is passed along.

" Only an iceberg! Barely grated it—side-swiped it—that is all! Ah, Ha!"

❡ The few on deck and some of those in cabins peering out of portholes, see a great white mass go gliding by.

A shower of broken ice has covered the decks. Passengers pick up specimens " for souvenirs to carry home," they laughingly say.

Five minutes pass—the engines start again—but only for an instant.

THIS story of the Titanic has a fascinating appeal, coming as it does from the pen of the man who, a short two years later, was destined to meet at sea the death which he here relates so vividly.

The reference to Mr. and Mrs. Straus, is particularly poignant for Elbert Hubbard himself was shortly to pass out as gloriously with his wife at his side to share his fate. "And Mr. and Mrs. Straus, I envy you that legacy of love and loyalty left to your children and grandchildren. The calm courage that was yours all your long and useful career was your possession in death." Had he indeed a presentiment of what was to be his destiny?

—*Editor's Note*

Again the steam is shut off ᴐᴏ Then the siren-whistles cleave and saw the frosty air ᴐᴏ ᴐᴏ

Silence and the sirens! Alarm, but no tumult—but why blow the whistles when there is no fog! ᴐᴏ ᴐᴏ

The cold is piercing. Some who have come up on deck return to their cabins for wraps and overcoats ᴐᴏ ᴐᴏ

The men laugh—and a few nervously smoke ᴐᴏ ᴐᴏ

It is a cold, clear night of stars. There is no moon. The sea is smooth as a Summer pond. The great towering iceberg that loomed above the topmost mast has done its work, gone on, disappeared, piloted by its partners, the darkness and the night ᴐᴏ ᴐᴏ

" There was no iceberg—you only imagined it," a man declares.

" Go back to bed —there is no danger—this ship can not sink anyway!" says the Managing Director of the Company ᴐᴏ ᴐᴏ

In a lull of the screaming siren, a hoarse voice is heard calling through a megaphone from the bridge—" Man the lifeboats! Women and children first!! "

❡ " It sounds just like a play," says Henry Harris to Major Butt.

Stewards and waiters are giving out life-preservers and showing passengers how to put them on.

There is laughter—a little hysteric. " I want my clothes made to order," a woman protests. " An outrageous fit! Give me a man's size!"

The order of the Captain on the bridge is repeated by other officers—" Man the lifeboats! Women and children first!! "

¶ "It's a boat-drill—that's all!" ❧ "A precautionary measure — we'll be going ahead soon," says George Widener to his wife, in reassuring tones as he holds her hand.

Women are loath to get into the boats. Officers not over gently, seize them, and half-lift and push them in. Children crying, and some half-asleep, are passed over into the boats.

Mother-arms reach out and take the little ones. Parentage and ownership are lost sight of.

Some boats are only half-filled, so slow are the women to believe that rescue is necessary ❧ ❧

The boats are lowered, awkwardly, for there has never been a boat-drill, and assignments are being made haphazard.

¶ A sudden little tilt of the deck hastens the proceeding. The bows of the ship are settling—there is a very perceptible list to starboard.

An Englishman tired and blasé, comes out of the smoking-room, having just ceased a card-game. He very deliberately approaches an officer who is loading women and children into a lifeboat ❧ ❧

The globe-trotting Briton is filling his pipe. "I si, orficer, you know; what seems to be the matter with this bloomin' craft, you know?"

"Fool," roars the officer, "the ship is sinking!" ❧ ❧

"Well," says the Englishman, as he strikes a match on the rail, "Well, you know, if she is sinking, just let 'er down a little easy, you know."

John Jacob Astor half forces his wife into the boat. She submits, but much against her will. He climbs over and takes a seat beside her in the lifeboat. It is a ruse to get her in—he kisses her tenderly—stands up, steps lightly out and gives his place to a woman.

"Lower away!" calls the officer.

"Wait—here is a boy—his mother is in there!" ❧ ❧

"Lower away!" calls the officer—"there is no more room."

Colonel Astor steps back. George Widener tosses him a woman's hat, picked up from the deck. Colonel Astor jams the hat on the boy's head, takes the lad up in his arms, runs to the rail and calls, "You won't leave this little girl, will you?" ❧ ❧

"Drop her into the boat," shouts the officer. The child drops into friendly hands as the boat is lowered.

Astor turns to Widener and laughingly says, "Well, we put one over on 'em that time." ❧ ❧

"I'll meet you in New York," calls Colonel Astor to his wife as the boat pulls off. He lights a cigarette and passes the silver case and a match-box along to the other men.

A man runs back to his cabin to get a box of money and jewels. The box is worth three hundred thousand dollars. The man changes his mind and gets three oranges, and gives one orange each to three children as they are lifted into safety ❧ ❧

As a lifeboat is being lowered, Mr. and Mrs. Isador Straus come running with arms full of blankets, brought from their stateroom. They throw the bedding to the people in the boat.

"Help that woman in!" shouts an officer. Two sailors seize Mrs. Straus. She struggles, frees herself, and proudly says, "Not I—I will not leave my husband." Mr. Straus insists, quietly and gently, that she shall go. He will follow later.

But Mrs. Straus is firm. "All these years we have traveled together, and shall we part now? No, our fate is one."

She smiles a quiet smile, and pushes aside the hand of Major Butt, who has ordered the sailors to leave her alone. "We will help you—Mr. Straus and I— come! It is the law of the sea—women and children first—come!" said Major Butt ❧ ❧

"No, Major; you do not understand. I remain with my husband—we are one, no matter what comes—you do not understand!" "See," she cried, as if to change the subject, "there is a woman getting in the lifeboat with her baby; she has no wraps!" Mrs. Straus tears off her fur-lined robe and places it tenderly around the woman and the innocently sleeping babe.

William T. Stead, grim, hatless, with furrowed face, stands with an iron bar in hand as a lifeboat is lowered. " Those men in the steerage, I fear, will make a rush—they will swamp the boats."
❧ Major Butt draws his revolver. He looks toward the crowded steerage. Then he puts his revolver back into his pocket, smiles. "No, they know we will save their women and children as quickly as we will our own."
Mr. Stead tosses the iron bar into the sea.
❧ He goes to the people crowding the afterdeck. They speak a polyglot language. They cry, they pray, they supplicate, they kiss each other in frenzied grief ❧ ❧
John B. Thayer, George Widener, Henry Harris, Benjamin Guggenheim, Charles M. Hays, Mr. and Mrs. Straus, move among these people, talk to them and try to reassure them.
There are other women besides Mrs. Straus who will not leave their husbands. These women clasp each other's hands. They smile—they understand!
Mr. Guggenheim and his secretary are in full dress. "If we are going to call on Neptune, we will go dressed as gentlemen," they laughingly say.
The ship is slowly settling by the head.
❧ The forward deck is below the water. The decks are at a vicious angle. The icy waters are full of struggling people.
Those still on the ship climb up from deck to deck.
The dark waters follow them, angry, jealous, savage, relentless.
The decks are almost perpendicular. The people hang by the rails.
A terrific explosion occurs—the ship's boilers have burst.
The last lights go out.
Darkness! ❧ ❧
The great iron monster slips, slides, gently glides, surely, down, down, down into the sea.
Where once the great ship proudly floated, there is now a mass of wreckage, the dead, the dying, and the great black all-enfolding night ❧ Overhead, the thousand stars shine with a brightness unaccustomed ❧ ❧
The Strauses, Stead, Astor, Butt, Harris,

Thayer, Widener, Guggenheim, Hays— I thought I knew you, just because I had seen you, realized somewhat of your able qualities, looked into your eyes and pressed your hands, but I did not guess your greatness.
You are now beyond the reach of praise —flattery touches you not—words for you are vain.
Medals for heroism—how cheap the gilt, how paltry the pewter!
You are beyond our praise or blame. We reach out, we do not touch you. We call, but you do not hear.
Words unkind, ill-considered, were some times flung at you, Colonel Astor, in your lifetime. We admit your handicap of wealth—pity you for the accident of birth—but we congratulate you that as your mouth was stopped with the brine of the sea, so you stopped the mouths of the carpers and critics with the dust of the tomb ❧ ❧
If any think unkindly of you now, be he priest or plebian, let it be with finger to his lips, and a look of shame in his own dark heart. Also, shall we not write a postscript to that booklet on cigarettes?
❧ Charles M. Hays—you who made life safe for travelers on shore, yet you were caught in a sea-trap, which, had you been manager of that Transatlantic Line, would never have been set, baited as it was with human lives.
You placed safety above speed. You fastened your faith to utilities, not futilities. You and John B. Thayer would have had a searchlight and used it in the danger-zone, so as to have located an iceberg five miles away. You would have filled the space occupied by that silly plunge-bath (how ironic the thing) with a hundred collapsible boats, and nests of dories ❧ ❧
You, Hays and Thayer, believed in other men—you trusted them—this time they failed you. We pity them, not you.
❧ And Mr. and Mrs. Straus, I envy you that legacy of love and loyalty left to your children and grandchildren. The calm courage that was yours all your long and useful career was your possession in death.
You knew how to do three great things—

you knew how to live, how to love and how to die.

Archie Butt, the gloss and glitter on your spangled uniform were pure gold. I always suspected it.

You tucked the ladies in the lifeboats, as if they were going for an automobile-ride. "Give my regards to the folks at home," you gaily called as you lifted your hat and stepped back on the doom-ed deck so so

You died the gallant gentleman that you were. You helped preserve the old and honored English tradition, "Women and children first." All America is proud of you. Guggenheim, Widener and Harris, you were unfortunate in life in having more money than we had. That is why we wrote things about you, and printed them in black and red. If you were sports, you were game to the last, cheerful losers, and all such are winners.
⁋ As your souls play hide-and-seek with sirens and dance with the naiads, you have lost interest in us. But our hearts are with you still. You showed us how death and danger put all on a parity. The women in the steerage were your sisters—the men your brothers; and on the tablets of love and memory we have 'graved your names.

William T. Stead, you were a writer, a thinker, a speaker, a doer of the word. You proved your case; sealed the brief with your heart's blood; and as your bearded face looked in admiration for the last time up at the twinkling, shining stars, God in pardonable pride said to Gabriel, "Here comes a man!"

And so all you I knew, and all that thousand and half a thousand more I did not know, passed out of this Earth-Life into the Unknown upon the unforgetting tide. You were sacrificed to the greedy Goddess of Luxury and her consort the Demon of Speed.

Was it worth the while? Who shall say? The great lessons of life are learned only in blood and tears. Fate decreed that you should die for us.

Happily, the world has passed forever from a time when it feels a sorrow for the dead. The dead are at rest, their work is ended, they have drunk of the waters of Lethe, and these are rocked in the cradle of the deep. We kiss our hands to them and cry, "Hail and Farewell—until we meet again!"

But for the living who wait for a footstep that will never come, and all those who listen for a voice that will never more be heard, our hearts go out in tenderness, love and sympathy.

These dead have not lived and died in vain. They have brought us all a little nearer together—we think better of our kind so so

One thing is sure, there are just two respectable ways to die. One is of old age, and the other is by accident. All disease is indecent.

Suicide is atrocious.

But to pass out as did Mr. and Mrs. Isador Straus is glorious. Few have such a privilege. Happy lovers, both. In life they were never separated, and in death they are not divided.

so so

SAFETY lies in living like a poor man, no matter how much money you have; and above all things, bring your children up to be useful, to perform the necessary tasks of life, never to be above doing good, plain, old-fashioned work so so

Any one who uses the term "menial" is touched with intellecticism. There are no menial tasks. The necessary is the sacred, and the useful is the divine. Keep your feet on the earth, even though your head is in the clouds. Do not be exclusive, and set yourself apart, as something special and peculiar. The high and lofty attitude we often see in the poet, the artist and the musician all token the defective. Have intellect, of course, but build it on a basis of common-sense.

so so

The duels between our celestial and terrestial natures often take place at so deep a point in our souls that we are not aware of the conflict — but still the fight if on.

so so

All my gods dwell in temples made with hands so so

USIC is the youngest of the arts. ❡ Modern music dates back only about four hundred years. It is not so old as the invention of printing ✒ ✒

As an art it began with the work of the Church in endeavoring to arrange a liturgy ✒ ✒

The medieval chant and the popular folk-song fused, and the result was our modern science of music.

Sculpture reached perfection in Greece, painting in Italy, portraiture in Holland; but Germany, the land of thought, has given us nearly all the great musicians and nine-tenths of all our valuable musical compositions.

Art follows in the wake of commerce, for without commerce there is neither surplus wealth nor leisure. The artist is paid from what is left after men have bought food and clothing; and the time to enjoy comes only after the struggle for existence.

When Venice was not only Queen of the Adriatic but of the maritime world as well, Art came and established there her Court of Beauty. It was Venice mothered Giorgione, Titian, the Bellinis, and those masterful book-makers, and the men who wrought in iron and silver and gold; and it was beautiful Venice that gave sustenance and encouragement to Stradivarius (who made violins to the glory of God) up at Cremona, only a few miles away.

But there came a day when all those seventy book-makers of Venice ceased to print, and the music of the anvils was stilled, and all the painters were dead, and Venice became but a monument of things that were, as she is today; for commerce is King, and his capital has been moved far away. So Venice sits sad and solitary, a pale and beautiful ruin, pathetic beyond speech, existing on the sale of souvenir postal-cards and by taking in boarders, patroled by petty pilferers, degenerate sons of the robbers who once roamed the sea and enthroned her on her hundred isles.

All that Venice knew was absorbed by Holland. The Elzevirs and the Plantins took over the business of the seventy book-makers, and the art schools of Amsterdam, Leyden and Antwerp reproduced every picture of note that had been done in Venice. The great churches of Holland are replicas of the churches of Venice. And the Cathedral at Antwerp, where the sweet bells have chimed each quarter of an hour for three centuries, through peace and plenty, through lurid war and sudden death—there where hangs Rubens' masterpiece—that cathedral is but an enlarged Santa Maria dei Frari, where for two hundred years hung the *Assumption* by Titian.

In these churches of Holland were placed splendid organs, and the priests formed choirs and offered prizes for the best singers and the best composition. Music and painting developed hand in hand, for, at the last, all of the arts are one—each being but a division of labor. The world owes a great debt to the Dutch. It was Holland taught England how to paint and how to print, and England taught us; so printing, painting and music came to us by way of the Dutch ✒ ✒

The march of civilization follows a simple trail, well defined beyond dispute. Viewed in retrospect it begins in retrospect. It begins in a haze thread stretching from Assyria into Egypt, from Egypt into Greece, from Greece to Rome, widening throughout Italy and Spain, then centering in Venice and tracing clear and deep to Amsterdam, widening again into Germany and across to England, thence carried in "Mayflowers" to America.

That remark of Grover Cleveland that there is no culture west of Buffalo was indelicate if not unkind; and residents of Kansas City aver that it is open to argument. But the fact stands beyond cavil that commerce and art have traveled westward ✒ ✒

From the rocky shores of New England civilization moved toward the setting sun.—*Art and Commerce*.

✒ ✒

Writer's Cramp is caused by undigested ideas and unpronounceable words.

HE rubber tire made the automobile possible, just as the iron rail made the locomotive a fact. If Doctor Goodrich had invented the rubber tire before Stephenson utilized the steel rail, the railroads would never have been built ❧ Possibly yet the streak of rust and the right of way will live only in history, passing into the realm of things that were, like the high-wheel bicycle, the beaver, the wild pigeon the buffalo, the dodo and side whiskers ❧ ❧

Transportation is the second most important thing in the world; and he who lubricates transportation is a world-builder, a benefactor of his kind, and will live in the hearts of humanity.

❧ ❧

THREE hundred twelve years before Christ, Appius Claudius began the making of the Appian Way. When this European War is over and you go Abroad with your White Car, you may have the pleasure of motoring over parts of the original Roadbed of the Appian Way. ❧ It was a Roadway eighteen feet wide, extending south from Rome to Capua— and thence on and on to Brundisium; parts of it are still in daily use.

The Appian Way was the symbol of abundance. It made the Oil and Wine accessible. It became the Milky Way of Roman Commerce. It was a Great White Way of Prosperity.

The Romans, two hundred fifty years later, while occupying Britain, constructed Watling Way, leading from Dover to York, and the great North Road from London to Edinburgh; and of this road, too, portions still remain. ❧ Cæsar's Legions, by establishing that broad stretch of Roadway, endowed the Britons with one of the primary principles of Civilization. Also, it may have suggested to them that thoroughness is a

quality that commends itself to all men. ❧ Undoubtedly the American more than the Roman or the Briton will live in History as a Roadmaker; at least he deserves to. In the year Nineteen Hundred Fifteen we have ten thousand Appian Ways and as many Watling Ways here on this continent; ribbons of brick and stone and macadam stretching from County Seat to County Seat; from State to State. All of which effect for good the lives of one hundred million people.

These Ways are memorials to great builders. They show Vision, and Courage, and Stick-to-it-iveness. They bespeak an intelligent desire to "get there!" They animate the spirit of the times—"Forward! March!" ❧ The evolution of Roadways depends upon modes of transportation. The modern automobile has been the greatest factor in scientific highway construction. Perfection in the one has brought perfection in the other.—*Roadways*.

❧ ❧

THERE is no damnation for any one—there never was, and never will be—and there is no defeat except for those who think defeat. Success is for you. Life is good!

SYMPATHY, Wisdom and Poise seem to be the three ingredients that are most needed in forming the Master Man.

No man is great who does not possess Sympathy ❧ ❧

Sympathy and Imagination are twin sisters. Your heart must go out to all men: the high, the low, the rich, the poor, the learned, the unlearned, the good, the bad, the wise and the foolish; it is necessary to be one with them all, else you can never comprehend them. ❧ Sympathy!—it is the touchstone to every secret, the key to all knowledge, the open sesame of all hearts. Put yourself in the other man's place, and then you will know why he thinks certain things and does certain deeds.

Put yourself in his place and your blame will dissolve itself into pity, and your tears will wipe out the record of his misdeeds. The saviors of the world have simply been men with wondrous Sympathy ✖ ✖

But Wisdom must go with Sympathy, else the emotions will become maudlin and pity may be wasted on a poodle instead of a child—on a field-mouse instead of a human soul. Knowledge in use is Wisdom, and Wisdom implies a sense of values—you know a big thing from a little one, a valuable fact from a trivial one. Tragedy and comedy are simply questions of value; a little misfit in life makes us laugh; a great one is tragedy and cause for expression of grief ✖ ✖

Poise is the strength of body and strength of mind to control your Sympathy and your Knowledge. Unless you control your emotions they run over and you stand in the slop.

Sympathy must not run riot, or it tokens weakness instead of strength. In every hospital for nervous disorders are to be found many instances of this loss of control. The indiviual has Sympathy, but no Poise, and therefore his life is worthless to himself and to the world.

❦ Poise reveals itself more in voice than it does in words; more in thought than in action; more in atmosphere than in conscious life. It is a spiritual quality, and is felt more than it is seen. It is not a matter of bodily size, nor of bodily attitude, nor attire, nor of personal comeliness; it is a state of inward being, and of knowing your cause is just.

❦ I know a man who is deformed in body, but who has such Poise that to enter a room where he is, is to feel his presence and acknowledge his superiority ✖ ✖

To allow Sympathy to waste itself on unworthy objects is to deplete one's life-forces ✖ ✖

To conserve is the part of Wisdom, and reserve is a necessary element in all art, as well as in life.

Poise being the control of our Sympathy and Knowledge, it implies a possession of these attributes, for without Sympathy and Knowledge you will have nothing to control but your physical body. To practise Poise as a mere gymnastic exercise—just as to study etiquette—is

to be self-conscious, stiff, preposterous. Poise is a question of spirit controlling flesh, heart controlling attitude.

Get Knowledge by coming close to Nature. That man is the greatest who best serves his kind. Sympathy and knowledge are for use—you acquire that you may give out; you accumulate that you may bestow. And as God has given unto you the sublime blessings of Sympathy and Wisdom, there will come to you the wish to reveal your gratitude by giving them out again; for the wise man is aware that we retain only as we give. Let your light shine. To him that hath shall be given. The exercise of Wisdom brings Wisdom; and at the last the infinitesimal quantity of man's Knowledge, compared with the Infinite, and the smallness of man's Sympathy when compared with the source from which ours is absorbed, will evolve a humility that will lend a perfect Poise.

The Master Man is one with Sympathy, Wisdom and Poise. And such are always learners, as well as teachers.—*Sympathy, Wisdom and Poise.*

✖ ✖

THE Science of Eugenics is no passing, transient fad. It is receiving an earnest, sincere, serious attention from many very great and noble minds. It has been taken out of the hands of theology, the fortune-teller and the sensational reformer, and is being dealt with as it deserves, by men and women intent on leaving this world a better place than they found it, and who are not afraid to follow a reason to its lair.

✖ ✖

STRONG men are in demand. You can always hire men, plenty of them, for two dollars a day. When you want a man, however, to fill a ten-thousand-dollar position, you have to hunt for him; and when you want a fifty-thousand-dollar man, you find that he already has a good job and is not anxious to give it up.

✖ ✖

To fail to win the approval of one's other self is defeat, and there is none other.

✖ ✖

Talk less and listen more ✖ ✖

MAN seeks happiness: all men seek happiness. There is no other goal or intent in life, and whether men seek it through license or asceticism, through selfishness or sacrifice, it is the one eternal quest.

There is no other aim in life for any man or any woman than this—happiness. Even the suicide seeks happiness, his act slips the cable of existence, being always an attempt to flee from misery, which is the opposite pole from happiness.

In man's search for happiness his perceptions pass through three separate and distinct forms of reason. The first and lowest form is rather a condition of unreason than reason. The man does not yet comprehend that life is a sequence, that this happens today because that happened yesterday—that effect follows cause. He seeks happiness, and he wants it now. He knows nothing of the pleasures of anticipation, the beauty of patience, the splendid reward for self-control.

The second stage is the period of virtue. The man has caught glimpses into the law of consequences. He knows that headache follows debauch, that satiety follows license, that notes come due, and that there is a difference between right and wrong.

That is, in fact, his distinguishing feature—he knows right from wrong. He thinks much on this subject, he talks about it, writes about it, preaches about it—right and wrong. He separates this from that, eschews evil and cleaves to that which is good: his life is given up to separating good from bad, and all that which he thinks is good he desires to appropriate, and what he thinks is bad he discards.

If he has the power he passes laws forbidding under severe penalties this, that and the other. He sees that certain things are "sins" and so he would stamp them out. He knows what is best (or he thinks he does), and for the good of men he would restrain them, and compel them to follow in the straight and narrow path. Such were the Puritans, the Huguenots, the early Methodists and all that excellent class that exists now and have always existed, known as Primitive Christians.

A man in this second stage lives a life of struggle—he wrestles with the spirit for a blessing, he struggles with the world of wrong, and he tussles with the demon within. He believes that his own nature is rooted in evil, and to eradicate this devil within is the chief thought of his life. His energies are given over, in great degree, to "resisting temptation." He is an abstainer, and to abstain from certain things he thinks constitutes "virtue." His life is largely negative, not positive; and to suppress and repress he believes is the duty of every one. In fact, the idea of "duty" is forever strong upon him.

¶ The first stage does not distinguish between right and wrong.

The distinguishing feature of the second stage is, it separates right from wrong.

¶ The third stage resembles the first to the uninitiated, for it does not seek to separate right from wrong. It recognizes that at the base of evil lies good; and that right and wrong are relative terms and easily shift places. It believes more in the goodness of bad people than the badness of good people. It sees that sin is misdirected energy, and also that often through sin do men reach the light, and it recognizes that that which teaches can not be wholly bad.

Of course, these three stages that I have outlined are to a degree arbitrary classifications, for they all overlap more or less, and a man may be in one stage one day and in another the next. Yet true types of stages number one and number two exist on every hand, and can easily be recalled by all observing men. Stage number three is not so sharply defined; men in this class are often unknown to those nearest them, and to the uninitiated they are sometimes pigeonholed with class one—they are branded "infidels." But you need not be disturbed by this, for if you have read history you know that the "infidel" has often been a person with faith plus.

He is ahead of his fellows, when they are quite sure he is behind.

The true type of man in stage three believes in all religions and in all gods. He sympathizes with every sect, but belongs to none. He recognizes that every religion is a reaching out for help, a prayer for light, and that a sect is merely a point of view. He recognizes that there is good in all, and that a man's "god" is the highest concept of what he would like to be—his god is himself at his best, and the devil is himself at his worst ◦◦ ◦◦

Yet the wise man does not cavil at the multiplicity of beliefs and strife of sects. For himself he would much prefer a religion that would unite men, not divide them. Yet he perceives that denominations represent stages of development in the onward and upward spiral of existence. There is much clay in their formation, and all are in a seething state of unrest; but each is doing its work in ministering to a certain type of mind. Birds moult their feathers because they are growing better feathers; and so in time will these same "orthodox" believers gladly moult the opinions for which they once stood ready to fight ◦◦ ◦◦

The wise man not only believes in all religions, but in all men—good, bad, ignorant, learned, the weak, the strong. He recognizes that night is as necessary as day; that all seasons are good; and that all weather is beautiful. The fierce blowing wind purifies the air, just as running water purifies itself. The winter is a preparation for summer.

Each and every thing is a part of the great whole. We are brother to the bird, the animal, the tree and the flower. Life is everywhere—even in the rocks—"a square foot of sod contains at least two hundred separate forms of existence," said Grant Allen. Life is everywhere, and it is all one life, and we are particles of it.

And this life is good.

Of all human reason none is more valuable than that higher understanding which comprehends that in nature no mistakes are made; and that all the seeming errors of men—so-called "sins"—are stepping stones that can be used to reach a higher good. Every truth is a paradox, and every strong man supplies the argument for his own undoing; each truth is only a half truth—and the statement of truth always involves a contradiction. Wise men realize these things and so they cease to quibble. They know you can explain nothing to any one—if the man does not already know it, your anxious efforts to make him see will all be futile.

MINIMIZE friction and create harmony. You can get friction for nothing, but harmony costs courtesy and self-control.

Every man does what he does because he, at the moment, thinks it is the best thing for him to do. He believes he makes a choice, but the truth is, his nature succumbs to the strongest attraction; and he is as much under the dominion of natural laws as if he were pure oxygen or nitrogen. Schopenhauer once said if you saw a stone rolling down hill and you would stop it and ask it why it rolled down hill, if it had conscious life, it would undoubtedly answer, "I roll down hill because I choose to."

Any man of certain temperament, who has had certain experiences, and is possessed of certain qualities, will always do a certain thing under certain conditions. And if you can find another man like him, he will also do exactly the same thing as the first under like conditions. ❧ Knowing these things, the man of wisdom does not blame. He may pity, but he does not attempt to punish, for he knows that the law of consequences sees that exact justice is done and he never makes the mistake of supposing that he is divinely appointed to act the part of a section of the day of judgment. He will influence if he can—he will reform, educate and lead out, but he will not try to repress nor chastise.

His life will be one long pardon, one inexhaustible pity; one infinite love and therefore, one infinite strength.

Anchorage is what most people pray for,

when what we really need is God's great open sea. The command, " Sail on, and on, and on, and on!" comes only to those who are in stage three, or the stage of enlightenment.

It is almost too much to expect that the period of insight and perfect poise should be more than transient. Yet it does exist, and there is no reason why it should not in time become a habit of life. Most free souls who have reached this state of " cosmic consciousness," will testify that insight came first as a thrill, and the periods then gradually extended as mastery became complete. It was a matter of growth—an evolution. Yet growth never proceeds at an even, steady pace, either in the realm of spirit or matter. There are bursts and bounds—throes and throbs—and then times of seeming inaction. But this inaction is only a gathering together of forces for the coming leap—the fallow years are just as natural, just as necessary as the years of plenty.

" Who shall relieve me of the body of this death? cried the prophet. He had in mind the ancient custom of punishing the murderer by chaining him to the dead body of his victim. Wherever the man went he had to drag the putrefying corpse—he could not disentangle himself from the result of his evil act. No more horrible punishment could possibly be devised; but Nature has a plan of retribution that is very much akin to it. What more terrible than this: The evil thing you do shall at once become an integral part of what you are.

You can not escape it—no concealment is possible, you are what you are on account of what you have done.

The man who imagined that scene of the " Final Judgment" where the righteous file into paradise and the wicked are tumbled into perdition, had a certain conception of life. And this conception was that separation of good people from bad, with an impassable gulf between, was a good thing. Yet the man to whom is attributed this parable did not believe in extrication, for his life was a living protest against it. He deliberately associated with so-called bad people, and surely had more love for the sinner than he had for the so-called righteous ❧ ❧

The law of consequences works both ways; by associating with the sinner and recognizing the good in him you unconsciously recognize the good in yourself. The love you give away is the only love you keep—by benefiting another you benefit yourself ❧ ❧

I T is a great man who, when he finds he has come out at the little end of the horn, simply appropriates the horn and blows it for evermore.

The thought of getting safely out of the world has no part in the life of the enlightened man—to live fully while he is here is his problem—one world at a time is enough for him. He believes that that which is good here is good in every star, and the Power that is caring for him here will not forsake him there.—*Man's Search for Happiness.*

❧ ❧

THE public school is life; the private school is a preparation for life.

Just take this matter home to yourself: You are a banker, merchant or railroad manager: you need a young man to help you in your business; two boys apply, seemingly of equal intelligence. One boy has been educated in the public schools, the other is fresh from a boarding academy—now which boy do you choose?

I 'll tell you—you 'll take the public school boy without a second thought, for the reason that you consider he probably knows the world of work, business and things much better than the other. You want a helper who can go after things and bring them, and you assume that the private school boy has been cared for and protected while the other boy has had to care for himself.

❧ ❧

A creed is an ossified metaphor.

THE other day a lady asked me this question: "What is your best book?" And I was going to say, *The Essay on Silence,* but the earnestness expressed in the lady's eyes indicated that persiflage was tabu, and so I answered truthfully, " The best piece of writing I ever produced is a little booklet entitled, *How I Found My Brother.*

THE Reformers tell us that this country needs this, that and the other, to save it from dire dissolution. ℂ These things are true, or not, as the case may be, but to my mind the one vital thing needed in America is an increase in the 'Gene Field Letter. We are suffering from epistolary elephantiasis. ℂ Every college should have a 'Gene Field Chair. Very few folks know how to write a letter, what to say or when to stop

A 'Gene Field Letter always contains an element of joy.

Next, it bears a message of wisdom. ℂ Third, it has a jigger of wit that gives the wisdom flavor. Fourth, it closes when it is done, and there is no postscript. ℂ A 'Gene Field Letter breathes kindness, appreciation, friendship, love, truth. The owner clings to it, shows it to friends, preserves it. If you own an original, you'll not part with it any more than you would sell your mother's portrait.

'Gene Field may not have been a great man, but he had a great heart. He knew the secret of friendship. To live so you will love and be loved is a fine art. Field was a friend.

Now let the world learn at his feet and follow his example.

The age demands it. Sensible people do not go around putting everything straight. Things will not stay put, anyway, unless it is in their nature to do so. 'Gene Field never called you down. He always called you up—up out of the mire of selfishness and despondency, up into the sunlight.

KNOWLEDGE is the distilled essence of our intuitions, corroborated by experience

NEVER write a grouchy letter— telephone. The grouchy word passes, and if you write in the mood it is fixed, and only the charming should be perpetuated

Of all living men no writer's letters are so valuable as those of James Whitcomb Riley. Jim may say foolish things, but he never writes them. Riley's letters are like bunches of violets with the morning dew upon them. Jim caught the idea from 'Gene

As a relief to pent-up emotions, the writer of a nasty letter has its use and purpose. So, if you must, then write it, fold it up, put it in the envelope, direct it in a bold hand, and mark it *Personal.* .

Next, stamp the envelope, placing the stamp upside down in the left-hand corner of the envelope. Then tear the whole thing into bits and throw them into the wastebasket.

THE chief value of life-insurance seems to be that it gives the man insured an increased capacity for meeting the natural and inevitable trials, difficulties and obstacles of life.

We fight the cussedness of inanimate things, the stupidity and inappreciation of the public—also, we fight our own limitations. But to meet these things with faith and fortitude and know in advance that you are victor—this is to live

That is the big thing at last—to live! ℂ And all that which helps us to live is good

The man who lives rightly will die gracefully when his times comes.

And he'll not die a hundred deaths before

WRITING is a matter of inspiration. You get your inspiration from your environment, but if the environment is not right, the little balance of brain upon which you do business is vapid. When you want peace, and poise, and power, choose the conditions that give the perfect environment.

Your friend is the man who knows all about you, and still likes you.

HE extension of the peace area is what constitutes progress, and nothing else does or can ✦ ✦

It was a mighty achievement when King Arthur brought about peace over an area as big as New York State, by dividing the country into districts, and over all of these having a central government or " court," to whom all grievances must be submitted.

Likewise it is a mighty and almost miraculous achievement when the whole of North America is a place of peace and prosperity, all through the matter of wise organization.

✦ ✦

JAMES WHITCOMB RILEY once told me that when he is about to begin a lecture he always expects to commence in a squeak or a squawk. He doubted himself—would memory fail, voice go on a strike, and thought sit silent, stupid, sullen in the brain cells? I know the feeling. And what an atrocious, brazen, brass-plated presumption on the part of any man to call from fields, parks, libraries, and homes of the great, the good and the strong of a big city and ask them to sit still and listen to him prate for two hours concerning this and that ✦ ✦

✦ ✦

IT is a mistake to raise false hopes— 'ware of the reaction.

But now comes a new style of advertisement, founded on the old idea of luring the reader on, but without its disappointing features ✦ ✦

I write advertisements for rest and recreation. But I only write about the things I know have merit plus.

If your heart is in a theme, when you write about it, the product is easy to read, instructive and amusing. These publicity articles, I frankly head, " An Advertisement." ✦ ✦

Thus at the start, I disarm disappointments and make peace with prejudice. Some of these advertisements are readable. A few are read from the first word to the last, and some of them impress good people and great, with the truth, beauty and desirability of the thing advertised.

I LOOK for a day when education will be like the landscape, free for all. Beauty and truth should be free to every one who has the capacity to absorb. The private school, the private library, the private art gallery, the exclusive college, have got to go. We want no excellence that is not for all. My brother must have all that I have—for my brother is myself and I am here. There must be no educated class, no superior class—every man must feel that he is superior to taking and enjoying a thing from which others by birth or ill-fortune are debarred.

A good man in an exclusive heaven would be in hell.

As long as other men are in prison, I, too, am in bonds.

But the world is getting better: go and visit your village school—any school— and compare it with the school you attended twenty-five years ago! There is beauty on the walls, cleanliness, order, fresh air, light and gentle consideration. Do not expect to find perfection— there is much work yet to do, but we are looking out towards the East! And I expect to see the day when all the great colleges of the land will be absorbed into the general public school system of America ✦ ✦

We are looking toward the East.

✦ ✦

IT is, of course, very necessary that when you are entrusted with a message you deliver it to the right person in the least possible time.

The man, however, who entrusts another with a message has a duty quite as much as the man who is given one.

There are men who can never get messages carried; and other men there be who inspire messengers with loyalty, fidelity and courage.

It is a somewhat curious thing that the most able men are never good teachers. " The great teacher," says Emerson, " is not the man who supplies the most facts, but the one in whose presence we become different people."

Too much individuality repels, overawes, subdues. An overpowering personality is a willopus-wallopus, or a steam-roller that flattens anything and everybody in the vicinity. A great actor seldom surrounds himself with able actors. In fact, a great actor usually reduces the whole company to a nullity. In his presence animation subsides, ambition declines, originality takes to the tall uncut, and initiative becomes apologetic.

In the United States there are a few merchants who are discoverers of genius, but most are served by the mediocre, not to mention the timeserver, the hypocrite and the lickspittle.

One great merchant in the United States lives in history, not only because he was a great merchant, but because he discovered to the world fully a half-dozen other great merchants. That is, he took young men, gave them an opportunity, and under his beneficent guiding influence these country boys mentally bloomed and blossomed.

When you expect a messenger to deliver a message it is well not to hamper him with too many instructions, nor scare him into innocuous desuetude by retailing the dangers that he will encounter, describing for him the punishment he will receive if he fails to "make good."

❡ It is a great man who knows when and how to place reliance in another; to relegate and delegate and keep discipline out of sight. To let one line of figures at the bottom of the balance-sheet tell the tale—this is genius. Of course, if you repose confidence in the wrong man you will rue it, but genius turns on selection. Big men, nowadays, are big because they get others to do their work.

Napoleon said, "I win my battles with my marshals." And then, when he was asked where he got his marshals, he said, "I make them out of mud!" What he meant was that he took obscure men and lifted them into positions of prominence by throwing responsibility on them. Note the loyalty and love of Bertrand, who followed his master to Saint Helena, giving up home, religion, family and all of his own private interests that he might serve his master—even refusing to leave his master when he was dead, but remaining at Saint Helena in order that his own dust might be buried in the grave of this man he loved. Any man who can inspire another with such love can not be obliterated by the scratch of a pen or the shrug of the shoulder ❧ ❧ Napoleon certainly had personality;

WE become robust, only through exercise, and every faculty of the mind and every attribute of the soul grows strong, only as it is exercised ❧ ❧ So you had better exercise your highest and best only, else you may give strength to habits and inclinations that may master you, to your great disadvantage ❧ ❧

at the same time he did not use it to destroy the personality of others.

Great is the man—supremely great—who does not bestride the narrow world like a colossus and cause other men to run and peep about under his huge legs to find themselves dishonorable graves.

❡ The world is big enough for all of us, and a very good slogan is, "Make room! Make room!" And if you are bound to give an order, let it be this: "Open up that gangway!"

When President McKinley gave that message to Rowan, he trusted Rowan to carry it. There were no instructions, no threats, no implied doubts, no injunctions. Rowan asked no questions; neither did McKinley.

The big man is not the man who wants to live not only his own life but the life of others, but he is great who reposes faith in others, and thus brings out the best there is in them, that which was often before unguessed.—*The Other Side.*

I AM going to content myself here with the mention of one thing, which so far as I know has never been mentioned in print: the danger to society of exclusive friendsips between man and man, and woman and woman.

No two persons of the same sex can complement each other.

¶ We should either have a good many acquaintances or else none at all.

¶ When two men begin to " tell each other everything," they are hiking for senility ৯ ৯

There must be a bit of well-defined reserve ৯ ৯

In matter—solid steel, for instance —the molecules never touch. They never surrender their individuality.

¶ We are all molcules of Divinity, and our personality should not be abandoned. Be yourself; let no man be necessary to you; your friend will think more of you if you keep him at a little distance. Friendship, like credit, is highest where it is not used. I can understand how a strong man can have a great and abiding affection for a thousand other men, and call them all by name, but how he can regard any one of these men much higher and closer to him than another, and preserve his mental balance, I do not know.

Let a man come close enough and he 'll clutch you like a drowning person, and down you both go. In close and exclusive friendships men partake of others' weaknesses ৯ ৯

৯ ৯

Enthusiasm is the great hill climber.

WE often hear of the beauties of old age, but the only old age that is beautiful is the one the man has been long preparing for by living a beautiful life. Every one of us is right now preparing for old age.

There may be a substitute somewhere in the world for Good Nature, but I do not know where it can be found.

The secret of salvation is this: Keep sweet, be useful, and keep busy.

৯ ৯

DO not lean on any one, and let no one lean on you ৯ The ideal society will be made up of ideal individuals. Be a man and be a friend to everybody.

When the Master admonished His disciples to love their enemies, He had in mind the truth that an exclusive love is a mistake—love dies when it is monopolized—it grows by giving. Love, lim., is an error.

¶ Your enemy is one who misunderstands you— why should you not rise above the fog and see his error and respect him for the good qualities you find in him?

৯ ৯

WE want the competent man. Self-reliance, patience, good cheer—the ability to be useful—these are the things we are working for in the public schools of America. And we are all working for them—the man or woman in a community who does not take a pride and interest in his public school has a very small and insignificant soul. And this general interest of the best minds token a continual betterment—we are going somewhere.

ARE you in the treadmill? Well, the only way you can get out is by evolving mastership. We are controlled by our habits. At first we manage them, but later they manage us. Habits young are like lion cubs—so fluffy and funny! Have a care what kind of habits you are evolving—soon you will be in their power, and they may eat you up. It is habit that chains us to the treadmill and makes us subject to the will of others. And it is habit that gives mastership—of yourself and others.

AM the tireless servant of man.
❡ To the intelligent merchant or manufacturer—the man who prizes economy, efficiency, sanity, sanitation and safety—I am a necessity. No animal that lives has strength and endurance such as I possess.

Congested highways cried aloud for me, that the channels of commerce might be cleared, delays to distribution destroyed—and the quicker enjoyment of life's luxuries might be yours.

Then Inventive Genii waved a wand, and I CAME!

I—WHO am more powerful than fifty horses—swifter than flesh and blood—tireless and sleepless;

I—who eat little and drink seldom—who feel not the lash of the driver and fear neither heat nor cold;

I—who ask no mercy—expect no kindness—to whom day and night are as one;—born full grown and full strength, as Minerva leaped from the brain of Jove, full armed;

I—whom age does not weaken nor illness harm;

I—who lengthen the reach of the merchant's arms a thousandfold, and daily help him win the battles of life;—bring from the fields and marts of plenty the overplus that feeds the rest of the world;—to the factories the food from the field—to the stores the cloth from the looms—from the press the news of the world;—to your home what you wear, eat or drink—the music you play, the books you read;

—to the trains the passengers who ride and the goods whose shipment is the commercial life of a community;

—to you the wealth that comes from bridging space bring I, compressing time, saving money, eliminating uncertainty.

❡ Various imitators have I, but no competitors ❧ ❧

The brains of a thousand inventors have seethed, dreamed, contrived, thought, so as to bring me up to my present form.

❡ I render useless the Society for the Prevention of Cruelty to Animals;

❡ I represent a maximum of carrying power with a minimum of cost—

❡ I symbol safety, surety, sanity, sanitation;

I carry the White Man's Burden!

❡ I AM THE MOTOR TRUCK.
—*The Motor Truck.*

❧ ❧

MOST certainly not all Socialists are shirks, but many shirks are Socialists. I have hired dozens of them, and when they agree to work eight hours they cross their fingers. They know little of obligation and nothing of responsibility. They regard their employer as their enemy. They do not know that a great industrial institution is a matter of conservation, eternal vigilance and sleepless persistency. This talk about bloated bond-holders and millionaires indulging in champagne suppers and exceeding the speed is Number Six tommyrot. Your captain of industry works sixteen hours a day, often sweats blood to make up a pay-roll, drinks tea and is satisfied with a baked apple and one egg on toast.

❡ He is the man at the helm—chained to Ixion's wheel—and his business is like unto that of Jim Bludsoe, " to hold her nose to the bank, till every galoot is ashore." He is the one man who cannot take off his apron, and throw down his tools. Only a free man can do that. Your so-called capitalist has to stay, face the deficit and bear the disgrace of defeat, if defeat it be, and often is.

❧ ❧

OUR hope now lies in business men and women.

It is the businessman—the economist—who constructs houses, builds railroads and irrigates the waste places. And the farmer of today is a businessman—he is no longer a serf. Of all men, he is an economist. You can get along without lawyers, but the farmer is a necessity. We all lean on the farmer—and sometimes heavily.

❡ Dreadnaughts add nothing to your wheat crop. They take from the ranks of production some of our brightest, strongest and best young men, and make of them consumers, not producers. The work of the soldier, the lawyer, the doctor, is all palliative, not creative or constructive. And it all has to be paid for by the men who dig it out of the ground.

EPILEPSY is a very ancient disorder. It was known in the time of Hippocrates as the "Sacred Disease," because the priests had it—victims we would say of trances or religious frenzy. In Rome it was frequent. We are told of a man who came to Christ saying, "Lord have mercy on my son, for he is a lunatic and sore vexed; for often he falleth into the fire, and oft into the water, and I have brought him unto thy disciples and they could not cure him."

The seizure or spasm of epilepsy is a remedial endeavor on the part of Nature to throw off a poison in the system. The primal cause of the immediate explosion is hidden in the secret recesses of infinity—no microscope can find it. But there is always an immediate cause—a pushing of the button—the current goes off with a bang—the vital fluids are short circuited, and the burning out of the fuse saves the patient's life

But the tendency is always toward dementia, for the wear and tear on the machinery that races, when the governor is on a strike, is terrific.

Epileptics are, almost without exception, gluttons. Here epilepsy and apoplexy are twins. Gourmands sleep too much, and at the wrong time. Bolt your food and you are beckoning for the barrel-stave of Nemesis. Fear, hate, worry, alcoholism, and all psychic trolley-rides that exceed the speed limit, make for epilepsy

Whether epilepsy is hereditary or not is a question, but the tendency toward it surely is.

Epileptics should not marry. For a healthy person to mate with an epileptic is a sin. For two epileptics to mate should be a crime—it is to cross chaos with a blizzard

TOO much emphasis is no emphasis — raise your voice too loud and no one hears you. Hit too hard and you excite sympathy for your victim. Draw your indictment too sweeping and it becomes suspicious

Possibly, if we could see the cells of the brain, we would find the secret of epilepsy in a lesion. But as it is, to treat a brain-storm with ether, bromides, calabar bean, nitroglycerine, chloroform, arsenic, and continued narcosis with opium, are all futile. The relief is bought with a price. For the time you may paralyze the patient, but quiet is not cure. The cause is faulty elimination and the return of the norm must be by the turnpike of God—sunshine, work, equanimity, moderation

EVERY sanitarium, every hotel, every public institution—every family, I was going to say—has two lives: the placid, moving life that the public knows, and the throbbing, pulsing life of plot and counterplot—the life that goes on beneath the surface. It is the same with the human body: how bright and calm the eye, how smooth and soft the skin, how warm and beautiful this rose mesh of flesh! But beneath there is a seething struggle between the forces of life and the forces of disintegration—and eventually nothing succeeds but failure.

TO cultivate concentration, practise relaxation. Lie down on the floor for three minutes on your back, breathe deeply, lie still, and turn your mind in—think of nothing.

To concentrate on your work, you must enjoy your work. And to enjoy your work, you must drop it at certain hours. He lasts longest, and soars highest, who cultivates the habit of just being a boy for an hour a day. Take a vacation every day, if you want to do good work.

I think that in Literature the man who wins in the future can not afford to be diffuse or profound. He will be suggestive, and the reader must have the privilege of being learned and profound.

HOSE who are given to the luxuries of the table are preparing for the pleasures of the operator's table.

The average length of life would be increased immensely if we would just begin to "Know Thyself."

¶ As it is now, we depend on the doctors to cure us if we are sick, and if worst comes to worst, we are fully prepared to go to the hospital and have the surgeon remove the inflamed organ. Would n't it be better to so live that no inflammation would follow?

Disease comes only to those who have been preparing for it. Disease is a sequence postponed by Nature as long as she can, and then, discouraged, she says, "Let 'er go—back to the Mass!" Beginners on the bicycle run into the object they seek to avoid. The doctor and the hospital are in our minds: we think disease, not happiness and health.

Health is within our reach—it costs nothing—only the effort which soon grows into a pleasurable habit. Ask any doctor of any school if I am not right!

¶ Why not acquire the Health Habit?

¶ Here is the formula:

First, deep breathing in the open air with your mouth closed.

Second, moderation in eating—simple dishes—fletcherize.

Third, exercise at least an hour in the open each day, walking, working in the garden, playing with the children.

Fourth, sleep eight hours in a thoroughly ventilated room.

Fifth, don't bother to forgive your enemies—just forget them.

Sixth, keep busy—it is a beautiful world, and we must and will and can leave it more beautiful than we found it.

✸ ✸

EMERSON says, "A great institution is the lengthened shadow of one man." ✸ ✸

That is, one man's spirit runs through and pervades every successful institution. He keys the symphony.

Is the store a jumble of rush, push, grab, graft and disorder? That is the soul of the manager you see. He is not big enough to make an atmosphere.

CONTINUALLY there comes to every thinking man a Voice which says, "Arise and get thee hence, for this is not thy rest." All through life are these way stations where man says, "There, now I've found it; here will I build three tabernacles." But soon he hears the Voice, and it is ever on, and on, and on. He came into life without his choice and is being hurried out of it against his will, and over the evening of his dream steals the final conclusion that he has been used by a Power, not himself, for unseen ends.

But the novelists, and politicians, and economists, and poets are continually telling us that man's trouble comes from this or that, and then they name their specialty. They are like catarrh doctors who treat every patient, no matter what the ailment, by nasal douche.

Marriage is only a way station.

Trains may stop two minutes or twenty minutes for lunch. The place may be an ugly little crossroads, or it may be a beautiful village ✸ ✸

Possibly it's the end of a division, but egad, dearie, it's not the end of the journey! ✸ ✸

Very young people think it is, but they find their mistake. It's a nice place, very often, but not the place they thought it was. They bought one thing and when they got home found something else in the package, and Nature won't change it ✸ ✸

But woman should n't be blamed for that—that's God's fault, not hers.

✸ ✸

THERE is a disease known as factory melancholia. If there is a depression of spirit in the front office it goes out through the foreman, the superintendent, and reaches everybody in the employ of the institution. Even the horses that deliver the goods to the railroad station will catch it. They will moderate their pace, and no longer will they frolic in glee. The brass on their harness is not receiving attention. The ivory rings are being lost. Indifference is showing itself in every department. Everybody is saying, "What's the use!"

WHEN a guinea sees a hawk or any big bird flying around, he gives the alarm and all the fowls but the guineas scoot for cover. The guinea just flies up on the gate and shoots forth a torrent of Billingsgate defiance. No bird that wears feathers has a vocabulary equal to the guinea—it is so profane that it is unprintable. Epithet, ridicule, sarcasm and cussword are sent forth in rapid fire. When a guinea is a little excited you can hear him a mile. As before intimated, it is Mr. Guinea himself who makes most of the noise, but his wife is a good imitator, and she always echoes the sentiments of her liege—political, social, religious. On the subject of hawks, weasels, skunks and strange cats, old Mr. and Mrs. Guinea are absolutely one. On non-essentials they occasionally differ and exhibit these differences as to what constitutes wit by many interesting little physical-culture exhibitions. In other words, they fight.

But with guineas a foreign disturbance always makes peace at home so so

The guinea has surpassed man in this— he has abolished fear. He sounds warning notes, but as for himself, he resembles Fuzzy-Wuzzy, his former owner, and does n't give a damn.

Mr. Guinea is boss of the barnyard. Even a game-bird considers discretion the better part of valor. A guinea will tackle an English bulldog. If the dog knew his power he might win, or at least get a slice of the gate-receipts, but when a guinea begins to say things at a bulldog —or any other dog for that matter—Mr. Pup stipulates all the facts concerning his lineal descent to be as stated, and hikes so so

so so

ANY man who plots anothers' undoing is digging his own grave. Every politician who voices innuendoes, and hints of base wrong about a rival, is blackening his own character. For a time he may seem to succeed, but the end is sure—it is defeat and death. All those plotters of the French Revolution who worked the guillotine in double shifts were at last dragged to the scaffold, and pushed under the knife.

The hate we sow finds lodgment in our hearts, and the crop is nettles that Fate unrelentingly demands we gather. Who lives by the hammer shall perish by the hammer.

If you work in a department-store, a bank, a railroad-office, a factory, I beg of you, on your life, do not knock. Speak ill of no one, and listen to no idle tales. Whether the bitter things told are true or not, has no bearing on the issue. To repeat an unkind truth is just as bad as to invent a lie. If some one has spoken ill of me, do not be so foolish as to hope to curry favor by telling me of it. The "housecleaning" that occurs in the offices of companies and corporations, every little while, comes as a necessity. In a small establishment the head of the house can usually pooh-pooh the bickering out of the window; but in large concerns where many men are troubled with lint on the lungs, and everybody seems to have forgotten his work, just to "chew," then self-protection prompts the manager to clean house. It is the only thing he can do to preserve the life of the concern.

THE individual busy at work, at work he likes, is safe. This way sanity, health and happiness lie so so

Through the proper exercise of the three H's—Head, Hand, Heart—are we educated. And to be educated is to live, for education means development, unfoldment. There is only one thing worth praying for, and that is to be in the line of evolution —growth. There is no happiness elsewhere, save in the consciousness that we are tunneling toward the light, slowly but surely. To know this is to live. We are all Sons of God, and it doth not yet appear what we shall be. Our Windows are open toward the East!

WHAT this country has got to do is to retain the good and valuable services which lawyers and doctors have to give; and this can only be done by making them attaches of the State, and putting them on salaries ✒ ✒

The doctors must find it to their interest to destroy their business. They must keep people well and show them how to banish the demons of disease. ❡ Every lawyer should be a conciliator. He should thrive through diffusing justice, harmony, peace, good will and love, and not through distributing their opposites, like the termagant woman distributing the dust, dirt, bacteria, by violently agitating a broom.

We must make it easier for lawyers to do what is right, by making it for their interest so to do; and exactly the same thing applies to doctors. We must fix the doctor's ideal on health, happiness and usefulness, and take his gaze off the warts, tumors and inflamed appendices ✒ ✒

People who live rightly are well; and it is for the doctor to show us how to keep well, and this he will do when he thrives through health and not through our disabilities.

The world is being made over, it is true; but there are a few things that yet need a little buffing and a bit of sand-papering. ✒ ✒

PUBLIC opinion will not tolerate in America a heartless judiciary. At last the people judge the judge. The court of last resort is not the Supreme court at Washington ✒ ✒

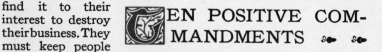

TEN POSITIVE COMMANDMENTS ✒ ✒

I. Thou shalt think well of thyself and well of thy neighbor.

II. Thou shalt add to the health, wealth and happiness of the world ✒

III. Thou shalt be on good terms with sunshine, fresh air and water ✒

IV. Thou shalt get eight hours' sleep a day.

V. Thou shalt eat moderately, and exercise every day in the open air ✒

VI. Thou shalt love the memory of thy mother, and be true to the friends that have done so much for thee ✒ ✒

VII. Thou shalt recognize the divinity in all men.

VIII. Thou shalt remember the week-day to keep it holy.

IX. Thou shalt remember that thee can only help thine by helping other people, and that to injure another is to injure thyself, and that to love and benefit others is to live long and well.

X. Thou shalt love the stars, the ocean, the forest, and reverence all living things, recognizing that the source of life is one.

The judge who is not a gentleman is now the rare exception; and a gentleman is one who is gentle toward the friendless. He realizes that the person who has failed to be a friend to himself, needs a friend. The instincts of the typical American judge are all in the direction of pity and helpfulness. He is not a sanctimonious bigot. Jeffreys is dead.

The wide experience of a judge dealing with humanity in every phase, makes him slow to condemn. He realizes that the major habit or the minor sin trips its victim over the bank at an unguarded point, and to get back to safety, strong and friendly hands must reach out.

That man who, when any one fell in the canal opposite his house, put up the price of lumber, was not fit timber for the wool-sack ✒ ✒

How any man can look into the mirror and blame any man or woman for anything, I do not know.

We fight on forever and fail; we are

mauled to the earth and arise; we stumble forward with feeble vision and tired feet, and only the love that lives in lenient hearts makes life tolerable. When mankind repudiates us and fellowship is dead, we then turn for surcease to the welcoming waters of the lake and find peace ❧ ❧

Our common lot is not to succeed, but to struggle, persevere and fail.

❧ ❧

ANY law that can be easily broken is a bad law. Any tendency in life that is wrong, which is palliated and perpetuated by society, is unethical.

Every one is agreed that we should make it easy for everybody to do what is right, and difficult to do what is wrong. That is, we should reward, by a natural automatic process, everything which tends to human betterment; and we should discourage, by withholding a reward, everything which tends to double-dealing, falsity, finesse, chicanery.

❧ ❧

ONCE, in my callow days, I accepted a wager that I could wear a prison suit and walk from Buffalo to Cleveland without serious molestation. It took me over four days to get thirty miles, I was arrested nine times, and at Dunkirk I came near being mobbed by Sunday School picnickers, and was compelled to give up my uniform for citizens clothes. Yet I was a free man and innocent of crime, and there was no law defining what I should wear, so long as it was male attire.

But there are unwritten laws, and to a great degree society dictates what its members shall wear, just as in feudal times, and much the same today, the master dictates to his servants what their clothing shall be.

And the master himself is caught in the mesh that he has woven, and this soulless something we call Society dictates to him what he shall do and what not. There are limits beyond which he can not go. So the men who make fashions are caught and held captive by them, just as the children who play ghost get badly frightened themselves.

ANYTHING you prepare for, you get. Nations that prepare for war will find an excuse for fighting.

The Law of Compensation never rests. There was no such thing as civilization until individuals ceased carrying arms, and agreed to refer their differences to the courts ❧ ❧

If Ohio and Pennsylvania have a misunderstanding, they do not go at it tooth and nail to destroy property— they have agreed on a way to adjust their misunderstandings ❧

The good sense of the world says today that nations should mediate and arbitrate ❧ ❧

The War-Lord spirit is an anachronism. And no matter what it was once, it today is a detestable thing.

War preparedness leads to war.

The coast-line between Canada and the United States, from the Saint Lawrence River to Lake Superior, is about two thousand miles.

In the year Eighteen Hundred Twelve, there were forty-six forts, big and little, on the United States side, and about the same number frowned at us from Canada.

❡ At Fort Niagara alone there were at one time six thousand troops. Altogether we had on the Great Lakes over a hundred craft devoted to the art of fighting—this in the interest of peace.

❡ In one little battle we had with our British cousins, on Lake Erie, Commodore Perry, a rash youth of twenty-seven, captured six British ships and killed three hundred men. A little before this the British destroyed ten ships for us and killed two hundred Americans ❧ ❧

After the War of Eighteen Hundred Twelve was ended and peace was declared, both sides got busy, very busy strengthening the forts and building warships ❧ ❧

At Watertown, Conneaut, Erie, Port Huron, Cleveland and Detroit were shipyards where hundreds of men were working night and day building warships. Not that war was imminent, but the statesmen of the time said there was nothing like " preparedness." In Canada, things were much the same, and there were threats that Perry's famous message, "We have met the enemy and they are ours," would soon be reversed ❧ ❧

Suddenly, but very quietly, two men in Washington got together and made an agreement. One man was acting Secretary of State, Richard Rush of Philadelphia; the other was Charles Bagot, Minister to the United States from England. Rush was of Quaker parentage, and naturally was opposed to the business of war.

Bagot had seen enough of fighting to know that it was neither glorious nor amusing ❧ ❧

Rush wrote out a memorandum of agreement which he headed "An Arrangement." ❧ ❧

The document is written on one side of a single sheet of paper and is dated April Twenty-eight, Eighteen Hundred Seventeen. Here is a copy:

" 1. The Naval Forces henceforth to be maintained upon the Great Lakes shall be confined to the following vessels on each side ❧ ❧

" 2. On Lake Ontario one vessel, not to exceed one hundred tons burden, carrying not more than twenty men and one eighteen pound cannon.

" 3. On the Upper Lakes two vessels, of same burden, and armed in a like way.

" 4. On Lake Champlain one vessel of like size and armament.

" 5. All other armed vessels to be at once dismantled, and no other vessel of war shall be built or armed along the Saint Lawrence River or on the Great Lakes." ❧ ❧

This agreement has been religiously kept. Its effect was to stop work at once on the fortifications, and cause disarmament along the Great Lakes.

So far as we know, the agreement will continue for all time. Both parties are satisfied, and in fact so naturally has it been accepted very few people know of its existence ❧ ❧

Here is an example that our friends in Europe might well ponder over. If those forts on the frontier had been maintained, and had the ships of war continued to sail up and down, it would have been a positive miracle if there had not been fighting ❧ ❧

Probably they would have forced us into a war with England before this. We have had several disputes with Canada when it would have been very easy to open hostilities if the tools had been handy. Men who tote pistols find reasons for using them, and the nations that have big armies will find excuse for testing their efficiency ❧ ❧

If two countries can make an " arrangement " limiting the extent of armament, and this arrangement holds for a hundred years, can not nine countries do the same? ❦ Then all that is needed is a few soldiers to do police duty.

Nations can not afford to be savages, any more than individuals.

❧ ❧

AS a rule, I have noticed that Jews treat their wives, children and aged parents with a deal more tenderness and consideration than we Hittites. I wonder if this is a fact, or is it a mere coincidence in my experience? I have had a good deal to do with the Chosen, but I never yet heard one of them refer to his father as the Old Gent; and I have noticed, very often, in Jewish families that the grandfather and grandmother were the loving equals of the children and the pride and pet of the household ❧ ❧

A full-grown Jew might put up a good company bluff, but a child is no hypocrite; and mark you this, the child gets its cue for manners and behavior from its parents. If the mother has little patience the child is a little worse, and if the father is a boor in his home his boys are hoodlums. Jewish children respect their parents and grandparents.

I do not believe that you can teach a child under fourteen anything by admonition; you do teach him, however, most emphatically, by example. If you scold a child you only add to his vocabulary, and he visits on doll or playfellow your language and manner.

The Jew may hang on to a dollar when dealing with the Enemy, but he does not dole out pittances to his wife, alternately humor and cuff his children, nor request, by his manner, that elderly people who are not up-to-date shall get off the earth ❧ ❧

❧ ❧

ET me relate a somewhat sad but true incident: In New York, years ago, there used to live an elderly gentleman with long white whiskers, a linen duster and patriarchal ways ❧ ❧

He was known as the "Bum Peter Cooper." At conventions, mass-meetings and public gatherings, his services were in demand at two dollars per. All he had to do was to applaud the speakers by pounding vociferously on the floor with his cane, say nothing and look like the real Peter Cooper.

Finally, through the applause that always greeted him when he appeared upon the stage at public meetings, a buzzing bluebottle got into his bonnet, and he became possessed of the idea that he was the Sure-Enough Peter Cooper, and the other man, who built the Cooper Union was a Bum. He grew garrulous and fell into the habit of referring to the Real Peter Cooper as a freak, a fake and a fraud. As long as the Bum was quiet, all was well, but when he began to talk, his supporters were obliged to throw him into the Irish Sea.

❧ ❧

THERE is just one objection to Yellowstone Park and that is, it exhausts your supply of adjectives.

Usually we describe things by saying they are like this or they remind you of that.

But the Yellowstone Park reminds you of things you have seen and experienced in dim eons past and ages gone. You look upon the gushing geysers, the towering crystal peaks, the dashing streams, the limpid lakes, the mountains lifting themselves to the skies, cold, solemn and imperturbable, and your eyes turn at last to the eternal blue overhead, and you are hushed, awed, subdued, and the Sense of Sublimity holds you fast. Tears come as a great relief.

No one can ever describe Yellowstone Park, because what you see and feel there is beyond compare, and therefore beyond speech. The eyes reveal the soul, the mouth, the flesh, the chin stand for purpose, the nose means will. But over and behind all is that fleeting Something we call "expression." This Something is not set or fixed, it is fluid as the ether, changeful as the clouds that move in mysterious majesty across the surface of the Summer sky, subtle as the sob of rustling leaves—too faint at times for human ears—elusive as the ripples that play hide-and-seek over the bosom of a placid lake. You feel there as did Leonardo when he tried to portray the face of his lady-love. To do so would have been to picture his own fleeting, changing, moving mood.

You see Niagara Falls and you go away and talk about it; you see Yellowstone Park and you go away and think about it ❧ It is an Experience, and never again are you quite the same person. You have been close to Infinity.

Robert Browning tells us of Lazarus, who, having come back from the confines of Death, could not speak of what he had seen, because there was nobody he could talk with who had had a similar experience ❧ ❧

The person who has been to Yellowstone Park can only talk about it with those who, too, have seen, known and felt.

❧ ❧

ANY man who is unfamiliar and out of sympathy with the simple, little, common, every-day things of life, who is not in touch with the multitude and whose heart does not go out to the many, is a good man to let alone. No matter how plausible his arguments, give him absent treatment. Flee any man who does not have commonsense, no matter how great his mental attainments.

❧ ❧

BROOK FARM disbanded because the man at the head of it had no head for business, nor did he have the capacity to select a man who had. But its "failure" was a success, in that it was a rotting log that nourished a bank of violets.

A CORRESPONDENT asks me this:—" Do brilliant men prefer brilliant women?" ᔒ ᔒ
First, disclaiming the gentle assumption that I am brilliant, I say, yes ᔒ ᔒ

The essence of marriage is companionship, and the woman you face across the coffee urn every morning for ninety-nine years must be both able to appreciate your jokes and to sympathize with your aspirations. If this is not so the man will stray, actually, or else chase the ghosts of dead hopes through the grave-yard of his dreams ᔒ ᔒ

By brilliant men is meant, of course, men who have achieved brilliant things—who can write, paint, model, orate, plan, manage, devise and execute.

Brilliant men are but ordinary men, who at intervals are capable of brilliant performances. Not only are they ordinary most of the time, but often at times they are dull, perverse, prejudiced and absurd ᔒ ᔒ

So here is the truth: Your ordinary man who does the brilliant things would be ordinary all the time were it not for the fact that he is inspired by a woman.

❧ Great thoughts and great deeds are the children of married minds.

When you find a great man playing a big part on life's stage you 'll find in sight, or just around the corner, a great woman. Read history!

A man alone is only half a man; it takes the two to make the whole.

Ideas are born of parents.

Now life never did, nor can, consist in doing brilliant things all day long. Before breakfast most men are rogues. And even brilliant men are brilliant only two hours a day. These brilliant moments are exceptional. Life is life to everybody. We must eat, breathe, sleep, exercise, bathe, dress and lace our shoes. We must be decent to folks, agreeable to friends, talk when we should and be silent when we ought.

To be companionable—fit to live under the same roof with good people—consists neither in being pretty nor clever. It all hinges on the ability to serve. No man can love a woman long if she does not help him carry the burden of life. He will support her for a few weeks, or possibly years, then if she does n't show a disposition and ability to support him, her stock drops below par. Men and women must go forward hand in hand— single file is savagery. A brilliant man is dependent on a woman, and the greater he is the more he needs her.

The brilliant man wants a wife who is his chum, companion, a " good fellow" to whom he can tell the things he knows, or guesses, or hopes, one with whom he can be stupid and foolish—one with whom he can act out his nature. If she is stupid all the time, he will have to be brilliant, and this will kill them both. To grin and bear it is gradual dissolution; to bear it and not grin is death.

Robert Louis, the Beloved, used to tell of something he called " Charm." But even his subtle pen with all its witchery, could not quite describe charm of manner—that gracious personal quality which meets people, high or low, great or small, rich or poor and sends them away benefited, blessed and refreshed.

❧ Ellen Terry, turned sixty, has it. The Duse, homely, positively homely in features, rests her chin in her hand and looks at you and listens in a way that captures, captivates and brings again the pleasures of past years.

We are all just children in the Kindergarten of God, and we want play-fellows.

❧ If a woman is pretty I would say it is no disadvantage unless she is unable to forget it. But plainness of feature does not prohibit charm of manner, sincerity, honesty and the ability to be a good house-keeper and a noble mother.

There are many degrees of brilliancy, but as a general proposition this holds.

❧ A brilliant man wants a wife who is intellectually on his wire—one who, when he rings up, responds.

This is PARADISE!—*Men and Women.*

ᔒ ᔒ

❧ This incapacity for independent action, this moral stupidity, [this infirmity of the will to catch hold and lift, are the things that put pure Socialism so far into the future.

HE habit of Self-Confidence is a result of the habits of Industry and Concentration. And I hope I've made it clear that Concentration is the result of pleasurable, useful effort, or Industry. Also, I hope I've made it clear that for Industry to be of the first quality the person must at times relax and find rest in change through play—be a child—run, frolic, dig in the garden, saw wood—relax. When you have reached a point where your work gives you a great, quiet joy, and through this joy and interest you concentrate, then comes Self-Confidence. You are now well out on the road to Mastership.

Robert Louis Stevenson said, "I know what pleasure is, for I have done good work."

❧ The recipe for Self-Confidence is: Do good work.

"Courage," says Emerson, "comes from having done the thing before."

❧ A man who does good work does not have to talk, apologize or explain—his work speaks. And even though there be no one to appreciate it, the man feels in it a great, quiet joy. He relaxes, smiles, rests, fully intent on taking up his labors to-morrow and doing better than ever.

The highest reward that God gives us for good work, is the ability to do better work. Rest means rust.

So we get the formula: Acquire and evolve physical and mental Industry by doing certain things at certain hours, ceasing the effort before it becomes wearisome. In mental work keep in touch with people who are a little beyond you.

The joy and satisfaction of successful effort—overcoming obstacles, getting lessons, mastering details which we once thought difficult, evolves into a habit, and gives Concentration. Industry and Concentration fixed in character as habits mean Self-Confidence.

Industry, Concentration and Self-Confidence spell Mastership ❧ ❧

So from the man we get the Masterman ❧ What lies beyond I do not know ❧ Perhaps when I become a Master I shall know—one stage at a time is enough. If there isn't time in this life, perhaps there will be hereafter.

❧ ❧

IF I were an employee I would never mention wages. I would focus right on my work and do it.

❧ The man that endures is the man that wins. I would never harass my employer with inopportune propositions. I would give him peace, and I would lighten his burdens.

Personally, I would never be in evidence unless it were positively necessary—my work would tell its own story.

The cheerful worker who goes ahead and makes himself a necessity to the business —never adding to the burden of his

LIFE is beautiful, and for all we know, death is just as good. And death, science shows, is in itself a form of life.

The man who lives well is the one who is willing to go or stay. And the man who is willing to go or stay, stays quite a while. John Calvin and John Knox had a deal to do with devising and formulating a religion of sorrow, and each died old at fifty-seven. Unfortunately, they took themselves seriously, attempting to say the final word. And any one who does this is suffering from arterio-sclerosis of his think-cells. Life is fluid; and nothing is permanent but change.

superiors—will sooner or later get all that is his due, and more. He will not only get pay for his work, but will get a bonus for his patience and another for his good cheer. This is the law of the world *so so*

The man who makes a strike to have his wages raised from fifteen to eighteen dollars a week may get the increase, and then his wages will stay there. Had he kept quiet and just been intent on making himself a five-thousand-dollar man, he might have gravitated straight to a five-thousand-dollar desk.

I would not risk spoiling my chances for a large promotion by asking for a small one. And it is but a trite truism to say that no man ever received a large promotion because he demanded it—he got it because he was wanted to fill the job. Ask the man who receives a ten-thousand-dollar-a-year salary how he managed to bring it about, and he will tell you that he did his work as well as he could *so so*

Never did such a man go on a strike. ⫟ The most successful strike is a defeat; and had this man been a striker by nature, sudden and quick to quarrel, jealous of his rights, things would have conspired to keep him down and under. I do not care how clever he may be or how well educated, his salary would have been eighteen a week at the furthest, with a very tenuous hold upon his job.

so so

LOYALTY is that quality which prompts a person to be true to the thing he understands. It means definite direction, fixity of purpose.

Loyalty supplies power, poise, purpose, ballast, and works for health and success. ⫟ Nature helps the loyal man.

If you are careless, slipshod, indifferent, Nature assumes that you wish to be a nobody and grants your prayer. ⫟ Loyalty, in one sense, is love, for it is a form of attraction.

A vacillating mind is a sick mind in a sick body. Vacillation is lack of loyalty— and it is a disease.

Loyalty is not a mere matter of brain capacity; success does not go to those who know the most—it gravitates to those who are true to the cause which they undertake. " This one thing I do."

⫟ The human mind can be likened to a tract of land divided into lots. These mental lots are made up of say, business, religion, education, love, art, music, work, play—a single lot being given to each subject—then each of these is also subdivided *so so*

In some of these town lots the man has a devout, loyal interest; for others he is neutral; and toward others he may have an indifference bordering on repulsion. No man has ever lived who had an equal loyalty toward every department of life, and if a person is absolutely loyal to one he does well. If he can show himself equal to being true to several, he is a genius. The more worthy things to which you are loyal, the greater are you.

⫟ Unloyalty is very much more common than disloyalty. Unloyalty means simply indifference. For instance, most church members are quite indifferent to truth. Their belief is supplied hand-me-down. They join the church for social reasons— in response to mild coercion or family pressure, and so are moving in the line of least resistance. The person of intelligence who does not join a church is usually one who resists this polite social blackmail, because his religious conscience forbids his being disloyal to truth. Such were the martyrs—Tyndale, Wyclif, Ridley, Latimer, Savonarola, Bruno. These men all preferred the fagots to social favor and intellectual slavery, just as there are women who prefer death to ease, gauds and baubles and disloyalty to their ideal of love.

⫟ All artists who succeed are loyal to their art. That maxim " false in one, false in all," is as false a commonplace as was ever launched. Gladstone was true in his domestic affairs, and loyal as a statesman, but he could not possibly imagine how and why Ingersoll could not accept the Book of Genesis.

Gladstone's loyalty to England was the keystone in his arch of triumph. And we forget his sophistry in Bible argument, just as we forget the book written by Sir Isaac Newton, proving the literal truth of the Old Testament prophecies.

And so it is that every man who succeeds in anything wins through his unflinching, unfailing, tireless loyalty to that particular thing ❧ Byron made bargains with Barabbas, but he never wrote a muddy slipshod line, nor could he be bribed nor bought to do so ❧ He had the "artist conscience," whether he had any other kind or not ❧ ❧ Michelangelo was ever and always loyal to his art, and this was why six popes, under whom he worked, all kissed his big toe. And this is why we, too, kiss his big toe, even yet.

Lincoln was loyal to the land of his birth, but disloyal to the niceties and proprieties of thought and language ❧ ❧

Success hinges on loyalty. Be true to your art, your business, your employer, your " house." Dalliance is defeat. ❧ " All is fair in love and war," is a maxim that may be true as regards war, but never as to love. Love is founded on faith, and he who violates faith vitiates his own nature and wrecks the venture ❧ ❧

❧ Loyalty is for the one who is loyal. It is a quality, woven through the very fabric of one's being, and never a thing apart. Loyalty makes the thing to which you are loyal, yours. Disloyalty removes it from you. Whether any one knows of your disloyalty is really of little moment, either one way or the other. The real point is how does it affect yourself! ❧ Work is for the worker. Love is for the lover. Art is for the artist. Acting is for the actor, and he who does not know that Richard Mansfield's success was due to his "artistic conscience,"

IF you are defamed, let time vindicate you—silence is a thousand times better than explanation. Explanations do not explain. Let your life be its own excuse for being—cease all explanations and all apologies, and just live your life. By minding your own business you give others an opportunity to mind theirs; and depend upon it, the great souls will appreciate you for this very thing. I am not sure that absolute, perfect justice comes to everybody in this world; but I do know that the best way to get justice is not to be too anxious about it ❧ ❧

As love goes to those that do not lie in wait for it, so does the great reward gravitate to the patient man.

and not through a furtive eye on the house and a canny peep-hole in the curtain has not traveled far.

No man ever succeeded in business, or can, who wears the dial off the clock. Such an one may not be disloyal — he may be merely unloyal — but he is ever ripe for a lay-off, and always imagines some one has it in for him.

And he is right—everybody and everything, including Fate and Destiny, Clio and Nemesis, have it in for him. The only man who goes unscathed is the one who is loyal to himself by being loyal to others.

❧ The ship that starts from New York to Queenstown and arrives safely and on time, is the one that flies the Queenstown signal, that has a Queenstown purpose—whose every package and letter and post-card is marked "Queenstown." She fights wind and wave and tide and current, always and forever with Queenstown in mind. ❧ Should the captain and mate, just outside of Sandy Hook, shake dice to see where they should go, or the wheelmen all say, " To 'll with Queenstown," it is quite likely the ship would not go to Queenstown, but instead would go to Davy Jones' Locker.

The hospitals, jails, asylums, and sanitariums are full of disloyal people—folks who have been disloyal to friends, society, school, business, work. Never say, " That will do," or " This is good enough," or " Who cares? " Nothing but your best is good enough. Stick! you rogue, and if you quit, quit to tackle a harder job ❧ ❧

God is on the side of the loyal!—*Loyalty.*

HOMAS DE QUINCEY was saved from despair and death by Ann of Venusberg. De Quincey lived for full fifty years after that—always looking for Ann. ❡ Some folks say that he was looking for his Ideal, and that he simply called her "Ann," but this is mere quibble ❧

❡ DeMusset translated the *Confessions of an Opium-Eater* and transformed Ann into a conventional society belle, lest the Faubourg D'Upper be shocked.

Let that pass, if the Hepburn Bill does not forbid ❧

❡ Every man whose life and aspirations are touched with the Spirit, spends his life, perhaps unconsciously, looking for the Ideal Woman—the woman whose soul will make good the deficiencies in his own. He feels his weakness, his incompleteness; he is conscious that alone he is but half a man, but if he could only find Her—his other half—all would be as God designed it.

Thus sought Dante, thus sought De Quincey, thus sought Le Gallienne in his Quest. And Le Gallienne found Her —the Golden Girl—found her just where De Quincey found his Ann.

Ann of Venusberg was not a vampire; the Golden Girl was not a vampire ❧

Each was the Woman who Understands.

❡ And having an understanding mind and a willing heart each gave life and healing and complemented the soul of a strong man, instead of sucking his heart's blood.

The man of Spiritual Impulse is to a degree an ascetic; perforce, he must be, for Spirituality is sex manifesting itself in religious or artistic fervor. I will grant

if you insist on it, that asceticism is a form of sensuality that finds its gratification in denial. I will also grant that your Artist is not a celibate, and all I claim is that his highest pleasures are to him a symbol. He knows that the things which endure are spiritual ❧ ❧

❡ And so the woman who is to complement this man of intellect and soul must be the Woman who Understands. He can not teach her, life is too short. She should comprehend without explanation that sex must not run rampant; neither need it be subdued, but it must be spiritualized ❧

If she allows mere intuition to lead she is a vampire, and in a very short time will hold her mate only by a statutory bond ❧

❡ And even though a bishop in full canonicals has solemnized a riot of passions, and little girls in white have gone before strewing flowers, love's death surely follows license. Can law sanctify sensuality? ❧ ❧

Do all the "bad women" live in this "quarter" or that?

The police do not know, for they are but the tools of that ignorant, blundering, blind thing, the law; and the preachers who conventionally bless certain things, and curse others, lift an eyebrow and ask in affected surprise, "What does the gentleman mean?" But the law of antithesis exists, the paradox lives, life is a spiral; and possibly when all Things are Made Plain, we who have glorified in women but a single virtue, will find that De Quincey and Le Gallienne were right, and that the Woman who Understands is the Magdalene, who from out of the purging fires of purgatory completes the circle and arises pure and

LOYALTY is the great lubricant in life. It saves the wear and tear of making daily decisions as to what is best to do. It preserves balance and makes results cumulative. The man who is loyal to his work is not wrung nor perplexed by doubts—he sticks to the ship, and if the ship founders, he goes down a hero with the colors flying at the mast, and band playing.

spotless, recognizing Deity incarnate when all others blindly fail. I really do not know ✌ ✌
Walking through the gallery of statuary of the Luxembourg I saw the white carved nude figure of a man—a man in all the splendid strength of youth. Standing behind him on a higher part of the pedestal was the form of a woman; and this woman was leaning over, her face turned toward him, her lips about to be pressed upon his. I moved closer and to one side, and saw that on the face of the youth was an expression of deathly agony; and then I noted that the muscles of that splendid body were tense with awful pain. And in that one glance I saw that the woman's body was the body of a tigress —that only her face was beautiful—and that the arms ended in claws that were digging deep into the vitals of the man as she drew his face to hers. Suddenly feeling the need of fresh air I turned and went out on the street.

That piece of statuary gave Philip Burne Jones the suggestion for his painting, " The Vampire."

Now one might suppose from that awful sermon in stone that woman is the cause of man's undoing. But for the benefit of henpecked and misunderstood husbands I 'll call attention to the fact that the men who have achieved most in literature, music, painting and philosophy are men who knew from sad experience the sharpness of woman's claws: Socrates, Dante, Shakespeare, Rousseau, Milton, Wagner, Paganini and so many more that were I to name them all the world would not be large enough to contain the books in which they were printed. Of course I 'll admit that the men who have been flayed by women have usually been greatly helped by women, and this sometimes accounts for the flaying. But the point that I make is that all experi-

THE menial is a man who is disloyal to his work. ❧ All useful service is raised to the plane of art— When love for the task— Loyalty—is fused with the effort ✌ ✌

ence is good—the Law of Compensation never rests and the stagnation of a dead-level " happy married life " may not be any more to the strong man's advantage than a long course of stupid misunderstanding. Milton bewailed the fact that he could get freedom from marital woes on no less ignoble grounds than by violating his marriage vows. Milton did not get his freedom. His wife sat on him, silent and insensate, and so did her whole family of seven persons. And his sharp cry made him the butt of jibes and jeers innumerable. Milton was at one time an obscure school teacher and clerk; but if any of those great men who sought to humiliate and defeat him are mentioned nowadays in history it is only to say " they lived in the Age of Milton."

" His life ruined by a woman "—Pish! you flatter her; she has n't the power. ❧ And the end of the whole matter, Brother, is, it does n't much matter what your condition in life is: all things are equalized. Even pain, grief and loss are good, if you are big enough to take your medicine. When the Prophet said, " God is good and His mercy endureth from everlasting to everlasting," he certainly understood himself.

✌ ✌

AMERICA is a giant; it is well to have a giant's strength but not well to use it like a giant. This is the richest country the world has ever known—in treasure and in men and women. If we mind our own business and devote our energies to the arts of peace we can solve a problem that has vexed the world from the beginning of time.

✌ ✌

Young man, don't get groggy over girls, religion, words, art or politics. They are all good in moderation, but bad if you get an overdose ✌ ✌

T is a great man who can introduce us to the divinities that surround us, and make us realize our sacred relationships. I met such a man some months ago.

His life and work so appealed to me that I grew suspicious of myself, and refused to write of him until I knew him better. That is to say, the very excess of my regard for this man made me go slow. In the past the man with a surface-show has occasionally caused me to ebulliate and then stand in the under-tow and apologize for my rashness and unfounded zeal. You remember all the complimentary things I said about What's-his-name? He wasn't worth it, was he? He could not live up to the mark I set for him.

The Messianic Instinct is in us all. Like Carlyle and Emerson we are hero-worshipers ✒ And our expectancy of meeting the exceptional person constantly leads us astray.

And this is no tragedy, either, provided we are not led so far afield that we are lost in a miasmatic mental swamp, and turned misanthropes.

It is a terrible thing to lose faith in mankind. And it is a glorious and refreshing thing to meet a person who restores our faith in humanity and enables us to forget the fools who have done us dirt. ❡ A year has passed since I first heard of this man of power whom I would discover to all Roycroftia and the lands that lie beyond. " Now there was a man sent from God, and his name was John." This man's name is John—John Davey. He is sixty years old, but looks forty, and at times acts twenty. In figure he is slight and slender, but in strength he is like the silken cord that held the god Thor—it stretched but never broke. ❡ John Davey is the Tree-Man, or the Tree-Doctor, or the Father of Tree-Surgery. I like to call him the Tree's Brother. No man I ever saw so mixed him with the elements—no man I ever knew was so blended with the leaves— no man I ever knew possessed such a sympathy for waving, swaying saplings as this man. His life is all so bound up

in trees and the birds that live in their branches, that he would forget his own needs, if some one did not look after him with the same loving care that he bestows on the trees. Fortunately, John Davey has a very practical wife and they have four sons and one daughter, all tree-folks, who realize that it is not quite time to adopt the Elijah habit of life, and bank on the ravens.

John Davey is a genius, for a genius is one who has the faculty of abandonment to an idea, or a cause. He is a genius without a taint of degeneration—a genius with the innocence of childhood, and the intellect of a man.

The actions of men have two effects— primary and secondary. Often the secondary effect is of more importance than that of the primary .

John Davey calls himself a tree-surgeon. His treatment of decayed trees is parallel to the work of a dentist on a decayed tooth ✒ ✒

He arrests decay, and works for health. ❡ This is Davey's primary work. The secondary result of his work is not its effect upon the tree and the owner of the tree, but the influence of his work on society ✒ ✒

This, to me, is the vital issue.

In carrying forward this work of looking after sick trees, Davey is assisted by several hundred young men, whom he has selected and educated for the business ✒ ✒

When you hear of a " Davey gang" being at work somewhere, go and see them ✒ ✒

They are a type. Bare of head and of arm, brown, small or of medium size, silent, they work with a precision, an intelligence and an earnestness that is a delight to see.

If they use tobacco it is not during work-hours; if they frolic and play it is never at their employer's expense. Their zeal is the zeal of John Davey. " This one thing I do."

John Davey has created a new breed of men—athletes all—who climb trees like troglodytes, and yet have the sensibility of artists. They are big factors in reclaiming the earth for the joy of man. As the years go by there will be more John Davey men, and every Davey man is a teacher—an educator. This widens the circle. " So far does that little candle throw its beams."—*The Tree-Surgeon.*

STRONG men are in demand. You can always hire men, plenty of them, for two dollars a day. When you want a man, however, to fill a ten-thousand-dollar position, you have to hunt for him; and when you want a fifty-thousand-dollar man, you find that he already has a good job and is not anxious to give it up.

THAT expression, "sinking self," is only a figure of speech. At the last the true artist never sinks self: he is always supreme and towers above every subject, every object that he portrays.

Farmers did not trust the bankers as a rule, and certainly, as a rule, bankers did not trust the farmers. I can swear to that!

SAMUEL M. JONES was elected Mayor of Toledo four times. Even when the Democrats and Republicans made a deal and combined on one candidate to beat the Golden Rule Man, he won. When he ran for Governor of Ohio he was defeated. He won in his own city because he was beloved by the poor, the plain, the ignorant. The fact that he was elected by the submerged one-half, can not be denied. The submerged did n't understand Sam Jones any more than we understand God, but they believed in him. To Sam, we were all submerged, more or less, and those who claimed to have reached the sunlight, really had n't. ❡ Sam Jones planned, at the expense of the city, a comfortable and safe place where working women could leave their children—a sort of club house for over-worked women—with a competent matron in charge. The demagogs were shocked. They lifted a howl of dissent that could be heard in Toronto—" What business has a working woman to have a baby?" they asked

with injured accent. And not waiting for an answer to their conundrum they began to talk about the downtrodden taxpayers Sam said that if the city could provide palatial places where thieves and other rogues could be locked up, fed and looked after, it should also supply a place where poor women could go and give their children a bath. And Sam had his way

Sam had no sympathy with cruelty, injustice, poverty, and misery even admitting that these things were hoary with age. In my various talks and walks with him, I noticed he discussed principles, not persons—things, not individuals. And this characteristic, be it noted, is the distinguishing mark of greatness. "He always talked of things not people," said Huxley in his eulogy of Darwin. ❡ The fear of Death was not in the formula that made Sam Jones. Death was to him the deliverer, and life he often regarded as a jailer that holds us captive. This view does not tend to longevity—this nostalgia of the soul does not make for length of days. It is a fever that consumes. I have heard him repeat Beecher's words: " When I die do not place crepe— the emblem of gloom—on the house, but rather hang a basket of flowers at the door as an emblen that a soul has passed from death unto life." And again he would quote the clown in *Twelfth Night,* " The more fool, Madame to mourn because your brother's soul is in heaven." Gladly would Sam Jones have given his life for his race—he yearned for his kind as a mother yearns for her babe. ❡ He had in him a strain of the madness of the old Hebrew prophets. He was Malachi and Isaiah, Koheleth and Daniel, Walt Whitman and Tolstoy by turn. He lacked the placidity and poise

AN is a detached portion of the Divine Life," says Chunder Moozamdar. Like a planet flung off by the sun, and following its own orbit for a time, he will return again to the central mass from whence he sprung. Man is a lonely creature. In his heart there is a craving for sympathy and companionship, and the unrest that drives him on and on is only a search for his own. Leonardo da Vinci felt sure that the love of animals was a manifestation of this same desire. Unconsciously man often turns to a horse or a dog and finds in the brute a complement for his own nature that he never does in his own kind. And so Leonardo, the sanest and least morbid of men, could see no distinction in the " divinity " of life in the man and the divinity of life in the beast.

The loyalty of the dog for his master so excited the admiration of a certain man in Italy, a long time ago, that as he walked through the field, his faithful dog with him, a prayer came to his heart that he might be as loyal and unselfish in his service to God as the dog was to him. The idea grew upon him, and he explained it to several other men, and they formed a society, calling themselves " Domini Canes," literally, the Dogs of the Lord. Soon the name was written " Dominicans," and Dominicans it is, even unto this day. And I wish to emphasize the fact that the original idea of the Dominicans was not one of abjectness, but of loyalty.

THE beast makes no demands upon you. His affections and loyalty are complete, he has no sinister motives, he holds nothing back. The proud, strong horse that carries me over the miles, and responds with his entire nature to my slightest wish, rests me as no man who argues ever can. My dog whines piteously if left behind, and only asks to go that he may be near me; he runs ahead and then barks for an encouraging word, and getting it leaps and quivers in pure joy; and I lift up my heart in gratitude for the privilege of life and health and conscious oneness with the Life that is Universal.

—*Domini Canes.*

AY what you will of the coldness and selfishness of men, at the last we long for companionship and the fellowship of our kind

SWIMMING uneasily in my inkbottle is an essay on the benefits and advantages of Sin. As yet I do not feel myself competent to fish it out. I am waiting, hoping that some one else will do the task for me. It is a delicate and elusive bit of work, and no matter how well done, I know that the man who does it will lay himself open to the charge of being an advocate of the Devil.

¶ Yet the grim fact remains that Sin has in very many instances led the way to saintship. No woman happily married to the man she loves ever recognized divinity incarnate, breaking over his head the precious ointment of her loyalty and wiping his feet with the hairs of her head

There is something startling in the truth that the woman who preserves her " virtue " pays a price for the privilege

¶ And where is the preacher who dare face the fact that the " honest " man or woman with fixed income, happily situated, is to a degree isolated from all sympathy and fellowship with the great mass of beings who suffer and endure the slings and arrows of outrageous fortune? Prosperity is not all prosperity: there is even a penalty in traveling successward, although Samuel Smiles knew it not. Men are great only as they possess sympathy, and that which causes a man to center in himself, taking a satisfaction in the security he has attained for the good things of this, or another world, is not, can not be, wholly good.—*Sin.*

¶ Joyous are the busy.

HE first necessity in organization is initiative.

And initiative is imagination in action ✍ ✍

Initiative does not imply merely the suggestion of the right thing; men of initiative are men who can carry their plans to a successful issue. ¶ Intelligent supervision of the labor of other men is a rare gift. Nine out of ten men do not possess it at all. Only one in ten thousand can do it well ✍ ✍

Sir Humphry Davy said his finest discovery was Michael Faraday.

Donald G. Smith—Lord Strathcona—said his one great achievement was the discovery of James J. Hill. Andrew Carnegie made Charles M. Schwab possible. ¶ And Schwab distributes seventeen thousand pay-envelopes every Saturday night ✍ ✍

To wisely encourage initiative is a necessity. Otherwise the Dark Ages are at the door. That which would destroy initiative would destroy civilization ✍ ¶ The ability to plan a thing that has never been done before, to organize great numbers of men and use great masses of materials in an intelligent way, is a gift valuable beyond the ability of men to compute.

Theoretically, socialism is beyond argument, but if put to actual test it would prove the decline of individuality, the death of initiative. " Liberty "—all the liberty a man can use—this America has supplied, and this is why we lead the world ✍ ✍

A man of initiative must work out his own plans in his own way. Curtailment of his liberties breaks his wings and imagination languishes.

No man knows his capacity for initiative. Great men are always surprised at their achievements.

✍ ✍

NY system can be defeated by one single man who places himself out of harmony with it.

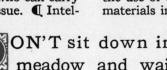ON'T sit down in the meadow and wait for the cow to back up and be milked — go after the cow ✍

IVILIZATION is a matter of the organization of men and materials.

Civilization lays out roadways, builds factories, equips them with machinery, educates men to the use of this machinery, converts raw materials into useful commodities ✍ ✍

¶ Men and materials are organized so as to manufacture, distribute and transport the necessities of life. ¶ Transportation is the first great factor in civilization.

Savages get enough to eat by killing animals and using raw fruits and vegetables. To preserve, pack, transport and distribute are beyond their power. ¶ The barbarian may plant, and he may take care of a limited number of livestock, but the savage does not transport; and until men organized so as to safely transport, famine was just around the corner ✍ ✍

Both men and materials have to be moved before they are of much value.

✍ ✍

HE men who manage big utilities now everywhere realize the necessity of going in partnership with the people. A public utility thrives only as it is backed up by the best people in the town. A public utility stands for permanence. It is always a booster. It joins hands with everybody who is in a good business, and the financial advantages that it enjoys over any local concern put it in a position where it can render a great, important service to the community. It siphons capital from a thousand towns and cities and centers it in places where it will do the most good.

✍ ✍

HE thought of getting safely out of the world has no part in the life of Enlightened Man—to live fully while he is here is his problem—one world at a time is enough for him.

✍ ✍

Be moderate in the use of all things, save fresh air and sunshine.

HERE are big institutions which never produce big men. In many shops there is a general tendency to keep down all originality. Strong men, if they are secured at all, have to be imported from the outside.

If any man in the place suggests a new thing the whole proposition is gently pooh-poohed ⚶ ⚶

Too much discipline destroys individuality; and mediocrity is the rule.

Marshall Field is one of the big businessmen who discovered latent genius. Marshall Field produced a few big men, and he did it by paying men a commission where they increased the business above a certain amount.

There are at least ten men who are millionaires several times over who began employment with Marshall Field and Company on very moderate salaries ⚶ ⚶

You can not bring out the powers in a man unless you offer proper incentives.

⚶ Had James J. Hill been kept on a salary he never would have evolved. He would today not be known outside the city of Saint Paul.

Edison's genius came from the fact that he had a full and free field and opportunity to make millions for himself.

⚶ Money is the measure of power. Men do not especially prize money for the sake of money, but they prize it as a tangible recognition of their ability.

⚶ Socialism with its restrictions on what any man shall receive would never have produced a Marshall Field, a James J. Hill, a Commodore Vanderbilt, a Henry Ford, a John H. Patterson, a Charles M. Schwab.

The end of socialism would be when a strong man emerged out of the mass and ruled through the autocratic exercise of power. Then we would have a monarchy.

⚶ Democracy is a compromise between socialism and monarchy. It seeks the greatest good to the greatest number.

⚶ Also, it places no limit on individual achievement ⚶ ⚶

That which would iron out men to one common level, and cease to offer reward to initiative, would reduce the race to nullity. Communism only succeeds where there is a strong, just and efficient leader.

⚶ Successful communism is beneficent autocracy ⚶ ⚶

Great industrial leaders set large numbers of men to work. They plan and execute great engineering schemes. They take vast quantities of raw materials and manufacture them into forms of use and beauty ⚶ ⚶

These organizations give work to millions. And this work, with the distribution of the pink and pudgy pay-envelope, makes prosperity possible.

When you make war on men of initiative you paralyze the pay-roll.

That power unrestrained tends to tyranny is a fact. Therefore, supervision of our great organizations is necessary. But this supervision must be conducted intelligently, and not as an inquisition.

⚶ And it should be taken entirely out of the guiding hands of political parties. Otherwise we get a condition where party obligations are paid for in offices, and we get a government of grafters, by grafters, for grafters.

Industrial leaders today understand that they can help themselves only as they help humanity. To work for self alone is fatal to any business enterprise.

But liberty to sell your labor, either collectively or individually, must be granted, otherwise we get the rule of the walking delegate, who rides in a taxi and never works ⚶ ⚶

This way tyranny lies, for all professional reformers are tyrants in false whiskers.—*Producing Big Men.*

⚶ ⚶

IT must not be supposed that the mere amount of money a man possesses gives him any claim on the loving remembrance of his fellows. But in the interest of truth I might here relate a little anecdote that seems to illumine the subject in hand. A young woman, from Memphis, who had been engaged in College Settlement work, was with us for a few weeks, and grew quite interested in Baba as she saw him working around the place. Being philanthropic she concluded it would be nice to start a bank account for the old man, and thus encourage him in habits of economy. Ali was consulted and made no objection, only stating that he already had a bank book, issued by the Erie County Savings Bank of Buffalo. The young woman was a bit surprised, but concluding that some other charitable person had anticipated her, congratulated Baba on the fact, and said if he would let her take the bank book she and others would add something to it *so* The book was given to her the next day. She looked at it and when she discovered that there was a credit balance of just $2,385.50, she nearly threw a Double Arab backward over the book-binder's glue pot *so so*

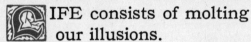

LIFE consists of molting our illusions. We form creeds today only to throw them away tomorrow. ¶ The eagle molts a feather because he is growing a better one *so so*

The mistake made by the charitably disposed young woman was that she took Ali Baba's beautiful brick-dust complexion as a consequence of intoxicants used to excess; and his impossible hat, the reinforced trousers and picturesque coat for tokens of poverty. The complexion of the Baba is merely the result of a plentiful supply of ozone, and betokens iron in the blood—a vigorous red corpuscle. The impossible hat and the rags reveal nothing more than the eccentricity of genius.

so so

STRONG men can always afford to be gentle. Only the weak are intent on " giving as good as they get."

so so

THE man who lives truth, if such there be, does not think it worth while to formulate it. He knows no more of truth than the fishes know of the sea. It is the gyve and the fetter that make a man formulate truth. Only prisoners meditate. And so does the philosopher forever meditate upon plans of escape— escape from his own limitations, and the bonds of custom, prejudice, ignorance and pride *so so*

RAVEL, as a means of broadening one's horizon, and giving a new point of view, has no substitute *so so*

It is easy to call attention to Immanuel Kant, who was born at Konigsberg, and was never more than ten miles from that city in all of his life of more than eighty years *so so*

But the very fact that we mention Kant proves the case. He was the rare exception.

We get rid of our whims, notions, prejudices and fears through travel.

Through travel we vitalize our ideas *so so*

Travel, transportation and transmission —these disseminators of things and ideas —are what is working the solidarity of the race. The villager is a man who is interested in just what is going on in his own town. Of necessity, he deals largely in gossip and vacuities.

The provincial is a man who does not get out of his own province, intellectually or otherwise *so so*

Immanuel Kant lived in one town, but he was neither a villager nor was he a provincial. His thought roamed, not only the world, but the universe. The strength of his imagination allowed him to stay at home and project himself to the farthest planet. His body dwelt in Konigsberg, but his soul was a citizen of the universe. He was one with the Milky Way. Not many of us have the ability to take a little journey from the safe and comfortable recesses of a Morris chair. We have to see, to feel, to touch, to come in contact with things in order to be impressed *so so*

These journeys are great educators, but I advise everybody, after taking a journey around the world, across the continent, to Washington, to Niagara Falls, to East Aurora, or even to the next town, to just take a look out of the window when he gets home.—*Travel.*

T has been said, " Man is the most wonderful of all the works of God," but no one ever said so but man. Bees can do things man can not, and they know things man never will. A queen bee will lay over a million eggs during the summer. The eggs she lays every day are about double her own weight. These eggs are all alike when they hatch, but by feeding the larva differently, bees produce drones, workers or queens, at will.

It only takes three days for the eggs to hatch. The young are then fed by the nurse bees, which are the bees under sixteen days old. These nurse bees feed the others from glands in their heads that secrete milk.

When the bee is sixteen days old she is of age and goes to work. The average life of the worker is only forty-five days. She just works herself to death, unless winter comes on and then she may live through until the next year.

There are about fifty thousand bees in a hive, thirty-five thousand workers and fifteen thousand nurse bees or housekeepers. Then there are six hundred drones and one queen. The queen often lives for five years, but the drones never live over winter. As soon as the first sign of winter comes and the flowers begin to wither, the bees have a St. Bartholomew's day and kill every drone. Drones have no stingers, but queens and workers have. The workers are females—undeveloped queens.

Bees have five eyes, three they use for seeing in the dark and for reading, and two for long distance hustling.

When a hive gets too full, the bees swarm, the old ones going away led by the queen. As soon as the old queen goes, the bees that remain at home immediately grow a new queen.

EES are very orderly and cleanly. They have inspectors that stay at the door of the hive and see that no bee comes in from the field without a good load of honey. Often if the bee has only a little honey, the inspector will turn him back and give him what is coming to

him. The drones buzz around and make a bluff at working, flying around in the sunshine near the hive watching for the queen. The workers do not like the drones and they always kill a great many before St. Bartholomew's day, if Br'er Drone gets too gay. Bees very seldom die in the hive: if they do, it is a sign the whole hive is weak. The bees clean out all dust and dirt with great care, and if a bug or mouse gets into the hive they will straightway kill the intruder. Then if the body is too big for them to drag out they will cover it over and seal it up with propolis, a sticky substance, which bees gather from buds or the bark of trees.

HIVE of thirty-five thousand workers will often bring in twenty pounds of honey in a day, if the flowers are just right; and one man I know who owns eighty-five hives, has had his bees make a ton of honey in ten hours. And yet one bee only gathers a grain of honey a day, and may visit three hundred flowers to get it.

The wax is a secretion from the bee's body, but the honey they get from the flowers. The object of the honey in the flower is that the insect will come and get itself dusted with pollen, which they carry to other flowers. So besides gathering honey, bees do a very necessary work in the fertilization of flowers. In fact, you can not raise white clover without bees, and bees do not thrive at their best excepting when they find white clover, so thus does nature understand her business.

Nature plays some rather mean tricks on men and birds and bees, just to get her work done. Nature seems to make use of man just as she uses bees, and all the time man chuckles and congratulates himself that he is using nature. But nature says nothing—just lies low and works, and man can only guess what the end of it all is.

The soul goes by leaps and bounds, by throes and throbs. A flash! and a glory stands revealed for which you have been blindly groping through the years.

A FADED flower flung from the grated window of a prison cell; it falls at the feet of a passer-by, a woman of the town ॐ ॐ

But why should I call her a woman? She is a creature of the night. She belongs to all and to none, her home is a hovel and she lives in hell—a hell of her own preparing ॐ ॐ

Once she was courted, flattered, petted, pampered. She had her nightmare of glory when gold was showered upon her, silks rustled, perfumes filled the air, bouquets burdened her table, carriages with footmen stopped at her door. Mansions, servants, joyous suppers laughter, diamonds, pearls—to do nothing and have everything, this was her ambition ॐ ॐ

She has drunk to its dregs the cup of nothingness. She has sought the potion that gives forgetfulness; for abandonment, desertion, death follow as an unerring sequence on all the gleam, glitter and glamour that have gone before ॐ

❧ And now she breathes only the sulphur fumes of Gehenna, and the scant silver that comes her way goes for the drug that brings oblivion.

With bloodshot eyes, disheveled hair, and burning thirst she hurries along—watched, hunted, hooted. She draws her tattered shawl closer about her benumbed frame as the cutting blasts of winter, rushing down alleys and from around sharp corners, hunt her out ॐ

❧ The flower drops at her feet.

She stops, looks around, no one is watching, she picks it up—yes, it is a spray of hyacinth. She looks up to see from whence it came, and high up she thinks she sees a hand thrust out from a grated window ॐ ॐ

Some one is waving a hand to her—to her. ❧ Who can it be—some one has

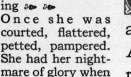

THE soul grows by leaps and bounds, by throes and throbs ॐ ॐ
A flash, and a glory stands revealed —
For which you have been groping blindly
Through the years.

thought of her—some one has sent her a flower! ॐ ॐ

She brushes her hand across her eyes, as if to clear her misty vision and looks up again ॐ ॐ

This time she sees nothing, only the sullen front of a great prison wall, jutting stone, grated windows, stone piled upon stone.

❧ She thrusts the flower into her bosom, and forgetful of where she was going, turns about and hastens to the den she calls home ॐ ॐ

Some one has thrown her a flower—not the flower such as patronizing women of the Flower Mission bring with tracts and words of advice—not that—a flower from the hand of a man, a man in trouble, a prisoner, disgraced like herself, in bonds. He has thrown her a flower. Who is this " he " of whom she thinks? ॐ ॐ

Alas, she does not know. Years and years, aye, centuries ago, when she wore pinafores and lived with her father, mother, brothers and sisters in the country, she dreamed of that man, this man who would come to her and love her and give her freedom.

It is the same dream come back—it is he. He will deliver her from the body of this death. He has flung her a flower. He is in trouble. What can she do to help him!

She is a woman. She is not old. God sent her into life and she has a right to love, to tenderness, to motherhood and a home. No chill of doubt can put out the eternal fire—she loves the Ideal.

❧ This is her misery, her disgrace and her crown. Illusions will not fade away, she has prayed and watched and longed for this—some one loves her. He has flung her a flower.

When he is released he will come to her and take her away, and they will leave this life of horror, and fly to the country and make themselves a nest as the birds do. ❡ Some one has flung her a flower. She belongs to him and him alone. She has loved him all these years. She has waited for him. God knows she has done wrong, but God knows, too, her heart is pure. She appeals to the Higher Law—a power greater than herself has been pulling her down to death—but God knows, God knows! For was it not God who allowed her to be tempted beyond her strength ᵍᵉ ᵍᵉ

Some one has flung her a flower. It has awakened in her the Ideal—she had thought it dead, dead and nailed down with the coffin nails of her crimes. ❡ But no, there is light there yet. She wishes to do penance, to condole, to succor, to sanctify herself to some one, to be kind, to be useful.

The refluxes of the heart are as sure and certain as the march of the planets. ❡ The desires of the heart are fixed stars—clouds may obscure, but wait and you shall see the light.

There is that in souls which never perishes ᵍᵉ ᵍᵉ

Some one has flung this woman a flower and she becomes happy with a horrible happiness. She sees a cottage, warmed and lighted; a kettle singing on the hearth; supper on the table for him who was even now coming to his home, their home, whistling from his work; she sees in the corner a cradle, and she begins crooning a lullaby to a babe that she has never pressed to her aching breast. Some one has flung her a flower.

In the direst gloom, in the chill of abandonment, in the black of darkest pathways, in the dim, gray light of prison cells where the sun never enters, before stern judges, while policemen leer and men restrain not their evil tongues; beneath the maze of pitfalls; in nights of horror and blackest chaos there is a gleam of light. It grows into a flame. What think you it can be?

It is love—it is the Ideal. It exists even in hell ᵍᵉ God never quite withdraws His Holy Spirit.

Some one has flung her a flower.
—*Wilted Hyacinths.*

HERE is a nervous disease called paranoia. Its first symptom is the belief that some one is plotting to undo you. ❡ The holding of such a thought feeds the malady. We believe things first and look for proof later; and when the idea is once fixed in a man's mind that some one is his enemy, reasons light as air are to him confirmation strong as holy writ. The individual who thinks he is hated, will be hated, in fact, very shortly.

❡ Hate is catching.

The person who thinks another hates him is, while in that mood, unlovable. ❡ Love only responds to love.

Incipient paranoia manifests itself in suspicion, distrust and jealousy. Acute paranoia reveals itself in pronounced hallucinations, and efforts in the line of revenge, even to the taking of lives of persons entirely disinterested.

Every police captain is familiar with the phase of paranoia where persons with staring eyes and cold sweat upon their foreheads demand protection from supposed enemies that are upon their track ᵍᵉ ᵍᵉ

The psychologist can look down the paranoiac's past and see the time when the disease was only the germ of a distrust or glimmering suspicion.

Gœthe said, " I have in me the germ of every crime." And just so are we all potential paranoiacs. To harbor the thought of wrong is to warm and vivify the germ ᵍᵉ ᵍᵉ

If a person injures me accidentally, I am quite willing to forgive him. If I think he did it purposely, I want to fight. The matter lies with me and not with him. My mental state controls the situation—it is violence or peace, just as I attribute an evil intent where none exists. If we can think wrong we bring wrong into being, and thus create a condition of hate out of nothing.

Then if we can attribute wrong intent to others, of course they can to us. Yet we know that, at the last, what we desire most is to be loved and trusted. And yet this person who attributes malice to us, can, if we are not guarded, control us through a wrong thought, so as to make us unlovely and unlovable. In certain physical conditions we think less of people than in others. I know a man who hates everybody and everything until about ten o'clock in the morning. By noon he is quite approachable, and for an hour or so after dinner he is usually gentle and generous.

Does not the amount of wrong and injustice in the world vary with us all according to the time of day and our physical condition?

We do not fear anything but evil. The fear of evil is largely, if not entirely, a morbid and therefore insane idea.

ℂ From these things I gather that each man is really the creator of the world in which he lives. And what is more, every man creates in his own image. Without an evil thought there never would have been any evil in the world. Banish evil thought, and thought of evil, and there would not now be an evil in the world.

ℂ The thought of evil is born of fear. Paranoia as a disease is the direct result of fear—we fear some one is going to harm us, and then we hate. Hate is a manifestation of fear, and therefore is a species of cowardice.

Fear affects the circulation, even at times to stopping forever and instantly the action of the heart. A faulty circulation affects every organ, and most of all, the organs of digestion. And impaired digestion at once affects the mind. Impaired digestion means impaired thought.

ℂ The treatment we receive at the hands of others is very largely the reflection of our own mental attitude toward them.

ℂ As a man thinketh, so is he.

THINK NO EVIL.

—About Right Thinking.

UT let us be honest—the man who is jealous is himself to blame most.

Each soul is a center in itself, and the mistakes of others—the follies of wife or child, husband or parent, are none of ours. We are individuals—we came into the world alone, we live alone, and we die alone, and we must be so girded round by right that no fault of another can touch us

And this I believe is true: The jealous person is really the one first at fault. Back of a result lies a cause. Before there is unfaithfulness, there is indifference, secrecy, repulsion, neglect.

The recipe for unfaithfulness—concrete selfishness

The jealous individual always considers himself wronged—all he thinks of is his own condition. And the epithet he applies to another usually fits himself best. He hugs his woe to his heart night and day, and shows it to every pitying passer-by. He centers on self.

Go back a way and you'll find he has caused the unfaithfulness of which he now so bitterly complains.

No one can harm you but yourself. Jealousy is a crop of nettles that is being garnered from seeds sown in darkness. For he who lives more lives than one, more deaths than one must die.

Nettles and dragons' teeth—Merciful Christ! Let us not sow in folly lest we reap in tears.

N all this Cuban business there is one man stands out on the horizon of my memory like Mars at perihelion.

When war broke between Spain and the United States, it was very necessary to communicate quickly with the leader of the Insurgents. Garcia was somewhere in the mountain fastnesses of Cuba—no one knew where. No mail or telegraph message could reach him. The President must secure his co-operation, and quickly. ℂ What to do!

Some one said to the President, " There is a fellow by the name of Rowan will find Garcia for you, if anybody can."

ℂ Rowan was sent for and given a letter to be delivered to Garcia. How the " fellow by the name of Rowan" took the letter, sealed it up in an oilskin pouch, strapped it over his heart, in four days landed by night off the coast of Cuba from an open boat, disappeared into the jungle, and in three weeks came out on the other side of the Island, having traversed a hostile country on foot, and delivered his letter to Garcia—are things I have no special desire now to tell in detail. The point I wish to make is this: McKinley gave Rowan a letter to be delivered to Garcia; Rowan took the letter and did not ask, "Where is he at?" ᴔ ᴔ

By the Eternal! there is a man whose form should be cast in deathless bronze and the statue placed in every college of the land ᴔ It is not book-learning young men need, nor instruction about this and that, but a stiffening of the vertebrae which will cause them to be loyal to a trust, to act promptly, concentrate their energies: do the thing —"Carry a message to Garcia."

LIVE so as to get the approbation of your Other
Self, and
Success is yours.
But pray that success
Will not come any faster than
You are able to endure it.

General Garcia is dead now, but there are other Garcias. No man who has endeavored to carry out an enterprise where many hands were needed, but has been well-nigh appalled at times by the imbecility of the average man—the inability or unwillingness to concentrate on a thing and do it.

Slipshod assistance, foolish inattention, dowdy indifference, and half-hearted work seem the rule; and no man succeeds, unless by hook or crook or threat he forces or bribes other men to assist him; or mayhap, God in His goodness performs a miracle, and sends him an Angel of Light for an assistant.

You, reader, put this matter to a test: You are sitting now in your office—six clerks are within call. Summon any one and make this requrst: "Please look in the encyclopedia aud make a brief memorandum for me concerning the life of Correggio."

Will the clerk quietly say, "Yes, sir," and go do the task? On your life he will not. He will look at you out of a fishy eye and ask one or more of the following questions:

Who was he?

Which encyclopedia? ℭ Where is the encyclopedia? ᴔ ᴔ
Was I hired for that?
Don't you mean Bismarck?
What's the matter with Charlie doing it? ℭ Is he dead?
Is there any hurry?
Sha'n't I bring you the book and let you look it up for yourself? ᴔ ᴔ
What do you want to know for? ᴔ ᴔ ℭ And I will lay you ten to one that after you have answered the questions and explained how to find the information, and why you want it, the clerk will go off and get one of the other clerks to help him to try to find Garcia—and then come back and tell you there is no such man. Of course, I may lose my bet, but according to the Law of Average I will not. Now, if you are wise, you will not bother to explain to your "assistant" that Correggio is indexed under the C's, not in the K's, but you will smile very sweetly and say, "Never mind," and go look it up yourself. And this incapacity for independent action, this moral stupidity, this infirmity of the will, this unwillingness to cheerfully catch hold and lift—these are the things that put pure Socialism so far into the future. If men will not act for themselves, what will they do when the benefit of their effort is for all? ᴔ ᴔ

A first mate with knotted club seems necessary; and the dread of getting the "bounce" Saturday night holds many a worker to his place. Advertise for a stenographer, and nine out of ten who apply can neither spell nor punctuate—and do not think it necessary to.

Can such a one write a letter to Garcia? ℭ "You see that bookkeeper," said the foreman to me in a large factory ᴔ ᴔ ℭ "Yes; what about him?"

"Well, he's a fine accountant, but if I'd send him uptown on an errand, he might accomplish the errand all right, and on the other hand, might stop at four saloons on the way, and when he got to Main Street would forget what he had been sent for."

Can such a man be trusted to carry a message to Garcia?

We have recently been hearing much maudlin sympathy expressed for the "downtrodden denizens of the sweat-shop " and the "homeless wanderer searching for honest employment," and with it all often go many hard words for the men in power. Nothing is said about the employer who grows old before his time in a vain attempt to get frowsy ne'er-do-wells to do intelligent work; and his long, patient striving after " help " that does nothing but loaf when his back is turned. In every store and factory there is a constant weeding-out process going on

The employer is constantly sending away "help" that have shown their incapacity to further the interests of the business, and others are being taken on. No matter how good times are, this sorting continues: only, if times are hard and work is scarce, the sorting is done finer—but out and forever out the incompetent and unworthy go. It is the survival of the fittest. Self-interest prompts every employer to keep the best—those who can carry a message to Garcia.

I know one man of really brilliant parts who has not the ability to manage a business of his own, and yet who is absolutely worthless to any one else, because he carries with him constantly the insane suspicion that his employer is oppressing, or intending to oppress him. He can not give orders, and he will not receive them. Should a message be given him to take to Garcia, his answer would probably be, " Take it yourself! "

Tonight this man walks the streets looking for work, the wind whistling through his threadbare coat. No one who knows him dare employ him, for he is a regular firebrand of discontent. He is impervious to reason, and the only thing that can impress him is the toe of a thick-soled Number Nine boot

Of course I know that one so morally deformed is no less to be pitied than a physical cripple; but in our pitying, let us drop a tear, too, for the men who are striving to carry on a great enterprise, whose working hours are not limited by the whistle, and whose hair is fast turning white through the struggle to hold in line dowdy indifference, slipshod imbecility, and the heartless ingratitude which, but for their enterprise, would be both hungry and homeless.

Have I put the matter too strongly? Possibly I have; but when all the world has gone a-slumming I wish to speak a word of sympathy for the man who succeeds—the man who, against great odds, has directed the efforts of others, and, having succeeded, finds there's nothing in it but bare board and clothes

I have carried a dinner-pail and worked for day's wages, and I have also been an employer of labor, and I know there is something to be said on both sides. There is no excellence, *per se*, in poverty; rags are no recommendation; and all employers are not rapacious and high-handed, any more than all poor men are virtuous. My heart goes out to the man who does his work when the " boss " is away, as well as when he is at home. And the man who, when given a letter for Garcia, quietly takes the missive, without asking any idiotic questions, and with no lurking intention of chucking it into the nearest sewer, or of doing aught else but deliver it, never gets " laid off," nor has to go on a strike for higher wages. Civilization is one long, anxious search for just such individuals. Anything such a man asks shall be granted. He is wanted in every city,

THE best preparation for good work tomorrow is to do good work today; The best preparation for life in the hereafter is to live now.

town and village—in every office, shop, store and factory. The world cries out for such: he is needed and needed badly —the man who can " Carry a Message to Garcia."—*A Message to Garcia.*

so so

OCIETY is in league against all of its members," wrote Emerson. And as once every clan was at enmity with every other clan, and every nation at war with every other nation, so yet does every man in his heart distrust every other man. Suspicion, hate, jealousy, apprehension —all forms of fear—fill the hearts of men. The newspapers that have the largest circulation are those whose columns bulge with tales of disgrace, defeat and death. If joy comes to you the news will go unheralded, but should great grief, woe, disgrace and hopes dashed upon the rocks be your portion, the wires will flash the news from continent to continent, and flaring headlines will tell the tale to people who never before heard of you.

And all that this proves is that it is a satisfaction to a vast number of people to hear of the downfall of others—it is gratification to them to know that disaster has caught some one in the toils.

❡ The newspapers print what the people want, and thus does the savage still swing his club and flourish his spear.

Ride in any American city, on the morning cars, or upon any suburban train, and note the greedy grab for the daily papers, and observe how the savory morsels of scandal are rolled beneath the tongue! so so

So long as most men glory in the defeat of other men, it is a perversion of words to call this a Christian Land.

But, as clan once united with clan, and nation with nation, for a mutual protection, so do a goodly number of people now recognize that men should unite with men—not only in deed, but in thought—for a mutual benefit.

Abolish fear and you can accomplish whatever you wish.

Reserve your best thoughts for the elect few so so

Idleness is the only sin. A blacksmith singing at his forge, sparks a-flying, anvil ringing, the man materializing an idea—what is finer!

so so

NATURE makes the crab-apple, but without man's help she could never evolve the pippin so so

Nature makes the man, but unless the man takes charge of himself, he will never evolve into a Master. He will remain a crab-apple man.

So Nature requires men to cooperate with her. And of course in this statement I fully admit that man is but a higher manifestation of Nature.

Nature knows nothing of time—time is for men. And the fleeting quality of time is what makes it so valuable. If life were without limit, we would do nothing. Life without death would be appalling. It would be a day without end—a day with no night of rest. Death is a change—and death is a manifestation of life. We are allowed to live during good behavior, and this is what leads men toward truth, justice and beauty, for these things mean an extension of time and happiness instead of misery so so

We work because life is short, and through this work we evolve. The Master is a man who has worked wisely and intelligently, and through habit has come to believe in himself.

Men are strong just in proportion as they have the ability to say NO, and stand by it. Look back on your own life—what was it caused you the most worry, wear, vexation, loss and pain? Was n't it because you failed to say NO at certain times and stick to it?

This vice of the inability to say NO comes from lack of confidence in yourself. You think too much of the opinions of other people and not enough of your own. And the real fact is that the good opinion of the best people comes from your saying NO, and not weakly yielding to a contract which is none of yours.

Cultivate self-confidence and learn to say NO. It is a great thing to be a man, but it is a finer thing to be a Master— Master of yourself.

E are finding out things right along; and one of the things we have recently discovered or rediscovered is that getting old is simply a bad habit. A man who thinks he is old, is. And the man who retires from business will shortly be retired by death. Nature has no use for the person who quits, so she just takes his word for it and lets him quit.

¶ And another rather curious thing is, that the fear of death is the monopoly of young people. The man who has lived lives long; and who has kept right at his work, living one day at a time and not bothering other folks any more than he had to, doing each task the best he could, keeping an interest in all good things—that man is not afraid to die. He is willing to go or stay, and the man who is willing to go or stay, stays quite a while ✺ ✺

✺ ✺

MENTAL work of a congenial kind is a great stimulus to bodily vigor —to think good thoughts, work them out like nuggets of gold and then coin them into words, is a splendid joy ✺ ✺ And joy is life ✺ ✺

I remember seeing Oliver Wendell Holmes when he was eighty-three at Emerson College of Oratory, where of course, he was dearly beloved by everybody. On the occasion I have in mind, he made a little speech and explained that he was just getting his affairs into shape, that he might come and join the school as a student. Then to prove his quality he recited, " Has there any old fellow got mixed with the boys? "

The man's enjoyment in life was complete—he was satisfied, grateful for the past, and he showed his gratitude by filling the present with good work ✺

MEN are rich only as they give. He who gives great service gets great returns ✺ Action and reaction are equal, and the radiatory power of planets balances their attraction. The love you keep is the love you give away.

BRAIN work is just as necessary as physical exercise, and the man who studies his own case and then plays one kind of work off against another, finds a continual joy and zest in life. The Greeks came near finding this just balance of things; Solon, Sophocles, Pindar, Anacreon and Xenophon lived to be over eighty, doing strong and excellent work to the last. When Gœthe died, past eighty, the doctors laid his naked body out on the table and Scheffler exclaimed, " It is the body of a Greek god," and burst into tears. There was no wastage, nor shrinkage nor signs of age in that heroic form. Michelangelo was writing love sonnets at eighty-nine, and Titian came within one year of making the century run, and his prayer at the last was that he might live to finish a certain fresco.

✺ ✺

WALTER SAVAGE LANDOR wrote his "Imaginary Conversations," picturing the love of Pericles and Aspasia, at eighty-five. Izaak Walton went a-fishing and wrote fiction about his luck at ninety. Fontenelle was as light-hearted at ninety-eight as at forty; Cornaro enjoyed better health at ninety-five than at thirty, and Sir Isaac Newton at eighty-five was still smoking the pipe that cost him his lady-love. Simon Cameron went to the Bermudas at ninety to investigate the resources of the Islands.—*On Getting Old.*

✺ ✺

BEES have a scheme whereby they eliminate the useless drones. That is where the bees set man a pace. But bees have no way of making a worker out of a drone; and possibly that is where we score one on Brer Bee.

✺ ✺

He has achieved success who has lived well, laughed often and loved much.

I TACK the following theses on every college bulletin-board, and every church door in Christendom, and stand ready to publicly debate and defend them, six nights and days together, 'gainst all comers—college presidents and preachers preferred.

1.—Man's education is never complete, and life and education should go hand in hand to the end.

2.—By separating education from practical life society has inculcated the vicious belief that education is one thing and life another.

3.—Five hours of intelligently directed work a day will supply ample board, lodging and clothing to the adolescent student, male or female.

4.—Five hours of manual labor will not only support the student, but it will add to his intellectual vigor and conduce to his better physical, mental and spiritual development ✒ ✒

5.—This work should be directly in the line of education, and a part of the school curriculum.

6.—No effort of life need be inutile, but all effort should be useful in order to satisfy the consciousness.

7.—Somebody must do the work of the world. There is a certain amount of work to do, and the reason some people have to labor from daylight until dark is because others never work at all.

8.—To do a certain amount of manual labor every day, should be accounted a privilege to every normal man and woman ✒ ✒

9.—No person should be overworked.

10.—All should do some work.

11.—To work intelligently is education.

12.—To abstain from useful work in order to get an education, is to get an education of the wrong kind.

13.—From fourteen years up, every normal individual can be self-supporting, and to be so is a God-given privilege, conducive to the best mental, moral and spiritual development.

14.—The plan of examinations, in order to ascertain how much the pupil knows, does not reveal how much the pupil knows, causes much misery, is conducive to hypocrisy, and is like pulling up the plant to examine its roots. It further indicates that we have small faith in our methods ✒ ✒

15.—People who have too much leisure, consume more than they should, and do not produce enough.

16.—To go to school for four years, or six, is no proof of excellence; any more than to fail in an examination is proof of incompetence ✒ ✒

17.—The giving of degrees and diplomas to people who have done no useful things is puerile and absurd, since degrees so secured are no proof of competence, and tend to inflate the holder with the idea that he is some great one when, probably, he isn't.

18.—All degrees should be honorary, and be given for meritorious service to society—that is, for doing something useful for somebody.

✒ ✒

E VERY preacher who preaches ably has two doors to his church: one where he attracts people in and the other through which he preaches them out. Still there is recompense in the thought that people who walk out with unnecessary clatter are often found after many moons tiptoeing in again. Yet I do not see how any man, though he be divine, could hope, or expect, to have as many as twelve disciples for three years and not be denied, doubted and betrayed. If you have thoughts and speak them frankly, Golgotha for you is not far away ✒ ✒

✒ ✒

Let us all pray to be delivered from whim: it is the poisoner of our joys, the corrupter of our peace, and Dead Sea fruit for all those about us.

✒ ✒

Better mend one fault in yourself than a hundred in your neighbor.

ILLIAM PENN was born with his hat on, and he never took it off even in church or at bed time. Happy man!

My hat cost me three dollars. I have worn this hat for three years, and while the original investment was only three dollars, as truthfully stated, the expense involved in safeguarding the dicer has been, constructively, one hundred twenty dollars a year.

In three years, three hundred sixty dollars was expended, or one hundred twenty times the original investment.

❡ If I had followed the law of natural selection, this hat could have been stolen one hundred times and I would still be no worse off than I am now.

I notice that in all first-class hotels a safe is provided in the office in which you can deposit your money, jewels and valuables, but when you endeavor to put your hat in the safe the landlord lifts unmanicured, pudgy paws in virtuous protest.

When you attempt to enter the dining-room, you will find yourself overpowered and your hat taken from you; and you can recover the property only by paying an indemnity.

Ladies wear their hats, even at breakfast, and thus elude the Hat-Snatcher. But when I attempted to wear my headgear in a fashionable New York hotel dining-room the foreign reservists were called in, and I was requested in eleven languages to abdicate.

I have repeatedly shied my castor into the ring, but so far have succeeded in getting it back, and in spite of wear and tear and natural deterioration, it costs me just as much to guard this ancient bean-protector now as when it was in the heyday of its youth.

In fact, my hat has reached a stage where no sane man would really annex it, and if he should make bold to wear it down the street he would be quickly overtaken by the hurry-up wagon.

❡ What we need is that Stetson shall issue an insurance policy with every hat, agreeing to replace it if stolen. Let Knox knock the Hat-Snatcher by guaranteeing that his commodity is exempt from theft—and all will be well. Then when we enter the dining-room we will simply fling the overhead into the corner, forget it and take a chance on recovery.

As it is, we submit to the Hat-Snatcher and pay the stipend, rather than risk social contumely. To successfully guard a hat in a first-class hotel requires a ten-per-cent insurance-premium on the cost of the tile per day.

And I submit that this is more than the service is worth, judged according to the rule of reason. If every one who goes up in an elevator in an office-building should be required to pay, we would lift an unholy howl of protest. Yet the service rendered in transporting an individual up four, five, six, or a dozen stories, and safely delivering him in apparently good order, is much greater than the act of simply taking care of his headgear while he is courting indigestion. Any institution that maintains this graft should be anathema in the minds of every honest person.

The first hotel that has the courage to come out against this pestiferous hold-up will receive the thanks of mankind, and the lasting gratitude of posterity.

❡ Just let one landlord come out strong, making an announcement to the effect that no charge is made, nor will an employee be allowed to accept a fee, for caring for hats and wraps, and the institution will get an advertisement valuable beyond the dreams of avarice. And if one hotel summons its conscience to the bar of public opinion, and meets this issue by officially decapitating the Hat-Snatcher, the flank will be turned, the combination broken, and all other taverns will be obliged to follow suit, or die in the trenches.

There are some optimistic people who say that if you do not care to disgorge cold cash to get your overhead released from chancery, you can defy the flunkey, boldly demand the dicer, and defiantly walk off with it without anything worse befalling you than the scorn of the hirelings ❧ ❧

This, however, is like that sophistical proposition of looking a lion in the eye

when he crouches to spring for you.
¶ Or, we are told that if a bear attacks you you must do everything the bear does, imitating his every gesture and action, and you will escape criticism and not even have your feelings hurt.

We are also told that when bulldogs are fighting and one gets another by the throat, the thing to do is to blow in the belligerent's ear, and this will cause him to relinquish his hold. It is very easy to give advice as to what we should do, but I notice that these men who supply suggestions move in the line of least resistance, finding discretion the better part of valor, and pay without any outward murmurs, rather than be socially disgraced in the eyes of the 'elp.

The worst about Hat-Snatching as a fine art is that we are hoodwinked into the idea that when we give the tardy dime or the elusive quarter, the worthy individual who guards the overhead is being recognized for heroic service rendered.

The fact is, however, that what is called the "Hat and Cloak Privileges" are sold to the highest bidder, and the man then employs Turcos, Cossacks, Uhlans and a few vivandieres, who are experts in social skullduggery, and skilfully extract from us the needed coin.

This money is dropped into a box that is hidden in some obscure corner, guarded by a bashi-bazouk, and the beggar is paid a paltry five dollars a week for his or her services. Over in London I have seen an old woman, disheveled, miserable, seemingly half-fed and underclothed, with a baby in her arms, crouching on a street corner. These babes, I am told by the police, are often borrowed, and the actual owner of the babe receives a percentage from the old crone who croons her witch-song. In Italy there is a beggars' trust, somewhat like the late Knickerbocker Trust Company, where cripples and deformed individuals are at a premium. They hire themselves out to a general manager and work both sides of the street.

This hat iniquity, which has grown up and established itself, is a piece of atrocious graft, an imposition on the plain people ❧ ❧

Most businessmen nowadays realize the necessity of giving full value. Reciprocity must be the rule.

To take money for a service, beyond what the service is worth, is petit larceny. If we wish to judge it in the bulk as to what is taken from the public, it then becomes grand larceny. I now propose that the Government take over all Hat-Snatching privileges, and thus meet the deficit caused by a bad guess on the income tax, and the hysteric tariff jump in the dark.

Then we will all gladly pay, realizing that we are pulling the Democratic Mule out of an inconvenient cavity.

❧ ❧

THE poor and the ignorant will continue to lie and steal as long as the rich and educated show them how. ¶ The lie is a mistake in judgment; it does not lead to the right place. It is a poor sort of defence, and usually no defence at all, since it is always calling on other lies to help it, and they break down by their own weight. Can't you get the preachers, lawyers and doctors to encourage the lowly to tell the truth by setting them an example?

❧ ❧

IS there some one who believes in the value of your mission? Ah, I am glad, for without that stimulus you were in a sorry plight. Professor Tyndall once said the finest inspiration he ever received was from an old man who could scarcely read. This man acted as his servant. Each morning the old man would knock on the door of the scientist and call, "Arise, Sir; it is near seven o'clock, and you have great work to do today." ❧ ❧

❧ ❧

I am not sure just what the unpardonable sin is, but I believe it is a disposition to evade the payment of small bills ❧ ❧

❧ ❧

Just how much discord is required in God's formula for a successful life, no one knows; but it must have a use, for it is always there.

❧ ❧

A friend is Nature's masterpiece ❧ ❧

HERE is no doubt that a teacher once committed to a certain line of thought will cling to that line long after all others have deserted it ๑ In trying to convince others, he convinces himself. This is especially so if he is opposed. Opposition evolves in his mind a maternal affection for the product of his brain, and he defends it blindly to the death ๑ Thus we see why institutions are so conservative. Like the coral insect, they secrete osseous matter; and when a preacher preaches, he himself goes forward to the mourners' bench and accepts all the dogmas that have just been so ably stated.

๑ ๑

NO one knows the vanity of riches save he who has been rich; therefore, I would have every man rich, and I would give every youth a college education that he might know the insignificance of it.

๑ ๑

THERE can be no secret in life and morals, because Nature has provided that every beautiful thought you know and every precious sentiment you feel will shine out of your face, so that all who are great enough may see, know, understand, appreciate and appropriate. You keep things only by giving them away ๑ ๑

๑ ๑

There is no freedom on earth or in any star for those who deny freedom to others.

๑ ๑

Women under thirty seldom know much unless Fate has been kind and cuffed them thoroughly.

๑ ๑

Peace comes to him who brings it; joy to him who gives it; but perfect understanding only to him who loves perfectly.

MAN never plots another's undoing except upon the stage. Because you do not like a man is no reason he is your enemy: this is a busy world, and no one has time to sit right down and hate you. The only enemies we have are those we conjure forth from our own inner consciousness ๑ One thing, we are not of enough account; and the idea that a man has enemies is only egotism gone to seed ๑ ๑

๑ ๑

TO recognize the accidentally impolitic from the essentially wrong is a step always taken first by a Philistine. The Chosen People damn him for his pains, after which they adopt and swear on their beards that they always held it.

๑ ๑

AMERICANS not only fill the teeth of royalty, but we furnish the Old World machinery, ideas and men ๑ For every twenty-five thousand men they supply us, we send them back one, and the one we send them is worth more than the twenty-five thousand they send us.

๑ ๑

GOD always gives us strength to bear our troubles of each day; but He never calculated on our piling the troubles past, and those to come, on top of those of today.

๑ ๑

No man wins his greatest fame in that to which he has given most of his time: it 's his side issue, the thing he does for recreation, his heart's play-spell, that gives him immortality.

๑ ๑

It is a great privilege to live, to work, to feel, to endure, to know: to realize that one is the instrument of Deity—being used by the Maker to work out His inscrutable purposes.

๑ ๑

The sad thing about the optimist is his state of mind concerning himself.

EDUCATION is simply the encouragement of right habits—the fixing of good habits until they become a part of one's nature, and are exercised automatically.

VERY man has moments when he doubts his ability. So does every woman at times doubt her wit and beauty, and long to see them mirrored in a masculine eye. This is why flattery is acceptable. A woman will doubt everything you say except it be compliments to herself—here she believes you are truthful and mentally admires you for your discernment.

∾ ∾

IN one of his short stories Anthony Trollope tells of a Sea Captain who fell in love with a Worthy Dame of discreet years and some property. All went well until the day before the wedding was to take place, when the Worthy Dame called in witnesses and stipulated as to which side of the bed she was to sleep on, arranged for a division of the bedclothes, and said she had heard as how sailor men liked to sleep in a breeze, and therefore she wanted it understood that she was to have sole say as to opening and shutting of all windows. She also told of a few things she would do, and gave a list of things she would n't do—there now!

Jack rolled his cud perplexed, then he scratched his head, and finally found voice to say that if he was to be captain of the matrimonial expedition, the craft in tow should n't have too much to say about the course. And as for sleeping on the right side or the left, she could have both sides, and sleep in the middle of the bed for all of him—he was going to put for open sea, and leave all gay-painted galleys to work their course alone ∾ ∾

And straightway he hove anchor and disappeared, never to be seen in that harbor again ∾ ∾

In the action for divorce in Newcomb vs. Newcomb, recently tried in New York City, the cross-examination of plaintiff brought out the following:

" Mr. Newcomb, when did the first lack of harmony between yourself and wife manifest itself?"

" At the altar."

" Indeed! how was that?"

" The bride, in the presence of the guests, requested the clergyman to omit the word ' obey.' "

Now there was nothing peculiar about that request of the soon-to-be Mrs. Newcomb. In fact, a clergyman, a good friend of mine, tells me that at least one bride out of five, where he officiates, makes the same demand.

And strange enough, that is the exact proportion of divorces to marriages in Indiana and Illinois!

The wife of Abraham Lincoln stipulated with her lord that the word " obey " be omitted, and she reminded him of the fact every little while for the rest of his natural life.

The woman who stipulates is lost— she is preparing for trouble ; and, has not a wise man whom we all know, recently said, we get anything for which we prepare? ∾ ∾

" The lie is the first blow;" and the woman who gives notice that she is not going to obey, illy masking the matter in merry smiles, is striking the first note of discord. She is serving notice that her own sweet caprice is to have precedence over the wishes of her husband— she has already begun to hedge, and the war is on.

At the time of marriage the idea of his wife obeying him is the farthest from the mind of the average man, and a lawyer-like request to strike out a certain word, of which he had never thought, savors so much of a cold matter of the head, that for the instant all the tenderness in his heart is chilled. " She is not going to obey me!" he inwardly gasps, and something clutches at his heart.

Now, very, very, very seldom does a man want his wife to slavishly obey him, but in the heart of even the most stupid of men, is a singular repugnance against having his wishes disregarded by his family ∾ ∾

Men idealize women more than women idealize men. That is to say, men do not understand women nearly so well as women understand men; but often a woman's cleverness and shrewdness and secrecy are her undoing—no good substitute has yet been found for simplicity and truth. In love affairs, centuries of serfdom have bred in the minds of women a sharpness and a smartness in love affairs that very few men possess. If a woman is big enough she will keep this shrewdness entirely out of sight, and then she may lead her liege and he will never be aware of it.

But if she is yet a little bigger she will not be a party to an alliance where there is not absolute trust, reverence and perfect faith. In which case, can you imagine her prompting the clergyman as to what he shall say or what omit? To accept the rites of the church, and then stickle at this or that implies that somebody is in doubt, and is getting ready for an emergency.

The woman who thinks a clergyman " marries 'em," is possessed of the mind of a microbe. She believes that if the preacher uses the word " obey," she will have to do it, and if he does n't use the word, she need n't. She is so soulless that she does not know that the spirit which actuates the couple, and not the words of the priest, or justice of the peace, controls the destiny of this man and woman.

No woman is worthy to be a wife who on her marriage day is not absolutely lost in an atmosphere of love and perfect trust; and the supreme sacredness of the relation is the only thing which, at the time, should possess her soul. Is she a bawd that she should bargain?

Women should not " obey" men, any more than men should obey women. There are six requisites in every happy marriage; the first is Faith, and the remaining five are Confidence.

Nothing so compliments a man as for a woman to believe in him—nothing so pleases a woman as for a man to repose confidence in her.

And at the last the desire of the man and woman who are mentally and spiritually mated is to obey each other.

Obey? God help me! Yes, if I loved a woman, my whole heart's desire would be to obey her slightest wish. And how could I love her unless I had perfect confidence that she would only aspire to what was beautiful, true and right? And to enable her to realize this ideal, her wish would be to me a sacred command; and her attitude of mind toward me, I know, would be the same.

And the only rivalry between us would be as to who could love most, and the desire to obey would be the one controlling impulse of our lives.

We gain freedom by giving it, and he who bestows faith receives it back with interest. To bargain and stipulate in love is to lose.

Perfect faith implies perfect love; and perfect love casteth out fear. It is the fear of imposition, and a lurking intent to rule, that causes the woman to haggle over a word—it is an absence of love, a limitation, an incapacity.

The price of a perfect love is an absolute surrender.

Keep back part of the price and yours will be the fate of Ananias and Sapphira ᕫ ᕫ

To win all we must give all.

ᕫ ᕫ

TO the clerk who would succeed, I say, Cultivate Charm of Manner.

❡ Courteous manners in little things are an asset worth acquiring. When a customer approaches, rise and offer a chair. Step aside and let the store's guest pass first into the elevator. These things, though little, make for finer work.

❡ To gibe visitors, or to give fresh and flippant answers, even to stupid or impudent people, is a great mistake. Meet rudeness with unfailing politeness and see how much better you feel. Your promise to a customer is your employer's promise. A broken promise always hurts; and it shows weakness in the character of a business organization, just as unreliability does in an individual.

❡ Most inaccuracies come from not really listening to what is said, or not really seeing what you put down.

❡ Having promised to obtain goods or information, or to deliver goods by a certain time, do not start the thing going and trust to luck for the rest. Do your own part in full, and then follow up to know that the rest is moving on schedule time. Remember that "accidents" and " hindrances " get after just those things with a keen scent.

Give each customer your whole attention, and give just as considerate attention to a little buyer as to a big one.

If asked for information, be sure you have it before you give it. Do not assume that the location or fact is so now because you once thought it so.

Don't misdirect. Make your directions so clear that they will be a real help.

❡ There are houses known by courteous telephoning. Telephone courtesy is a big thing, as courtesy always is. Loss of temper gains nothing.

The less you require looking after, the more able you are to stand alone and complete your tasks, the greater the reward. Then if you can not only do your work, but also intelligently and effectively direct the efforts of others, your reward is in exact ratio.

And the more people you direct, and the higher the intelligence you can rightly lend, the more valuable is your life.

The most precious possession in life is good health. Eat moderately, breathe deeply, exercise outdoors and get eight hours' sleep. And cultivate Charm of Manner as a Business Proposition.

—Courtesy As An Asset.

ॐ ॐ

The world has always acted on the principle that one good kick deserves another ॐ ॐ

ॐ ॐ

Do not lose faith in humanity: there are over ninety million people in America who never played you a single nasty trick ॐ ॐ

ॐ ॐ

FALLING in love is the beginning of all wisdom, all sympathy, all compassion, all art, all religion; and in its larger sense is the one thing in life worth doing ॐ ॐ

ॐ ॐ

Nature in her endeavors to keep man well has not only to fight disease, but often the doctor as well.

THERE are three kinds of friends: those who love you; those who are indifferent to you; and next friends, these being the people who want something that is yours.

SHE was not a suffragette. She lived in the days before there was talk of the rights of women, before women were supposed to need rights. Her name was Dorcas, and she was a spinster in both the primitive and the modern sense of the word; she went from house to house spinning and weaving. The children used to watch for her coming, for she was Aunt Dorcas, even then, before she committed the crime that helped to liberate her more fortunate sisters: a strong, straight, capable, little woman of good, tough English stock, who feared not loneliness, nor hunger, nor cold, and loved hard work ॐ ॐ

Nothing is said of her early life, of how she lost father and mother, sisters and brothers, perhaps. So far as anybody cared, she had always been Aunt Dorcas, who lived alone in the small house by the crossroads. Pine-forests shut her in on the North and East, beech and birch woods sloped away to the West; but South there was a clearing, and here the sun shone and ripened her small garden. And no matter how far she must tramp to her day's work of spinning, she always came back to this small house at night, sure of a welcome from her cat, Kittimaturus ॐ ॐ

It happened that in the village where Dorcas went to spin and weave, there lived a man who was afflicted with a bad son. He was an old man, older by twenty years than Dorcas. He had been a shoemaker in his youth, and fairly prosperous; best of all, a good man, gentle, " and loving, and giving." He had mended Dorcas' shoes for her often without pay, when she was a child. His one son was not like him. If the son had had a harsh and cruel father, he might have been cudgeled and disciplined into something resembling a decent citizen. Lacking this, he became a drunkard and a spendthrift. He married a wife whose dominant characteristic was parsimony. Having no standards of his own, he grew to accept hers, except only as they affected his own personal desires. As long as old Lazarus could earn a few cents each day as a cobbler, he was allowed a home, if it could be called a home, by his son's fireside. When rheumatism finally crippled his hands, the son, prompted by his wife, declared he was too poor to bear his father's support, and, as the saying was, "threw him on the town."

There were kings in those days, three in each town. They were called "The Selectmen." They were usually good men; but as far as the poor were concerned, they were absolute tyrants. King Number One, who lived in this part of the town, accordingly took Lazarus in his one-horse shay , and as he had business in another direction, he left the old man at the crossroads to walk the last quarter of a mile to the poorhouse.

It was early, and Dorcas was just starting for her day's work. She found the old man weeping by the roadside. It was a sight such as no woman could endure. She took old Lazarus to her house, gave him a good meal, her own supper, and told him he was welcome to stay as long as he liked.

She kept him three days before The Selectmen found it out. Instantly, there was a great buzzing of scandal throughout the town. King Number One, instigated by his wife, went to see about this.
¶ "It won't du, Dorcas," he said; "it won't du."

"He's old enough to be my father," said Dorcas; "and it'll break his heart if he has to go to the poorhouse."

"I know; it's a hard case, but we can't have sech duin's in this town. He can't stay here onless you marry him."
¶ "Then I will marry him," said Dorcas.

King Number One, being also Justice of the Peace, performed the ceremony then and there.

Old Lazarus never seemed quite to understand. Sometimes, he thought Dorcas was his daughter who had died when she was a child. Sometimes he called her Mother, as a child might; but as long as he lived, he was very happy and well content. When he died, Dorcas knew, for the first time in her life, what the bitterness of loneliness really is.

Stepson Peleg and his wife came to the funeral, quite decorous in borrowed mourning. The widow, softened by the solemnity of death, did not express her mind to him, as she had often threatened to do if they ever met. She wished to forget the bad son, for this day at least, and think only of the good father. But Peleg placed himself directly in her way.
¶ "I don't believe in putting things off," he said; "I guess you and I might as well talk a little business, Stepmother. I don't mean to be hard on ye, but my wife an' I have been talkin' things over, and we've decided to move into this house o' Fathers right away. We're willin' to board ye as long as your third lasts."

Dorcas glanced at him coldly. "This house is mine," she said.

"Used to be, I know; but it belonged to Father as soon as you married him. Married women can't hold property. That's the law."

Dorcas turned her back on him and walked away. She feared to profane the gentle dead, if she spoke in her anger.
¶ Next day, she went to see The First Selectman. She got no comfort from him. "I'm afraid it is the law, Dorcas," he said; "you orter thought o' that when you married Lazarus."

Dorcas went home. All through the night in her loneliness, she sat and thought. She thought as an ignorant

THERE are two kinds of thought: New Thought and Secondhand Thought. New Thought is made up of thoughts you, yourself, think. The other kind is supplied to you by jobbers.

woman thinks—on primitive lines of right and justice. She had no hand in the making of this law that had defrauded her, simply because she had obeyed the law of Christ. So she found a way out.

¶ In the morning, she arose and gathered all her poor household treasures in a heap in the middle of the floor. She laboriously carried her few sticks of wood into the house, too, with all the dry brush and kindling she could find. Then she set fire to the whole and watched it burn, as women of an older race used to watch the funeral-pyres of the dead ✼ Distant neighbors, who had seen the smoke, came and found her there beside the ashes of her home. They tried to make her understand that she had committed a crime. She only said: "I burned it mine."

¶ Her years in prison were not the least happy and useful ones of her life ✼ When she came out, people noticed that she carried her head higher than before. ¶ "I burned it mine," was all she would ever say of her crime. Presently, it happened that the worthy Justice of the Peace and First Selectman, otherwise called King Number One, was sent to the State Legislature. He was a man slow of thought, but clear-headed and just when he once understood. One day, quite unofficially in the pauses of the game, he told Dorcas' story.

"Now," he said, "I've got daughters growing up, and so, gentlemen, have some of you. Perhaps we hope to leave them a little money sometime, but you see how the law is. 'T ain't right."

"No," they agreed; "'t ain't right."

¶ They really took it seriously, considering that it had nothing whatever to do with keeping the Party together. That very day they fell upon that law, and fixed it so that it was much better ✼ Next year, they fixed it better still. In more than one sense, Dorcas had broken the law ✼ ✼

This is a true story. If you don't believe it — the cross roads are there still; and in a green clearing that faces the South, there is a deep dimple where catnip still grows. It was once the cellar of a house. — *The Woman and the Law.*

✼ ✼

AND here is the argument: The fear of death, as taught by the clergy; the fear of disease, as fostered by the doctors; and the fear of the law, as disseminated by lawyers, has created a fog of fear that has permeated us like a miasma, and cut human life short one-third, causing the brain to reel and rock at a time when it should be the serene and steadfast pilot of our lives. "What, then," you ask; "shall we go back to savagery?"

And my answer is: No, we must, and will, and are, going on, on to Enlightenment.

AMERICA can never become the Ideal Republic—the home and refuge of all that is best in art and science, the fulfilment of the dreams of seers and prophets—until we cease modeling our political policy after the rotting monarchies of Europe. ¶ Force expends itself and dies. Every army is marching to its death; nothing but a skull and a skeleton fill helmet and cuirass; the aggressor is overcome by the poison of his pride; victory is only another name for defeat—but the spirit of gentleness and of love is eternal. Only by building on that can we hope as a nation to live.

✼ ✼

Optimism is a kind of heart stimulant —the digitalis of failure.

OT long ago Prof. Edwin Markham spent a day with us. The title of Professor is too cheap for so excellent a man, and so, with your permission I 'll call him Mister, which means Master. Mr. Markham is the man who wrote " The Man with the Hoe." When Mr. Markham arrived at the Shop, Saint Gerome, Sammy the Artist, Ali Baba and I were just starting for the potato field, each armed with a hoe. Mr. Markham laughed heartily at our appearance and thought it was a planned reception; but it was not—it was all purely accidental.

I sent one of the boys to the barn to find another hoe. Mr. Markham did not shy, and when he was provided we started away.

We reached the field and hoed.

Mr. Markham is no stranger to the hoe. He is hearty, bronzed, and his white hair and beard quite belie his strong physique and boyish spirit. As we hoed we discussed the " hoe-man." Baba declared he knew more clearly than Mr. Markham does, himself, just what the author had in view when he wrote " The Man with the Hoe."

So Baba explained to Mr. Markham what he meant. Mr. Markham was grateful.

The trouble with the hoe-man, said Ali Baba, is too much hoe—it is hoe-congestion *

The hoe is all right, and all men should hoe. If all men hoed a little, no man would have to hoe all the time.

To hoe all the time slants the brow.

To never hoe tends to hydrocephalus and nervous prostration.

Many men never hoe, because, they say, " I don't have to." It is a fool's answer. ⁋ Then very many men are not allowed to hoe—the land is needed for game preserves. And in a country called Italy, where the true type of the hoe-man is found most abundantly, there is an army of two hundred and fifty thousand fighting men who have to be fed with the things the hoe-man digs out of the ground *

Wherever there are many soldiers there are also many hoe-men. Some one must

hoe. All food and all wealth are hoed out of the ground.

If you never hoe, and yet eat, you are slanting the forehead of the hoe-man and adding to that stolid look of God-forsaken hopelessness.

If you help the hoe-man hoe, he will then have time to think, and gradually the shape of his head will change, his eye will brighten, the coarse mouth will become expressive, and at times he will take his dumb gaze from the earth and look up at the stars.

Let us all hoe—a little, says Ali Baba. ⁋ I have not quoted my friend with slavish exactness, but substantially.

THE known may be alarming but the Unseen is terrible. It saps the springs of action and by it decision is shorn of strength. It is the miasma of the dismal swamp that shuts down and holds the victim in its soft embrace; the mist of the mountain top that conceals the precipice and yet says alluringly— " This way." It is the fog that hides the iceberg; the jungle that covers the tiger; the doubt that paralyzes will. We can cope with the defined: when Goliath comes forth on the open plain we fearlessly give him fight with nothing better than a sling and pebbles from the brook. But Goliath in a maze of mystery, Goliath shouting curses, guttural and deep, from out the blackness of a cloud —ah! that is different.

WHAT wonderful things we imagine we would do if we were off on an island somewhere where folks did n't bother so eternally! But why not consider the whole earth an island—a speck —and perform our wonders right here and now?

Violence is transient; hate consumes itself and is blown away by the winds of heaven; jealousy dies; but the righteous thought is a pressure before which malice is powerless

When you accept a present, you have dissolved the pearl of independence in the vinegar of obligation.

IT was only a few weeks ago that I had occasion to have an interview with a poet on a matter that was semi-business

The poet seemed to me unreasonable and unreasoning in his demands.

I learned, in the course of our conference, that to his mind there were degrees in obligations of indebtedness. He had a class which he called debts of honor; another class, debts of a gentleman; and some debts that were not worth mentioning. A loan of money fell under the last class.

What he called the debt of a gentleman—one which could wait an indefinite length of time—was payment for services rendered. Debts of honor were those which the sheriff compelled him to pay

When I asked him to which class debts to a grocer, baker or butcher belonged, he assumed the attitude of an injured soul and said they were too vulgar to speak of

In mentioning the conversation to two or three interested persons, the general summing up was that this was the artistic temperament, that the man was a great poet, and the situation must be endured. There was no remedy.

WHILE the subject was the topic of talk, a man told me of his experience with a great painter. The artist had been a guest in his house for many months. He had invited him to be his guest when the painter was in great distress, without decent clothing, food or shelter. More than that, he was intoxicated.

Through the personal care and ministration of my friend, who had fed, clothed and watched him as a mother her child, the artist had been able to paint one beautiful picture. A friend of the host purchased this picture, at a great price, and the artist came into possession of an abundance of money. He became unusually independent and arrogant. His demands upon his host were an insult. Yet he used his money only for his own gratification.

He bought himself a wonderful vase. He left a permanent order at the florist's for a bouquet of roses, a gardenia, an orchid rare, a cluster of lilies of the valley, to be delivered at exactly eleven o'clock each morning

He caroused, he went to places that he should not, he brought people to the home of his host who had no right there.

"What did you do?" I said to my friend

"Oh, I waited until he had used up all his money and was in debt, then I helped him to clean up and paint another picture."

"And the previous experience was repeated?" I inquired.

"To the minutest detail"

"And then what did you do?"

"I confess that I kicked him out," was this businessman's response. "He is an artist. I am a businessman. The artistic temperament is too much for me."

"But," said a lady present, "see what he does for the world! He is an artist, and artists are gifts from God for the inspiration of all the people. They should be supported by the State for the benefit of the State. Tell me where this poor artist lives and I will buy his pictures."

And the woman's eyes filled with tears.

IT was my responsibility at one time to get artists to do some necessary work in connection with manufacturing artistic goods that were to be put upon the market.

In order to sell goods, it seems necessary to have a definite price which you can name to a buyer. Unless this can be done, there is very little opportunity for exexchanging the product for money.

In order to make a just and equitable selling-price, one must know at least the cost of material and production.

"Do not ask me anything about the cost of material," said the artist. "I make a beautiful vase, that is enough."

"How much time did it take you to make this?" I next inquired, because this artist was on the payroll, and I could easily find the amount of money he did the firm the honor to accept each week

"Time! How can you ask me the time it takes to make a beautiful thing?" he petulantly responded. "You certainly do not understand art. An artist knows nothing about time nor expense. He creates. That is enough." And I knew instantly that I was properly classified in his mind as being plebeian, possibly proletarian.

However, this same artist had a work of art, which, in an unguarded moment, he offered to part with if I would pay a price which seemed to me beyond that of rubies. Because I was obliged to refuse to take it, he re-rated me a little lower than proletarian.

Then I realized that, latent within his being, there was a dim sense of price, time and material.

"Oh! It is the artistic temperament! You have to expect that," said a sympathetic friend. "Artists are all that way."

I felt a decided irritation and began to be a little nervous lest this artistic-temperament idea were contagious, and that I might be affected. I am blessed with a friend who knows the truth, and is gracious enough to tell me in a kindly but forceful way a few facts concerning myself, when it is most helpful and wholesome.

And this friend said: "You are getting cross and unreasonable. It might be a good plan to keep out in the sunshine all the afternoon and get all the sleep you need."

I followed the advice and noticed that I lost my artistic temperament, and I suppose my immediate chance of having any artistic qualities. During my afternoon out, I had a few experiences that gave me pause, and cause to think.

WORKING on the farm where I took my sunshine was a primitive, uncultured, uneducated son of the soil, German by birth.

He was an object of attention, because he was in our employ—a new helper, most interestingly poverty-stricken.

He had a wife and six children.

They owned a cook-stove, one steel knife, a fork, two plates, three cups, a spoon, two very hard and unwholesome beds, very little bedding, and the clothing which they wore.

I made inquiries of the farm superintendent concerning these people. How came they to be so poor?

In the farmer's recounting of the story of this man, I discovered the astonishing fact that this uncivilized, inartistic, ignorant, improvident creature has the artistic temperament. He has not the ability to philosophize, so he has not classified his indebtedness to grocer, butcher, baker, his employer nor the farm-boss. In fact, all debts are of one class to him. They are something to forget, to deny, and to go into a fit of rage over if questioned concerning them.

On pay-day he forgot that he had a wife and six children, bills to pay, or obligations to meet, if he *ever* knew it. He took time off, went to the city, and stayed as long as his money lasted.

When he returned and the foreman asked for an explanation, he was boorish. He had neither rhyme nor reason. He was simply insolent, stubborn, doggedly impertinent, sullen, and then silent.

I have never heard any one excuse his performances on the ground that it was due to his artistic temperament, however. In fact, quite other names were used. But so far as I am able to discern, he had the same artistic temperament that the painter or sculptor has.

THE artistic temperament has ceased to irritate and has begun to interest me. It has become a problem in science. I have watched its manifestation in the ditch-digger, the clown, the "menial," in the "wash-lady," the scrub-woman, the cook, the farm-boss, the supervisor, the superintendent, the management, myself included, and I find, upon careful scrutiny, that all have the artistic temperament just in proportion to their ignorance, to the area of their uncultured, undisciplined acreage. In other words, the artistic temperament is a common manifestation of ignorance. The artistic temperament is an expression of an undisciplined mind.

Brain, reason, intelligence, never express themselves in the form of the artistic temperament

The artistic temperament naturally belongs to the boor who will hold the handles of the plow poorly even under minute direction, who can dig a ditch only when it is marked out for him. ❡ It is the primitive expression of a young child, unskilled, unschooled, without reason or thought. It belongs to the animal who is peaceable only when its physical comfort is undisturbed

D O not dump your woes upon people—keep the sad story of your life to yourself

Troubles grow by recounting them

When the artist grows angry, has no sense of honor, is self-indulgent, he grades himself with the beasts of the field. He is advertising that he is a mongrel. He is most imperfectly cultured and uneducated

Weigh him in the balance, putting all his poetry, his beautiful dreams and lovely ideas, and all that they can be worth to humanity, all that he is into one scale, and his brute qualities in the other, and see if the scale stands at balance.

We have used the term "artistic temperament" to cover a multitude of sins, shortcomings, ignorance and unforgivable boorishness. It might be well for us to look at the facts and call this spade just plain "spade." When a poet, painter or musician is in a fit of temper, or manifests gross ignorance, or brutal, low self-indulgence, we might use those terms in connection with it that are hard facts

At least that is the way the artistic temperament looks to a disinterested person.

N ATURE'S best use for genius is to make other men think; to stir things up, so sedimentation does not take place; to break the ankylosis of self-complacency; and start the stream of public opinion running, so it will purify itself.

To pardon is the privilege only of the living

S YMPATHY is the first attribute of love as well as its last. And I am not sure but that sympathy is love's own self, vitalized mayhap by some divine actinic ray. Only a thorn-crowned bleeding Christ could have won the adoration of the world. Only the souls who have suffered are well loved. Thus does Golgotha find its recompense. Hark and take courage, ye who are in bonds!

G REAT organizers are men who are able to distinguish between initiative and "freshness." And quite frequently the difference is very slight

F OR the most part, the women who live in history are those who were mismated, misunderstood, neglected, abused, spit upon by Fate, scorned. They were sometimes loved, of course, but loved by those who had no business to love them—loved by the wrong man. But the men who loved them were no more potent factors for good in their evolution than the little men who taunted, harassed, scorned and neglected them

E VERLASTING life will be yours if you deserve it—your present belief or disbelief does not affect the issue. But make sure of this: if you are to be a great soul in Heaven, you have got to begin to be a great soul here.

Remorse is the form that failure takes when it has made a grab and got nothing.

T HE mind sees all, hears all, listens, sifts, weighs and decides Over against this there is something in man which sees the mind and watches its workings—which analyzes the mind and knows why it does certain things, which knows the mind is not the soul; and this something that knows the mind is not the soul, is the soul

CARLYLE tells of a certain village in the dominion of Peter the Great where a few Catholic families dwelt. The "best citizens" felt that these Catholics were a menace to the well-being of the place, as "they were worshipers of images and hopelessly given over to popery." So, for the good of the place, and the glory of God, the first citizens sent a commission to the King asking permission to kill the Catholics

The King heard their prayer and agreed to give them the desired permission, provided they would agree to his giving other Catholics permission to kill them.

"Oh, but your Majesty," replied the commissioners, "there is a difference—you seem to forget that we are in possession of the True Faith!"

THE dominant note observable in nature—observable only to the eye of the mind that has severed itself from the prejudices of the will—is blitheness. ❡ She seems always to be laughing; her most terrible moments are like the scowls that gran'pa puts on in front of naughty children who really amuse him —the mocking mask of mirth. Nature goes her way through her four seasons with a carelessness, an insouciance, a sang froid, such as men have who care nothing for death or who have learned the fine secret that the tomb covers, but does not hide. Life is a huge joke to the Immortal Mother. She laughs eternally because she is wiser than her children. She knows nothing is lost. She knows that death is recomposition and pain the way character is tooled.

THE one unethical thing in the universe is to "brand" any one with a bad name, especially so if this person happens to be in the same line of business as yourself. The business world no longer knocks a competitor.

RESPONSIBILITIES Gravitate to the Person Who can Shoulder Them; POWER Flows to the Man Who Knows How

A FROWSLED, towsled, greasy and shiny One, in battered dinky derby and tightly buttoned Prince Albert, blew into the Shop the other day and greeted me effusively. He was one of the Elect, he said, temporarily reduced and slightly disfigured by too much contact with a cold and cruel world. He glibly explained these things, although he needed not, for life writes its record on the face, and the record in this case was writ large. Society was all wrong—the rich were getting richer, the poor poorer—merit was never considered, all things went by favoritism—my friend longed for the Ideal Life. I started to say something, but the Lubricated One shut me off with the gracious wave of a hand unmanicured. "Oh, never mind that," said he, "I anticipate you—you are going to say that the Ideal Life is an iridescent dream, and that all the East Aurora there is is the East Aurora that one carries in his own breast. Truth, truth, shining truth, but you see I brought my East Aurora with me—my heart is right—I believe in the Brotherhood of Man!"

"And you have no money?" I mused aloud, trying to gain time to formulate a Scheme

"Money—money? Have I money? Why, Comrade, I am a feather! I trust I am in time for the quarterly dividend!"

"Yes," he continued, "and I never could have reached this Haven of Rest—I mean Work—were it not for Col. Smith of Cleveland—A. J.—great fellow, is n't he? He gave me a ticket here. Where's Ali Baba? I think I'll have him take me over to the Phalanstery and get a bite of something before I go to work. 'You can take no joy in your tasks if you are on half rations,' William Morris used to say, and wisely say. Ali Baba, he's the man I want to see!"

"There he is," I exclaimed, "out there on that wagon with the spotted pony, and the load of mail bags." I walked to the door, arm in arm, with my new found friend, and as we reached the steps I pressed a big silver dollar in his palm and called, "Oh, Baba, one moment, please —here is a gentleman going to Buffalo. He wants to catch the four o'clock train!"

❡ Baba reached out a big calloused hand, and gave the fellow a lift to the top of the mail bags.

"Hold on," called the Elect One, "just a second!"

We shook hands warmly.

"Give my regards to Col. Smith when you see him," I said, as the wagon moved away ◆ ◆

"That I will!" called the passenger astride of the mail bags—"that I will— he's our kind, is the Colonel—so long!" And he lifted the battered derby with a flourish that symboled sincerity, respect, good will, and told of the brotherhood of man. I now hear that the Frowsy One has given a not wholly complimentary lecture on "The Roycrofters as I Found Them."—*One of the Elect.*

◆ ◆

THE best service a book can render you is, not to impart truth, but to make you think it out for yourself ◆

◆ ◆

Health and happiness can be found only out of doors.

◆ ◆

FOR disobedience the man and woman were put out of the Garden —they had wandered far—and they can only return hand in hand.

◆ ◆

If you have not known poverty, heart-hunger and misunderstanding, God has overlooked you, and you are to be pitied.

◆ ◆

Theology is not what we know about God, but what we know we do not know about Nature.

◆ ◆

Men congratulate themselves on their position, no matter what it is; the world is wrong, not they.

 PICNIC party is a pretty good example of applied communism. The atmosphere on such an occasion is vibrant with good will and good cheer. Everybody wants to carry the baskets, and everybody is anxious to help everybody else over the fence and across the ditch. Reaching the place that the party has set out for, some get fuel, others water, still others arrange the tables. The spirit of co-operation and mutual service is supreme. There are no old, no young, no high, no low—the college-bred and homespun meet on an equality. There are no noses in the air; patronage is unheard of.

Did I say that all unite on this occasion. I forgot.

There is one couple that followed far behind on the way to the picnic-ground. They talked together soft and low. At the ground they did not gather fuel, nor did they wash the dishes after the meal. Instead they sat on a log, close together, but clear apart from the rest, almost lost in the dense foliage.

They were in love, very much in love—a fact patent to all observers.

All the rest were in love, too, but the many were filled with universal love, while this one couple focused their thoughts upon the personal and particular ◆ ◆

They were talking of the "home" they were soon to have—love in a cottage.

❡ Schopenhauer would explain that they were caught in the toils of the "genius of the genus." Nature was intent on using them for a purpose. This desire on their part to get off in secrecy by themselves, to hide away and exclude the world, was right and proper.

But to found a society on this transient and intense mood is not scientific.

This young man and young woman fully expected to perpetuate their mood— that is exactly what they hoped to do.

❡ They are going to have a perpetual trysting-place, and never for a moment will their cottage become irksome.

But life to them will only be possible as they mix with other lives. The home is founded on this momentary sex impulse of exclusiveness; and the reason joy and peace do not last is because the occupants cease to be individual and long to become universal. Exclusion has its use, and up to a certain point it serves, but a point is surely reached where it is not wise to say, " Here will we build three tabernacles"—not one.

The selfishness of individual love should give way to the universal.

Where the heart once went out to a person, it now goes out to mankind. The lesser love is absorbed by the greater.

HONEST people are those who have been lifted up into a more spiritual atmosphere. They exercise an attractive force, and the better they are, the stronger this silent force they exert works for good. Purity of purpose is a force, just as truly as is the Law of Gravitation. ❦ The man who can not take care of himself and think for himself, and act rightly for himself, will be a drag and a burden on any community. Self-reliance, self-respect and self-control are the three things needful—and these things will bring you success in a community, or out of it.

THE monks were the first of our modern bookmakers, and the volumes they made are even yet the hopeless tantalization of every aspiring printer and binder. They set us a standard of excellence so high that it almost discourages emulation. Italian art, from which our modern art is derived, was not a private affair—it was for the Church, and the Church was for all.

MEN who marry for gratification, propagation or the matter of buttons or socks, must expect to cope with and deal in a certain amount of quibble, subterfuge, concealments, and double, deep-dyed prevarication ❧ And these things will stain the fabric of the souls of those who juggle them, and leave their mark upon futurity.

When you see a tomcat with his whiskers full of feathers, do not say "Canary!"— he 'll take offense.

GENTLENESS, consideration and constancy are natural to the civilized, normal man —these things pay and are in accordance with his best welfare. They are a part of the great divine law that works for the self-preservation and evolution of the species. Enlightened self-interest means fidelity; and loyalty to your own is the only policy that pays compound interest to both borrower and lender. That which is natural is best; and what is best is most expedient; the expedient thing is the right thing; and righteousness is simply a form of commonsense. That is good which serves—and that which serves is sacred, and nothing else is.

TOO much intimacy repels. Propinquity is both the cause of love and its cure. The secret of human satisfaction lies in the just balance that separates indulgence and denial. Man in his heart feels that he was made to be free. Morever he compliments himself by thinking that he knows what is for his own good. When you tell him he does not, and issue threats and prohibitions, you sow the seeds of rebellion. Society is now existing under a condition of enforced monogamy, but " prohibition" does not prohibit, and the effects of force are always more or less neutralized by stealth. It needs no argument to prove that William Dean Howells is right in his assertion that " American society is imperfectly monogamous."

The man who does too much for others leaves himself underdone.

Meanness is more in half-doing than in omitting acts of generosity.

Not only does beauty fade, but it leaves a record upon the face as to what became of it.

People whose souls are made of dawn-stuff and starshine may make mistakes, but God will not judge them by these alone ❧ ❧

EN are not punished for their sins, but by them.

Expression is necessary to life ✠ The spirit grows through exercise of its faculties, just as a muscle grows strong through use. Life is expression, and repression is stagnation—death ✠ ✠

Yet there is right expression and wrong expression. If a man allows his life to run riot, and only the animal side of his nature is allowed to express itself, he is repressing his highest and best, and therefore those qualities not used atrophy and die ✠ Sensuality, gluttony and the life of license repress the life of the spirit, and the soul never blossoms; and this is what it is to lose one's soul ✠ ✠

❡ All adown the centuries, thinking men have noted these great truths, and again and again we find individuals forsaking, in horror, the life of the senses and devoting themselves to the life of the spirit.

❡ The question of expression through the spirit or through the senses—through the soul or the body—has been the pivotal point of all philosophies and the inspiration of all religions.

Asceticism in our day finds an interesting manifestation in the Trappists, who live on a mountain, nearly inaccessible, and deprive themselves of almost every vestige of bodily comfort—going with out food for days, wearing uncomfortable garments, suffering severe cold. So here we find the extreme instance of men repressing the faculties of the body, in order that the spirit may find ample opportunity for exercise.

Between this extreme repression and the license of the sensualist lies the truth. But just where, is the great question;

WOULD you have your name smell sweet with the myrrh of remembrance, and chime melodiously in the ear of future days?

Then cultivate faith, not doubt ✠ ✠

And give every man credit for the good he does,

Never seeking to attribute base motives to beautiful acts.

Actions count ✠ ✠

and the desire of one person, who thinks he has discovered the norm, to compel all other men to stop there has led to war and strife untold. All law centers around this point: What shall men be allowed to do? Most of the frightful cruelties inflicted on mankind during the past have sprung out of a difference of opinion arising through a difference in temperament. The question is as live today as it was two thousand years ago: What expression is best? that is, What shall we do to be saved? And concrete absurdity consists in saying we must all do the same thing.

❡ Whether the race will ever grow to a point where men will be willing to leave the matter of life-expression to the individual is a question. Most men are anxious to do what is best for themselves and least harmful to others. The average man now has intelligence enough. Utopia is not far off, if the folk who govern us, for a consideration, would only be willing to do unto others as they would be done by. War among nations, and strife among individuals, is a result of the covetous spirit to possess power or things, or both.

A little more patience, a little more charity for all, a little more devotion, a little more love, with less bowing down to the past, a brave looking-forward to the future, with more confidence in ourselves, and more faith in our fellows, and the race will be ripe for a great burst of light and life.

✠ ✠

ACADEMIC education is the act of memorizing things read in books, and things told by college professors who got their education mostly by memorizing things read in books.

HE other day I read in a printed book these words, " Some mocked, some shook their heads and some believed." And that is the universal experience of every man who ever thought anything or did anything, or was anything. People always mock the thing they are not used to. Afterwards their hilarious mockery may reduce itself to a dubious shaking of the head, and a cynical smile; then the smile may fade away into blankness, and the man may believe. Deborah standing in the doorway of her father's house and making fun of the moon-faced Benjamin as he walked up the street munching at his loaves and gaping on every side, is typical

Deborah had no flitting ghost of a thought that this strange, loaf-munching, mirth-moving youth would ere long humble her into the very dust; then when she had been flung adrift by fate, her arms would reach out to him and he would marry her and give her immortality by linking her name with his own—the greatest name America has produced

No, of course she had n't.

Saul of Tarsus, going down to Damascus to persecute the Christians, could not foresee that he would come back and henceforth be the Master Christian of all time

Some mocked, some shook their heads and some believed.

Yes, be you preacher, lawyer, physician, artist, writer, do your work the best you can and try to live up to your highest ideal, some will surely mock. If you have genius a great many will mock, and a great many will shake their heads. But although a great multitude may mock, so long as a few believe, all is well. No good life was ever lived but there was some one believed in it. These few people who believe in us make life possible. Without them, what should we do? But with them we are knitted to the Infinite

Let the mob mock, let the crowd shake their heads! There are a few who believe. ℂ I know a cottage whose door for me always stands ajar, and where the dwellers therein start with gladness when they hear the coming of my footsteps
—Some Mocked—Some Believed

O you know: That newspapers are managed by men; And that editors are men; And that doctors are men; And that lawyers are men; And that judges are men;

And that all laws are and have been made by men;

And that all priests and preachers are men;

And that all religions were made and formulated by men;

And that all books were written by men;

ℂ And that all the justice we know is man's justice;

And that what we call God's justice is only man's idea of what he would do if he were God;

And that this idea changes as man changes;

And that man's conception of God's justice has softened, refined, and become less severe than ever before;

And that all the love we know is man's love;

And all compassion, man's compassion; And all sympathy, man's sympathy; And all forgiveness, man's forgiveness; And that there is nothing finer, greater or nobler in the world than man;

And that all beings, spirits and persons greater than man have been, and are, the creation of man's mind;

And that man is not yet completed, but only in process of creation;

And that in his present transitional state he has partially abandoned intuition, without fully getting control of his intellect;

And that all laws, creeds and dogmas are of only transient value;

And should be eliminated when they no longer minister to human happiness

ℂ And that now, for the first time in the history of the world, a very large number of people know these things;

ℂ And are exercising their brains; And that the brain is an organ and grows strong by use, and only through use;

And that man's ability to think is a new acquisition;

And that very few people as yet are able to think at all, being moved by feeling—hunger, fear, and the hope of reward;

❡ And that most so-called educated men are those who have memorized things and can glibly repeat the things which other men have memorized and then glibly told them; for to think efficiently one must be logical, rational, scientific and philosophic; ❧ ❧

That to be logical one must be able to follow a sequence, or a cause and effect, step by step;

That to be rational one must be able to accept and use a unit of measurement, so as to ascertain proportions and to reason rightly concerning the simple movements of life and its tendencies;

That to be scientific one must be able to classify and coordinate the facts that logic and reason supply;

And that to be philosophic he must be able to unify and deduce right conclusions from science;

And that this faculty of efficient thinking is yet only in its infancy;

And that philosophic thinking gives wings to the imagination;

And that through right thinking we will gradually learn to control our bodies, our tempers, our desires, our imaginations, our environment; And that the trained imagination is a searchlight which reveals the future;

And that by the use of imagination we now see Paradise ahead;

A Paradise of increasing effort, work, endeavor, and increasing power;

A Paradise of this world, that is to come through health, work, simplicity, honesty, mutuality, cooperation, reciprocity and love?—*A Question—Do You Know!*

SCIENCE is simply the classification of the common knowledge of the common people. It is bringing together the things we all know and putting them together so we can use them. This is creation and finds its analogy in Nature, where the elements are combined in certain ways to give us fruits or flowers or grain ❧ ❧

Every living man is a salesman. We all have something to offer—doctors, lawyers, preachers, actors, teachers, painters, orators, poets, clerks, merchants—all sell their talent, their skill, their knowledge or the result and accumulation of their talent, their skill, their knowledge, their foresight, wit, cleverness ❧

THE man of violence has ever received quick recognition, but not a lasting fame. We deify only the Gentle Man—the man of heart. The sober good sense of the time, simply through the law of self-preservation, will not continue to push to the front the man who delights in a fight.

ORATORS have died practically unheard; writers have existed in garrets, and starved painters have committed suicide—all through an inability to command the attention of the public. One-half the battle is to get the speaker's eye; the other half is to have something to say ❧ ❧

The wrecks of the world are of two kinds, those who have nothing that society wants, and those who do not know how to get their goods into the front window ❧ ❧

Good luck is science not yet classified; just as the supernatural is the natural not yet understood.

Men who are successful in most of their undertakings we call "lucky dogs." ❧

Diagnose the case, however, and you find that these successful men all have certain qualities. Men succeed or fail through lack of positive qualities, or through the possession of certain negative qualities ❧ ❧

T is perfectly safe to say that ninety-nine men out of a hundred, in civilized countries, are opposed to war. Savages like to go to war; we do not. ¶ We are farmers, mechanics, merchants, manufacturers, teachers, and all we ask is the privilege of attending to our own business. We own our homes, love our friends, are devoted to our families, and do not interfere with our neighbors any more than is necessary—we have work to do, and wish to work while it is called the day. We recognize that life is short, and the night cometh. Leave us alone ✆ ✆ ¶ But they will not—these demagogues, politicians and rogues intent on the strenuous life. We wish to be peaceable and want to be kind, but they say this life is warfare and we must fight ✆ Of course we would fight to protect our homes; but our homes are not threatened, nor our liberties, either, save by the men who chew the ubiquitous clove and insist on the strenuous life. Leave us alone ✆ ✆

We wish to pay off the mortgages on our houses, to educate our children, to work, to read, to meditate, to prepare for old age and quick-coming, cool, all-enfolding death.

But they will not leave us alone—these men who insist on governing us and living off our labor. They tax us, eat our substance, conscript us, draft our boys into their wars to fight farmers whose chief offenses are that they wear trousers that bag at the knee and cultivate an objectionable style of whisker. ¶ They call themselves the superior class. They live off the labor of our hands. They essay the task of governing us for a consideration. They deceive us—this superior class—they hoodwink us; they betray us; they bulldoze us

CALM, patient, persistent pressure wins. It wins! Violence is transient. Hate, wrath, vengeance are all forms of fear, and do not endure. Silent, persistent effort will dissipate them all. Be strong! ✆ ✆

by the plea of patriotism. ¶ They deceive us, and oh, the infamy and the shame of it! They deceive us in the name of the bleeding Christ—the gentle Christ whose love embraced a world, and whose pitying eyes look down upon us from a cross—the Christ who distinctly taught that war was wrong, and that the only rule of life should be to do unto others as we would be done by ✆ ✆

In order to establish a reason for their domination this self-appointed superior class pretend to follow in the footsteps of Christ—they call themselves Christians ✆ ✆

Few people, comparatively, think for themselves, and so this deception acts as a hypnosis on the many, and being peaceably disposed, they accept it ✆ ✆ ¶ But Christ never endorsed war, not even a war of self-defense, much less a war of aggression. The Bible is the book we all talk about but seldom read. ¶ Christ opposed war, never took up a collection, accepted no salary, founded no church, had no ritual, wore no mitre nor robe of office. He did not belong to the superior class—did not ever take pains to associate with respectable people. He was a carpenter who felt certain truths so intensely that He left His bench for a time and went forth speaking to men in the streets, the market places and by the seashore.

War is hell ✆ ✆

We would like to obey the Golden Rule. ¶ But the superior class will not have it so—they pass conscription laws, and use the army thus conscripted to conscript other men ✆ ✆

War is the sure result of the existence of armed men. That country which maintains a large standing army will sooner or later have a war on hand. The man who prides himself on fisticuffs is going, some day, to meet a man who considers

himself a better man, and they will fight.
❡ So the people who wish to follow the teachings of Christ are not allowed to do so, but are taxed, outraged, deceived by governments—by the superior class who demand that we shall lead the strenuous life, when all we ask is the privilege of doing our work—and doing unto others as we would be done by ❧

❡ Christ taught humility, meekness, the forgiveness of one's enemies, and that to kill is wrong. The Bible teaches men not to swear, but the superior class swear us on the Bible in which they do not believe.

The only relief lies in education. Educate men not to fight, and that it is wrong to kill. Teach them the Golden Rule, and yet again teach them the Golden Rule. Silently defy this superior class by refusing to bow down to their fetich of bullets.—*Leave Us Alone.*

❧ ❧

COMMON question is this one, "Would you care to live your life over again?" ❡ Not only is it a common question, but a foolish one, since we were sent into life without our permission, and are being sent out of it against our will, and the option of a return-ticket is not ours. But if urged to reply I would say with Benjamin Franklin, "Yes, provided, of course, that you allow me the author's privilege of correcting the second edition." If, however, this is denied, I will still say, "Yes," and say it so quickly it will give you vertigo.

In reading the *Journal of John Wesley* the other day, I ran across this item written in the author's eighty-fifth year, "In all of my life I have never had a period of depression nor unhappiness that lasted more than half an hour." I can truthfully say the same. One thing even Omnipotence can not do, and that is to make that which once occurred never to have been. The past is mine ❧ ❧

What does life mean to me? Everything! Because I have everything with which to enjoy life. I own a beautiful home, well furnished, and this home is not decorated with a mortgage. I have youth —I am only fifty—and as in degree the public is willing to lend me its large furry ear, I have prospects. I have a library of five thousand volumes to read; and besides, I have a little case of a hundred books to love, bound in full levant, hand-tooled.

Then besides I have a saddle-horse with a pedigree like unto that of a Daughter of the Revolution; a Howard watch, and a fur-lined overcoat. So there now, why should n't I enjoy Life? ❧ ❧

❡ I anticipate your answer, which is, that a man may have all of these things enumerated and also have indigestion and chronic Bright's Disease, so that the digger in the ditch, than he, is happier far. Your point is well taken, and so I will gently explain that if I have any aches or pains I am not aware of them.

❡ I have never used tobacco, nor spirituous liquors, nor have I contracted the chloral, cocaine, bromide or morphine habit, never having invested a dollar in medicine, patented, proprietary nor prescribed ❧ ❧

In fact, I have never had occasion to consult a physician. I have good eyesight, sound teeth, a perfect digestion, and God grants to me His great gift of sleep ❧ ❧

And again you say, "Very well, but you yourself have said, 'Expression is necessary to life,' and that the man who has everything is to be pitied, since he has nothing to work for, and that to have everything is to lose all, for life lies in the struggle." All the points are well made. But I have work to do—compelling work—that I can not delegate to others ❧ ❧

This prevents incipient smugosity and introspection. For more than twelve years I have written the copy for two monthly magazines. During that time no issue of either magazine has been skipped. The combined paid-in-advance circulation of these periodicals is more than two hundred thousand copies each issue, giving me an audience, counting at a conservative rate of three readers to a magazine, of more than a half-million souls. Here is a responsibility that may well sober any man, and which would subdue him, actually, if he stopped to contemplate it. The success of Blondin in crossing the Niagara Gorge on a wire, with a man on his back, hinged on his not stopping to think it over.

In order to write well you require respite and rest in change. And so to keep my think-apparatus in good working order I dilute the day with much manual work —which is only another word for play.

❡ Big mental work is done in heats ❧ Between these heats are intervals of delightful stupidity.

To cultivate his dull moments is the mark of wisdom for almost every thought-juggler who aspires to keep three balls in the air at one time. In the course of each year I give about a hundred lectures ❧ ❧

But besides writing and public speaking, I have something to do with a semi-communistic corporation called The Roycrofters, employing upwards of five hundred people ❧ ❧

The work of The Roycrofters is divided into departments as follows: a farm, bank, hotel, printing-plant, bookbindery, furniture-factory and blacksmith shop ❧

The workers in these various departments are mostly people of moderate experience, and therefore more or less superintendence is demanded. Eternal vigilance is not only the price of liberty but of success in business, and knowing this I keep in touch with all departments of the work. So far, we have always been able to meet our payroll. All of the top-notchers in the Roycroft Shops have been evolved there, so it will be seen that we aim to make something besides books. In fact, we have a brass band, an art-gallery, a reading-room, a library, and we have lectures, classes or concerts every night in the week. Some of these classes I teach, and usually I speak in the Roycroft Chapel twice a week on current topics ❧ ❧

These things are here explained to make clear the point that I have no time for ennui or brooding over troubles past or those to come. Even what I say here is written on by-product time, on board a railroad-train, going to meet a lecture engagement, seated with a strange fat man who talks to me, as I write, about the weather, news from nowhere, and his most wonderful collection of steins. All of which, I hear you say, is very interesting, but somewhat irrelevant and inconsequential, since one may have all of the things just named, and also hold the just balance between activity and rest, concentration and relaxation, which we call health, and yet his life be faulty, incomplete, a failure for lack of one thing—Love ❧ ❧

Your point is well made. When Charles Kingsley was asked to name the secret of his success he replied, "I had a friend."

❡ If asked the same question I would give the same answer. I might also explain that my friend is a woman.

This woman is my wife, legally and otherwise. She is also my comrade, my companion, my chum, my business partner ❧ ❧

There has long been a suspicion that when God said, " I will make a helpmeet for man," the remark was a subtle bit of sarcasm. However, the woman of whom I am speaking proves what God can do when He concentrates on His work ❧ ❧

To this woman I owe all I am—and to her the world owes its gratitude for any and all, be it much or little, that I have given it. My religion is all in my wife's name ❧ ❧

And I am not bankrupt, for all she has is mine, if I can use it, and in degree I have used it ❧ ❧

And why I prize life, and desire to live, is that I may give the world more of the treasures of her heart and mind, realizing with perfect faith that the supply coming from Infinity can never be lessened nor decreased.

I have succeeded beyond the wildest ambitions of my youth, but I am glad to find that my desires outstrip my performances, and as fast as I climb one hill I see a summit beyond. So I am not satisfied, nor do I ever declare, " Here will I build three tabernacles," but forever do I hear a voice which says, " Arise and get thee hence, for this is not thy rest."

𝓣HEOLOGY is passed along by the law of parental entail. The persistency of the Jew in religious matters is owling in great measure to his filial piety.

ॐ ॐ

All separation of society into sacred and secular, good and bad, saved and lost, learned and illiterate, rich and poor, illusions which mark certain periods in the evolution of society.

ॐ ॐ

A sincere man: One who bluffs only a part of the time.

ॐ ॐ

On man's journey through life he is confronted by two tragedies. One when he wants a thing he can not get; and the other when he gets the thing and finds he does not want it.

ॐ ॐ

HAT the Jews are a joyous people and find much sweet solace in their sorrowful religion is proven by one fact too obvious to be overlooked — they reproduce. Children are born of joy. The sorrows of Jewry are more apparent than real. After every Black Fast, when the congregations used to sit shoeless on the stone floors of the synagogues, weeping and wailing on account of the destruction of Jerusalem, the youngsters and the grown-ups as well, were counting the hours before the Feast of Pentecost would begin. The sorrow over the loss of things destroyed a thousand years or so ago is reduced to rather a pleasant emotional exercise.

Fasts were followed by feasts, also pro and con, as Mrs. Malaprop would say, so in the home of an orthodox Jewish family there was always something doing. Fasts, feasts, flowers, sweetmeats, lights, candles, little journeys, visits, calls, dances, prayers, responses, wails and cries of exultation—" Rejoicing of the Law"—this prevented monotony, stagnation and introspection.

And these are the things which have pressed their pre-natal influences upon the Jew until the fumes and reek of the Ghetto, the rumble and squeak of the rabble and the babble of bazaars are more acceptable to him than is the breeze blowing across mesa or prairie, or the low moaning lullaby of lonely pine forests. The sense of separation is hell, and if continued, becomes insanity. The sense of separation is a thing that seldom presses upon the Jew, and this is why he seldom goes insane. His family, friends, clan, tribe are close about him. Zangwill, himself a child of the Ghetto, comes to the rescue of the despised and misunderstood Christain, expresses a doubt as to whether the Ghetto was not devised by Jews in response to their gregarious instinct and great desire to live their religious and family life undisturbed. For certain it is that the wall which shut the Jews in, shut the Christians out.

The first Ghetto was at Venice. It came into being during the Italian Renaissance, say about the year Fourteen Hundred and Fifty. The Jews had settled in one corner of the city, as they always have done, and are still prone to do. They had their own shops, stores, bazaars, booths, schools and synagogues. They built close but high. and they built well. There they were packed, busied with their own affairs, jostling, quibbling, arguing—taking no interest in the social life outside.

To be sure, they traded with the Christians, bought, sold, ran, walked with them, but they did not dine with Christians nor pray with them. There were Jewish architects, painters, printers, lawyers, bankers, and many of the richest and most practical men of Venice were Jews ॐ ॐ

Children born and brought up in the Ghetto always felt a certain pity for those who had to live beyond the gates, in the great selfish, grasping, wicked world. Those inside the Ghetto were the Chosen People of God; those outside were the Children of the Devil.

That the Jews kept aloof from the Gentiles and preferred to live apart is true, no matter who built the Ghetto wall. Also, no matter who built the wall, it is a fact that the Government of Venice, which was Christian and under the immediate jurisdiction of the Church, kept guards at the gates and allowed no Jew to leave after a certain early hour of the evening, nor on Sundays or holidays.

so so

GIBBON, who was a Deist or Mono-theist and really liked the Jews, intimates that it was lucky for the Christians that Constantine did n't embrace Judaism instead of Christianity, for if he had, the Jews would have treated the Christians exactly as the Christians have since treated the Jews *so* Of course, nobody claims that Christianity is the religion of Christ—it is the religious rule of pagan Rome, with Christ as a convenient la-bel. Gibbon, in this connection, says at least one irrefut-able thing and that is that the Jewish people are men and women. Christians are men and women, too; both are surely human beings, and it is quite likely that the race is not to the swift, nor the battle to the strong, but time and chance happeneth to them all.

I am not so sure that Gibbon was right when he says the Christians were lucky in that Constantine did not turn Jew. To be persecuted is not wholly a calamity, but to persecute is to do that for which Nature seemingly affords no compensa-tion. The persecutor dies, but the perse-cuted lives on forever. The struggle for existence which the Jew has had to make, is the one thing that has differ-entiated him and made him strong.

Those first Christians—Primitive Christ-ians—who lived during the years from the time of Paul to that of Constantine, were a simple, direct, sincere and honest people—opinionated no doubt, and ob-stinately dogmatic, but with virtues that can never be omitted nor waived. They were economical, industrious and filled with the spirit of brotherhood, and they possessed a fine pride concerning their humility, as all ascetics do. They have every characteristic that distinguish-ed the Jew of the Middle Ages—those characteristics which invite persecution, and wax strong under it.

Poverty and persecution seem neces-sary factors in fixing upon a people a distinctive and peculiar religion *so* Persecution and poverty have no power to stamp out a religion—all they do is to stain it deeper into the hearts of its votar-ies. Centuries of starvation and re-pression deepened the religious im-pulse of the Irish, and it has ever been the same with the Jew.

The downfall of primitive Christ-ianity dates from the day that Con-stantine embraced it and thereby made it popular. Prosperity is a form of disin-tegration—a ripening of the fruit. Things succeed only that they may die.

Liberal Judaism is fast becoming a Universal Religion, taught in fact, if not in name, by priests, preachers and muftis of all denominations. The end of the Jew is near, for we are adopting him, willy, nilly.—*The Jews.*

so so

THE man who is worthy of being a leader of men will never complain of the stupidity of his helpers, of the ingratitude of mankind, nor of the inappreciation of the pub-lic. These things are all a part of the great game of life, and to meet them and not go down before them in discourage-ment and defeat is the final proof of power.

THE wise man contains in himself every quality of the foolish person, plus the attributes and characteristics of the wise one. His foolishness is held in check by discretion, and instead of energy being blown about by caprice, it is controlled by judgment.

so so

The object of teaching a child is to enable him to get along without his teacher *so so*

so so

Chase your work or your work will chase you.

HE trouble with the hoe-man is too much hoe—it is hoe-congestion ✷ ✷

The hoe is all right, and all men should hoe.

If all men hoed a little, no man would have to hoe all the time.

To hoe all the time slants the brow.

To never hoe tends to hydrocephalus and nervous prostration.

Many men never hoe, because, they say, "I don't have to." It is a fool's answer.

❡ Then very many men are not allowed to hoe—the land is needed for game preserves. And in a country called Italy, where the true type of hoe-man is found most abundantly, there is an army of two hundred and fifty thousand fighting men who have to be fed with the things the hoe-man digs out of the ground. Wherever there are many soldiers there are also many hoe-men.

❡ Some one must hoe.

All food and all wealth are hoed out of the ground.

If you never hoe, and yet eat, you are slanting the forehead of the hoe-man and adding to that stolid look of God-forsaken hopelessness.

If you help the hoe-man hoe, he will then have time to think, and gradually the shape of his head will change, his eye will brighten, the coarse mouth will become expressive, and at times he will take his dumb gaze from the earth and look up at the stars.

Let us all hoe—a little.

✷ ✷

IGHTING according to Marquis of Queensberry rules with five-ounce gloves is not a dangerous sport. In the year past, not a single serious accident has occurred among all the many fights in the State of New York.

❡ Modern prize-fighting is not nearly so dangerous as football or even baseball. If a baseball goes through your hands, it will probably mar your classic features for the rest of your life, if the spheroid is flung with the emphasis that is usually put behind it. But no blows that even the most sturdy prize-fighter can land are likely to do damage; and one-half the business of the prize-fighter is to defend himself from any packages that may be directed to him.

Recently a noted prize-fighter has spent a month at Roycroft. This man is Freddie Welsh, Champion Lightweight of England, who is matched to meet Matt Wells in the near future.

Freddie Welsh is twenty-six years of age; he weighs one hundred thirty-five pounds; stands five feet, six. He has fought seventy-nine battles, and lost just two.

Freddie is a very kindly, good-natured, intelligent individual. He knows enough to keep good hours, not to overeat, not to underbreathe, and he carries a civil tongue in his Welsh head. He makes friends, and keeps them. He is a good mixer. The truth that he is an individual of intelligence is proven in the fact that he reads everything I write, and buys a copy of every book I fling into the literary ring.

At Roycroft, Freddie passed the medicine-ball with the girls, played baseball with the boys, and every evening, between five and six, he put on the mitts, over on the Roycroft playground, with any individual who announced himself as a candidate for honors.

At one of our little amateur seances in the squared circle, a husky farmer from South Wales was in attendance. It seems this man had been a sailor, and about ten years ago was a handy individual at polishing the anchor or splicing the main brace ✷ ✷

However, he has taken on a little avoirdupois, and now tips the beam at two hundred ten.

A right bold and manly specimen he was, and many a time when under the influence of apple-juice, he cleaned out the whole bunch at the General Store at the Crossroads. As he watched Freddie, the days of his youth came back. He was like unto the fire-horse who has graduated to the milk-wagon.

This son of the sad sea-waves begged permission to put on the gloves, and get into the ring and give the bloomin' Britisher a taste of the medicine that General Jackson gave the English at

New Orleans, or that Paul Jones passed out to the same on the High Seas.

He insisted on taking off his shirt and so wore buff to the umbilicus. This was against the rules, but we waived precedent and allowed the innovation.

He was a sea-monster all right, all right. ¶ His arms were beautifully tattooed with the American Flag; and a dancer in yellow and blue, with one foot on earth and the other pointed toward the stars, was worked in on his steamer trunk. This is probably why he took off his shirt, so we might study art and fisticuffs at one fell swoop.

I whispered to Freddie, begging that I might explain to the people that he had been taken suddenly ill, but Freddie only smiled and said, " No!"

Then the big man went after the little one, much as a big bulldog might go after a rat-terrier. It was a Marathon. The big man pushed Freddie at will all around the ring. However, he could not reach him.

The bull-moose charged. Freddie side-stepped, and the big 'un hit the void, always with a tremendous grunt. And once the little fellow said, " Friend, you can't fight a little, but I like your voice."

¶ Then the big fellow seemed to think it was a matter of catch-as-catch-can, every man for himself—a sort of Presbyterian prayer-meeting, with the Lord looking the other way, and Gabriel busy on his card system, marking up the sins of the many.

The big man went at it again, and as he came rushing, Freddie side-stepped. As the man-of-war went by, Freddie gave him a short-arm punch with the right on the point of the jaw.

The dreadnought spun twice around, and then Freddie landed him another. The man spun round and round like a turbine, and finally dived over the ropes on to the friendly soil, making a dent in the Roycroft lawn.

He was not hurt, merely surprised and grieved.

He sat up, trying to locate his latitude and longitude.

Much to the surprise of the whole assembly, he did not climb back over the ropes and go after the party who had administered the ether, but instead reached for the nearest man, who happened to be Deacon Buffum, and landed him one on the puss.

Then he waded through the crowd, striking left and right, and we might have had a stampede had not Ali Baba been there with a fence-rail. The Bab struck him over his No. 6 bean with the rail and sent him to the turf. The man was soon up, and Ali chased him down the road and clear off the quarter-section, thereby saving what might have been a tragic scene.

¶ After that, peace, kindliness and the sweet spirit of harmony prevailed.

As the bold buccaneer carried away a new pair of boxing-gloves, not having time to take them off, we mourn the loss of his friendship. We might go up where the fellow works and demand the gloves, but no one yet has volunteered to take his life in his hands and be a candidate for Carnegie medals.

Every good thing can be abused. Exercise can easily be carried to the point where it gives a diminishing return; continued, it may be fatal to life. But it must be admitted that man has a body that thrives only when it is properly exercised. We eliminate the cosmic slag only when we work.

Boxing is a game. It tends to give courage, to make the man a cheerful loser. It teaches him to keep his temper, and its general tendency is to put fear behind and make him carry the crown of his head high and his chin in.

While I have no desire to revive the Roman sports as practised in the Colosseum of old, yet I realize the important part that play and games form in a well-rounded universe.

I believe the man who knows how to counter is reasonably free from introspection and brooding. He is not looking for insults, slights and troubles; he is not eternally thinking about himself.

Life is no soft, silly, four-o'clock " tea." The business of man is to hustle, and when an individual has lost his fighting edge, he is out of the game, and the Great Timekeeper is about to give him the count ◈◈

OWN at Syracuse, where they take things *cum grano salis*, is a concern that does business under the unique name of " Mary Elizabeth."

The head of the firm is Fanny Reigel Evans, a widow anywhere between thirty and fifty. Five years ago she had sorrow, bereavement and a much tangled estate to fill up the void of leaden hours. ❡ The lawyers straightened out the estate—and kept it. This simplified matters ✺ ✺

The mother would have just laid down and died of a broken heart, for hearts are made to be broken, but she had a family of three girls and a boy just blooming into adult life, leaving childhood behind. ❡ It is easy to die, but to bravely live and face each new day—that often takes courage, indeed!

I think so.

And so we find Mrs. Evans in dire extremity revolving in her mind what she could do and do well, that she might earn a living for herself and brood. She thought she could not do anything, but it came to her that years before she had made candy for her brothers and sisters, and then for neighbors, and occasionally for fairs and bazaars.

So she made some candy and Mary Elizabeth, a bright slip of a girl, went out and sold it. Mary Elizabeth was genius enough to march her troops on a phalanx—the candy was wrapped, boxed, labeled and tied in a most tempting and appetizing way. Then Mary Elizabeth wrote her name with one hand on every package to show that the goods were genuine. ❡ People smiled and bought, and would have patted Mary Elizabeth on her flaxen head, but she was fourteen goin' on fifteen ✺ ✺

Orders came in for the Mary Elizabeth candy—people of taste and distinction liked it and liked the looks of it. Then they liked the looks of Mary Elizabeth —she was such a fine, strong, healthy youngster—so full of life and good cheer—so honest and genuine!

The business grew.

It continued to grow.

It is growing still.

It is managed by Mrs. Evans, her three daughters and her son. These five work together as one person. They man the ship ✺ ✺

This earnest, honest, healthy, intelligent, active, alert and loving little group produce candy of a most superior kind and quality. The candy they make is like themselves ✺ ✺

That is all we can do anyway—reproduce ourselves. Your work is a broken off piece of your own spiritual estate. If there are sleazy strands in the warp and woof of your character, they will reappear in the woven fabric. Everything we make, we manufacture right out of our hearts ✺ ✺

The name " Mary Elizabeth" stuck—it is still on the package.

If love writes all the good books, sings all the songs, covers the canvas with harmonious color, and liberates beauty from the marble block, why may it not make candy and do business!

I think it can and does. The more love you work up into life the better for you and the better for the world.

Starr King tried to trace the transforming of a beefsteak into a poem, and we can trace mother-love into a factory that makes an art out of a candy package. Here you get the true correlation of force—the divine transmutation of energy ✺ ✺

Art is the beautiful way of doing things. ❡ There is quite a list of things I do not know, but set this down as beyond dispute: There can be no art without love, and the love you keep is the love you liberate in your work.—*Mary Elizabeth.*

✺ ✺

LITERATURE is the noblest of all the arts. Music dies on the air, or at best exists only as a memory; oratory ceases with the effort; the painter's colors fade and the canvas rots; the marble is dragged from its pedestal and is broken into fragments; but the *Index Expurgatorius* is as naught, and the books burned by the fires of the *auto da fe* still live. Literature is reproduced ten thousand times ten thousand and lodges its appeal with posterity. It dedicates itself to Time ✺ ✺

IN England and America, every citizen with a grievance has the legal right to prosecute or defend his own case before the courts. If he can not do this in an intelligible manner, the judge, as in the Age of the Barons, will tell him he must have the services of a lawyer. Now, if the man has come into court of his own accord, he can go and hire a lawyer, or else it's "back to the woods." If he hasbeenbrought into court against his will, and he has no money to hire a barrister, the court is obliged to name a lawyer to assist him exactly, as in olden times. I state the fact for the benefit of any of my friends who may be brought before a Sunrise Court.

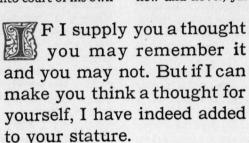

IF I supply you a thought you may remember it and you may not. But if I can make you think a thought for yourself, I have indeed added to your stature.

"The idea of justice, excepting as a legal fiction," says that eminent lawyer, Clarence Darrow, "has been long abandoned by the people of intelligence. We do the thing we want to do, if not thwarted by our neighbors, and hire men to get the courts to help us. A lawyer's business is to evade the law, quite as much as to comply with it."

Thus, by befogging judge and jury, and reading into the law new interpretations, are we arriving at peaceful anarchy by indirection. The danger of this process lies in the fact that while judges are not for sale, lawyers certainly are.

The "Rule of the People" is as yet a legal fiction, pleasing of course, but as rudimentary as that pocket on the back of a barrister.

Laugh with folks—not at them.

THE world is full of folks who are quick to ascribe an ulterior motive to every generous act. They ask with uplifted eyebrow: "Was Mary Magdalene sincere? Was n't it just a transient, hysterical spasm of repentance? And about that box of precious ointment— what proof is there that she did n't steal it?"

NOT long ago, a woman, going through from New York to Chicago, stopped off at Buffalo and came out to visit the Roycroft Shop. She had only recently come over to the Lord's side, so everything in Sun-up was very new and novel, just as it would be to a "sheep" recently arrived in heaven. ❡ Among other things that seemed curious to this woman were the notices on the bulletin board. One such announcement reads, "Class in Greekhistorymeets tonight at 7:30 in the Oak Room."

Now, this woman's husband is an instructor in History in Columbia University. And when she saw that particular notice she was especially interested.

"Who teaches that class?" she asked of the girl who was acting as guide.

"Mr. McVulcan, the blacksmith," was the answer.

"What! a blacksmith teaching Greek History?"

"Why, yes, of course."

"Show him to me."

So the two tramped back to the McVulcan studio, and there were the blacksmith and his busy helpers pounding away on the anvils.

"That is the man," said the guide, who thought the visitor wanted to talk with this volunteer school-teacher.

"No, I do not wish to speak with him, I might be disappointed. I just want to go away and remember that here a man may be a teacher of history and something more."

"You mean a blacksmith and something more," answered the guide with a smile.

❡ "No, I mean what I say, and it implies no slight upon my husband, either. He often bemoans the fact that he can only talk—he can not do things."

Another thing that surprised this visitor was that an East Aurora preacher was also there at work, handling the big

sledge, acting as the blacksmith's helper.
¶ And the woman went away full of the thought that she had caught a glimpse of Utopia ❧ ❧
But it was n't Utopia—it was only a finger on a mile-post pointing the way.
¶ If a man works ten hours at heavy manual labor, the probabilities are that he has little vitality left for thought. And who can wonder that if, too often, when the day's work is done, he seeks forgetfulness from his sore joints in strong drink! And then most certainly he has no mind for books.
So we look at the man as he nods in his chair at eventide and we say he is stupid—he lacks sparkle. And surely he does fall far short of being clever.
He has had too much of a good thing.
¶ And so has the soft, yellow, lily-fingered dyspeptic whom the world calls cultured ❧ ❧
These men must come together, and each bear a portion of the other's burdens. They must clasp hands for mutual respect and mutual support, and then we will have two strong men instead of a couple of defectives.
And everywhere are the fingers on mileposts pointing the way. We live in great times, Brother—your hand! your hand!
¶ Now why was this woman surprised that a man should be a blacksmith and still teach a class in Greek History?
Is the making of useful things out of iron degrading? ❧ ❧
Oh, no. Robert Collyer was a blacksmith. Elihu Burritt was a shoemaker. Paul was a tentmaker. Jesus was a carpenter.
¶ The woman's surprise was simply an involuntary indictment of the social and economic conditions under which we live ❧ ❧
We have so separated things and divided them up, that for the most part, carpenters and blacksmiths are excluded from " good society." How would a blacksmith look wearing white kid gloves at a reception perfunk?
The idea of culture until yesterday was that if a man were cultured it was quite enough—he need not be useful. If a woman were pretty, let her sit around and look pretty. You might have stains

on your soul, but God help you if you have any on your hands! This is extrication, separation—specialization carried to the limit of lunacy.
We are just getting back to sanity, and here was a woman surprised and delighted to find that culture and useful work were really not incompatible.
Manual training is a necessary part of every man's education. All men should work with their hands. The trouble has been that we have given all the work to one set of men, and the culture to another set, and the result has been the degradation of both. It is as if you should make your dinner of either pie or pickles.
—*Culture and Useful Work.*

❧ ❧

PLEASE bear in mind that the greatest dietetic sinners are not the poor and ignorant, but the so-called educated class. We all realize the dangers from strong drink, but strong meat that sets up its ferment after you eat it, is quite as bad as the product of the grain that is fermented first and swallowed afterwards ❧ ❧
The craving for stimulants is a disease, and never goes with Dietetic Righteousness. Crime follows mal-nutrition, as does night the day. Irritability, stupidity, touchiness are some of the results of food poisoning. The criminal is a sick man. You try to sip your Martini, Fletcherize it, hold it in your mouth and taste, taste, taste it, and you are a hero if you can empty the glass. Nature rebels after two or three very little sips and it tastes like kerosene.
Nature knows—trust her!

❧ ❧

IS there some one who believes in the value of your mission? Ah, I am glad, for without that stimulus you were in a sorry plight. Professor Tyndall once said the finest inspiration he ever received was from an old man who could scarcely read. This man acted as his servant. Each morning the old man would knock on the door of the scientist and call, " Arise, Sir; it is near seven o'clock, and you have great work to do today."

DENTIST to be successful must be a surgeon, an artist, a sculptor and a mechanic. He must have the same mental grasp of the laws of physics, chemistry and biology as is needed by the physician. He must have the manipulative skill that is required by the surgeon in his most delicate work. He must be able to take advantage of the finest requirements of the mechanic, and must have the ability to carry out those mechanical operations on living tissue in such manner as to cause no irritation thereto. His workshop is a hole in the face about two inches in diameter; in that hole he has to perform all of his operations and the patient takes the work away with him ✿ ✿ In nine-tenths of the work done by the physician or surgeon, Nature is expected to complete what he leaves. The dentist has to do his work. His failures stand out where he can always see them. The doctor buries his.

Most diseases are greatly aggravated by unsanitary oral conditions that some physicians ignore completely, but that every dentist appreciates. I venture the assertion that half the diseases that take toll of mankind will be controlled when dentistry has succeeded in teaching people to keep their mouths clean and their teeth in condition to masticate their food properly and vigorously.

The beauty, vigor and health of the human body and mind are greatly dependent on the possession of sound, useful, masticating apparatus. Isn't the man who is able to control this situation worthy of equal honor with the writer of prescriptions? ✿ ✿

There is another thing to which I want to direct your attention in connection with the dentist's shop. The man in his care is usually in bad humor. He does not go to the dentist until he has to, as a rule, and as soon as he gets there he begins to fuss about countless other things he would rather be doing; as a result he gets peevish and will not sit still. The dentist has to show consideration ✿ He must be tolerant. He has to do all the smiling, both for his patient and for himself. His best efforts are seldom appreciated. ❦ He is commonly regarded as a disagreeable necessity. His task is a thankless one, and because as a rule he is square and honest, and charges by the hour or by the operation, he does not make as much money as he ought to make. A surgeon can put up a bluff. He can make a mountain out of a mole-hill and charge the price for removing a tumor when he takes out a wart, and the patient will never be any the wiser. The most the physician has to do is to look wise and let Nature take her course. Nature has precious little to do with the restoration of teeth in the human mouth.

When I say a dentist has to be an artist, I mean he must have a knowledge of color, which enables him to properly match missing teeth with those remaining. When I say he must be a sculptor I mean he must have a knowledge of symmetry which will enable him to restore contours either in gold or silver or cement ✿ ✿

✿ ✿

As a general proposition, the community believes in the banker who believes in the community.

LEAVE the idle rich to Nemesis. Disease and death are at their heels. The men who operate our great enterprises—mills, factories, elevators, banks and department-stores—know nothing of ease. Their working-hours are not limited by the whistle. They sweat blood to meet payrolls and to keep the wheels of trade revolving.

HEN Theodore Roosevelt said that Elihu Root was "the most able man before the American people to-day, and probably the most able man ever before the American people," he slipped past the main entrance of the Ananias Club for once, and walked the open road of truth.

In all my acquaintanceship with so-called great men, I never met one who impressed me as being the genuine goods until I met Elihu Root. At that time he was Secretary of State.

Doctor Johnson said, " If I should meet William Shakespeare on the stairs, I would faint away."

If I had met Elihu Root in Washington in his office, my heart would have thumped fast.

Since the days of Thomas Jefferson, we have never had a man in America that was in Elihu Root's class.

The literal, cool fact is that Elihu Root and Thomas Jefferson each have the crystalline mind. I say " have," for, as far as I know, Thomas Jefferson is living yet, and his soul goes marching on. In what form it marches, I do not attempt to say ๑ ๑

But everything that Thomas Jefferson wrote was sharp, clear, lucid and logical. He was not an orator, but he was the best thinker who ever played a part in American politics. Read any of the State documents of Elihu Root and you will find the same lucidity. It is cold, clear, frosty, intellectual, with all soft sentiment eliminated.

Elihu Root's feelings never run over so that he stands in the slop. He is always in control of one man, and that is himself. Being master of his own spirit, he is also able to be master of many.

At the Chicago Exposition, it was the greatest sight of my life to see how this man, slim, slender, agile, graceful, managed that fifteen thousand seething, struggling, moving mass of humanity. Elihu Root let them run out, as a mask-inonge takes the hook and scoots for the rushes, oh. But when the Chairman wanted to bring them back, he did it. He never spoke until he had the large, furry

ear of that convention; and then his voice, exquisitely modulated, rang out clear as the song of an ax in the woods on an October morning.

Never can I forget how he walked down to the front of the stage and pointing with his gavel at one cheering, shouting, howling individual, who stood on his chair and endeavored to incite the mob to violence.

Root's attitude commanded silence, for just a second; but during that second, Root's voice rang forth. " If the gentleman continues his present conduct but a very little further, he will bring a disgrace upon the American People that time will not efface. I now order the gentleman to take his seat!"

And the silence that followed was vociferous ๑ ๑

If the man wanted to raise a riot, there was his opportunity. Root gave him his chance; but he failed to rise to the level of events. He sank sullenly, cowed, back into his seat.

Elihu Root has about him somewhat of the elemental indifference of Nature. He has the calm insouciance which realizes that nothing matters much; although, being wise, he knows that all things matter a little. The man possesses moral and physical courage. He has pride, poise, power—plus.—*Elihu Root.*

๑ ๑

EVERYBODY is really decent in spots; and I have seen the gentle answer completely disarm a grouch who was bent on chewing the red rag of wordy warfare.

Yes, courtesy is catching.

๑ ๑

THE fact is that so-called rich men are simply trustees. All they have, at best, is a life-lease on the property ๑ If these men are producing wealth—digging it out of the soil, cutting it out of the forest, fishing it out of the sea, digging it out of the mines, manufacturing it into forms of use and beauty—this wealth is the heritage of society. You will remember the question, " How much did the gentleman leave?" And the answer was, " All he had."

MY little girl, 'leven years old going on twelve, has been giving me a few lessons in lepidopterology, which she tells me, and I have no reason to doubt her, for she has never deceived me in anything, is the science of butterflies. I know lots of educated men, but only a-bout one out of a hundred ever heard of lepidoptera. I have always known a little about but-terflies but I never imagined they were lepidoptera until last week. I asked the best educated man in East Au-rora, the Baptist preacher, if he was a lepidopterologist, and he thought I was calling him bad names.

Among the things my little science teacher has taught me are these: There are more than ten thousand separate and distinct species of butterflies. The life of a butterfly is from three days to three months, but there is one species that migrates, like birds, and this one may live three years. No two butterflies of the same species are exactly alike, and the same species vary much in size. On account of the extremely fragile quality of its body a butterfly usually lives but a few days. A rain-storm always kills many, and col-lectors in order to get perfect specimens often prefer to breed them.

Moths and butterflies are very different. Moths fly at night and butterflies in the daytime. The reason moths fly at night is so to escape the birds—it is a habit. And the reason the whip-poor-will and some other birds fly at night is so to catch the moths—this is a habit, too. ❧ The male butterfly is much more brilliant in color than the female, but the female is much larger. She makes a nest and lays her eggs. These eggs do not hatch out butterflies—bless your soul! They hatch caterpillars. ❧ The cater-pillar is a worm. It can not fly; it can not run—it just can crawl. It has lots of legs, it has horns and feelers which are called antennæ, and on the ends of the antennæ some-times are eyes ❧ ❧ Antennæ are in place of eyes, so to keep from run-ning into things. When Nature got make a good eye she let up on an-tennæ. The eye is a mirror that re-flects things and at the back of the mirror is a tele-phone to the brain with little nerves for wires, so not only does the eye see but it tele-phones to the brain what it sees, so you always know whe-ther to run or stay. It took a long time for Nature to make an eye—it was a wonderful in-vention and God and Gabriel both turned somersaults and walked on their hands when they found the scheme would work. When the caterpillar has been a worm as long as it wants to— and finds out there is nothing in it— it wraps itself in a leaf and makes for it-self a cocoon. The silkworm is very parti-cular, so it makes its cocoon of silk in-stead of calico. It can make silk so well and so much silk, that man, who is a grafter, just steals this silk and fools the worm into making more silk, just as we steal the honey the bee makes, and also as we take advantage of the love of a cow for her calf and steal the milk. Man is the most wonderful grafter of all the works of God. All man gives the silk-worm

BUSINESS is a game, and we are all in it. It re-quires a terrific, unending en-ergy to succeed. But the men who do big things are those who occasionally get away from the mass and find rest and recreation where the winds blow and the soothing waters flow; where the odor of the pines is perpetual, and where Nature supplies every-thing in the way of health and healing that tired bodies demand ❧ ❧

in return for silk is its board. He gives it mulberry leaves and it eats and eats and eats, and spins and spins and spins, making a cocoon, so it can wind itself in the silk and turn into a beautiful moth ✄

But man keeps stealing the silk and fooling the silkworm and after a while it gets discouraged and dies while yet a worm without even having had the fun of being a moth ✄ ✄

Some butterflies are pure white, and there is one kind that is coal black. In this, butterflies differ from men, who are all a kind of slatey gray.

There are some butterflies that are so rare, they are worth a hundred dollars a piece; and some whole species have died out and become extinct within thirty-five years.

Men go from Washington to Borneo just to get butterflies. Linnæus traveled once over three thousand miles to catch a butterfly ✄ ✄

The most brilliant and beautiful butterflies are brilliant and beautiful only on one side of their wings. The Morphocypris butterfly, is a dazzling, brilliant blue, all lined off with tiny lines of gold on one side, and on the other side it is a plain dull dun, a kind of gray-brown. This is so it can fall on the ground when its enemies get after it and never be seen, or it can flatten out on a tree trunk so you would never find it. Then there is the owl butterfly that is very beautiful on one side, and on the other is brown with two black spots that look like the eyes of an owl. When pursued it just stops, turns itself upside down, and there you see the horns and the eyes of an owl, and this often scares the birds half to death. The most brilliant butterflies are the plainest when their wings are closed and they are in repose. A really wondrous butterfly only flashes in the sunlight and for those it loves, and in this it is like a genius. Most people declare a genius is nothing but a grub. A genius is a man who is plain brown like the earth or a tree-trunk, but he is n't brown all the time or to everybody.—*The Butterflies.*

✄ ✄

He who does not understand your silence will probably not understand your words.

HE very first form of property was the ownership of women. The Romans captured the Sabine women, because that was the regulation thing to do. Our pity need not be wasted upon the women—they simply exchanged owners—they were slaves in either case. Males were not at first made slaves, because it was inconvenient—there was danger of uprisings; it caused discontent among the slave women; and for a man there was no market, while a woman was in demand. She was valuable: first, as a wife, and second, as a worker. There are animals where the lordly male holds a dozen or more females captive, but it was man who first set his females at work.

Darwin says there is no doubt that marriage was at first a matter of coercion and purely a property-right. Certain ceremonies even now go with the transfer of real estate and most other property, and the marriage ceremonial was, in the beginning, a public notification of ownership and a warning to all parties to keep hands off. The husband had the power of life or death over the wife and her children. She, being a slave, performed all the menial tasks—she was the worker ✄ ✄

And the product of her labor belonged to her lord. Thus do we get the genesis of property. First, the man owned the woman. Second, he owned all that she produced. The man produced nothing—he was the protector. To be sure, he killed animals, but he did not deign to skin them nor prepare the flesh for food—woman did all this. For him to work would have been undignified and disgraceful—only slaves worked. And so to prove his prowess, his true greatness, he never did a thing but kill and consume. ❡ He was looked up to and reverenced—that is to say, he was respectable. And he took good care never to put his respectability in jeopardy by doing a menial thing. If high enough in the scale he had an armor-bearer, who carried his implements of death. The Polynesian chiefs do not even lift the food to their mouths, and the women dress and undress them. This, of course, is the extreme type, but I mention it to show the tendency. The outcrop is occasionally seen yet in the nobleman who has a valet. And we all know of men who never do a useful thing for fear of losing caste. The survival may even be seen in England, where no gentleman will " clean " his own shoes—this work is done by women. On the Continent, the care of public lavatories is all given to women. The woman is the scullion, the menial, the drudge, the vehicle of what is dirty, uncouth, inconvenient or disgraceful ๑๐ ๑๐

๑๐ ๑๐

THE property-right in marriage still exists, and the Common Law of America, which is founded on the Common Law of England, which is founded on the Common Law of Rome, provides that the property produced by the industry of the wife belongs, by legal right, to the husband. She may make blankets, beadwork, baskets, and her husband can take these things and do what he chooses with them ๑๐ ๑๐

Up to the year Eighteen Hundred Sixty-three, the custom of men selling their own children was common and well recognized in various States in America. And the children yet belong more to the man than to the woman.

๑๐ ๑๐

IN England the law still gives the husband the right to " reprove " a refractory wife—the same right that he has over his children. Yesterday he could kill her; and the right to " reprove " with a stick is yet conceded in London police-courts, but provision is made limiting the thickness and length of the stick ๑๐ ๑๐

We have seen that first women alone were enslaved, but later more workers were needed, and then men were made slaves also. Very often these were given charge of women slaves. And so the supervision of slaves by slaves, or the ownership of slaves by slaves, has, to a certain degree, still survived. These things are not noted here by way of criticism or reproach, but simply to make clear the proposition that personal

property began with the ownership of woman, and with that which she produced ๑๐ ๑๐

The fact is that every city, town and village has its self-appointed Superior Class, and this class gets its tone and takes its fashions from the extreme types just mentioned.

That these people in the smaller towns actually do work with their hands, and help carry the burdens of the world, is true, yet on Sundays and other holidays they delight in parading themselves in a dress which seems to advertise that they do not work.

Their raiment, when they can afford it, is the dress of those who habitually indulge in Conspicuous Waste.

Almost without a single exception they look forward to a time when they will not have to work. And those who do have to work unremittingly here, are offered an equivalent through a promise of endless rest and a mansion in the skies.

❆ No heaven has yet been pictured excepting as a place of idleness and Conspicuous Waste ๑๐ ๑๐

Your country storekeeper, if he is prosperous, straightway advertises his prosperity in Conspicuous Waste. He builds a house five times as big as he needs ๑๐

❆ One might at first suppose that the size of the house would give the beholder some idea of the number of people who live in it, and this is true: excepting that small families live in large houses and large families live in small houses. Indeed the number in any given family is usually in inverse ratio to the size of the house. If prosperity smiles, the wife has two servants, and the daughter ceases to work, in order to advertise the father's prosperity ๑๐ ๑๐

The mother will tell you her servant-girl woes, and of all she suffers, but what can she do? She was far happier when they lived in a cottage and she did her work, but now there are all these things to care for, and the social duties besides. Yet she is very happy in her misery. They are respectable and must advertise the fact; so the fashion that Paris decrees in dress is followed as it filters through New York, Chicago, Grand

Rapids, Galesburg and Des Moines, as the case may be ѕо And this fashion is always with a design of Conspicuous Waste ѕо ѕо

ѕо ѕо

A STILL further refinement of histrionic seizure of honors is sometimes seen among the descendants of geniuses, who have produced somewhat of a marked literary or artistic excellence. ¶ These people are like the descendants of Captain Kidd—they have everything but the great man's courage and ability. The dead ancestor was a writer, and a man of culture and kindness; the playactor descendants assume the gait and gesture, the manner and habit of this supposed greatness ѕо Theirs is the tone of kindness, minus the kindness; the thoughtful looks without the thought. ¶ They tell of literary tasks, and relate how busy they are at this or that great problem, but they never solve any problem, and the long-expected book dies a-borning ѕо ѕо

At the last the reverence of these degenerate descendants of great men for literature is a pretense—towards the living men who produce literature, this social Superior Class have only aversion and scorn. Their reverence is for the dead. Shakespeare, Browning, Keats, Rembrandt, Shelley, Thoreau, Whitman and Byron were not respectable; and the decayed gentility that holds letters in its custody would have scorned a genuine creator during his life.

That most sweet and gentle of all women writers, Elizabeth Barrett Browning, was accursed in the mind of her father to the day of his death, because she did not conform to his idea of what was respectable and right and proper. ¶ She sent him letters, but they were returned to her unopened; she dedicated to him books, but he refused to read them. And now he lives only because he sired this daughter, and his folly and his hate are his sole monument ѕо ¶ Our social play-actors have neither the ability nor the inclination to concentrate on chaos and make it concrete. They will not pay the price; they demand the honors, but they want ease.

HE Samurai stand for the entire list of military virtues which Thompson Seton has put before the world so vividly; that is to say, loyalty, truthfulness, honor, integrity, health, self-reliance, and the silent and prompt obedience of orders.

America as a country suffers from the proclivities of the genus buckwheat—that is, the native villager, who talks all day to everybody on any subject and seldom says anything. This kind of man lives either in his garret or in his sub-cellar, and a good deal of the time is talking through his roof.

All people who revel, roll and wallow in their emotions are cast down in defeat and exultant in victory. The Samurai accept everything as it comes and count it good—even death itself. And life itself is a small affair when it comes to giving it away in a good cause. This gives you a type of man that is pretty nearly invincible ѕо He can not be stampeded, bribed, bought or panic-stricken ѕо ѕо

ѕо ѕо

ROWN-UPS delight in make-believe. Count Leo Tolstoy, the greatest thinker in Russia, and a rich man, plays he is a peasant; and often gives his family goose-flesh by threats to give away his property. Those who threaten to dissipate their property never do, and those who do, do not intend to. ¶ Americans are rich people with big estates, who live the Simple Life five days each month and the rest of the time drive bangtail horses or ride in Red Devil automobiles, defying bucolic justice. Education, until yesterday, was of two kinds—priestly and military ѕо Roughly speaking, Harvard represents the one, West Point the other.

Harvard has departments of Theology, Law, Medicine and the Classics—all are non-productive, and largely make-believe. The simple fact that the education in Law, Medicine and Theology of twenty-five years ago is now regarded as inept, puerile and inconsequent, shows the make-believe in the pedagogics and science of the past.

As for the study of the Classics, its chief charm lay in its Futility—in the fact that it unfitted a man for useful life ❧ To know a dead language was a meritorious separation from life, and a thing desirable. Its desirability was an honor —you could use it so seldom and with so few. ❡ Education in the science of war, which is the science of carrying desolation and inflicting death, is still considered to be an honorable acquirement ❧ So everywhere we have Military Schools, where the martial spirit is instilled and encouraged, and where patriotism—the detestation of other countries—is inculcated. That this class of schools do good there is no doubt, but they minister largely to this habit of self-deception so common in the Superior Class. The people who patronize these academies joyously believe that they are fitting their boys to protect the toilers. ❡ Anyway, they unfit the boy for becoming a toiler.

Thus we hark back to the savage idea, which was that the best men should be set apart to protect the tribe. "In England," Gladstone once said, "there are only two honorable walks open to young men: the Army and the Church."

It is still the Warrior and the Priest, guised and glossed by a smug, complacent make-believe, carried out and refined by higher personal potencies ❧ Visit Old Point Comfort, Saratoga, Newport and Point of Pines and you will at once see the premium paid to ineptness and futility ❧ ❧

The inability and the disinclination to partake in useful effort is considered a virtue, in that it proves the prowess of the person—his power to make others do for him ❧ The Superior Class at Asheville, Saratoga and Newport have no power and reveal no prowess, but they take to themselves all the credit of prowess and parade their ability in killing time and following the aniseed make-believe trail, poetically speaking. The men of power who exploited labor or monopolized good things through force of arms or force of cunning and intellect were the ancestors of these men ❧ And, by a strange paradox, these descendants of men of power scorn a genuine, living man of power, and take to themselves credit on being one or two removes from a sure-enough person of prowess.

YOU had better learn to accept all the small misfits and the trivial annoyances of life as a matter of course. To allow them to receive attention beyond their deserts is to wear the web of your life to the warp. Be on the lookout for the great joys, and never let mosquitoes worry you into a passion.

❧ ❧

IF Captain Kidd were alive today he would not be considered Respectable, although, no doubt, he was, in the circle in which he moved. But I am told there are lineal descendants of Captain Kidd who are very proud of the name. So we have many descendants of Captain John Smith, who was no less than an outlaw. There are well-authenticated pedigrees of persons tracing a line direct to Pocahontas, and these people take much pride in saying they trace to a genuine American. But if Pocahontas were alive today they would hardly have the old lady in their homes and call her gran'ma ❧ ❧ ❡ It is somewhat like Anton Seidl, who claimed to be a natural son of Franz Liszt. When asked as to the truth of this claim, Philip Hale said, with a yawn, "Oh, but it is no great mark of distinction—there are so many claiming the honor, you know!"

Liszt is dead, removed from us by both time and distance, but, by a curious metamorphosis, we evolve the bar sinister into a virtue, and multiply honors by the square of the distance. Almost anybody traces back to William the Conqueror, and that he was a Natural Son of Nobody makes no difference ✺ Thus we have Societies of gentlewomen whose sole badge of distinction lies in that they had certain ancestors who fought in a certain war. No inquiry is made into this man's character, or as to why he fought.

✺ ✺

THIS idea of Respectability through Vicarious Virtue is an interesting subject for the psychologist, involving as it does the pretty make-believe of a histrionic benefit, where we play to the gallery of our own self-esteem. The idea of Respectability is a phantasmagoria contrived and created by the people that it controls. The desire is not to be, but to seem. The intent of life is to make an impression upon other people, and this, and this alone, is the controlling impulse in what is called Good Society. And so, to a great degree, we are all play-actors, and make-believe runs through the entire fabric of our lives. To the man who can get off at a little distance, so as to get the perspective, the whole thing is a comedy. But not wholly a comedy of errors, for it is all evolution—slow, perhaps, but necessary and very sure ✺

✺ ✺

DO away with Ancestor-Worship in China, and convert the Mussulman to the truth that if he prays to the South it will be just as effective as toward the East, and your task will be no greater than to show some men that the fact of Doctor Edward Everett Hale's partaking of the communion in Trinity Church is a matter of really no importance to anybody. Such trivial things as the privilege of a man to marry his deceased wife's sister has set the world by the ears. And suggestions to do away with the death penalty, to introduce the single tax, to bring about arbitration in place of war, have all been hotly denounced and their promulgators vilified. Suggest social changes such as these named and you will hear much talk about "the dissolution of society," "a reign of terror," "pulling out the keystone of society," "destruction of the hearthstone," a "return to savagery," etc. Yet changes occur and the morning stars still sing together.

✺ ✺

WITHIN twenty-five years men of sense have abandoned the idea of hell, and a personal devil is now only a huge joke even in orthodox churches. "Spare the rod and spoil the child," was once a great and vital truth, but now we spare the rod and save the child. ❦ Love, patience and kindness are answering the purpose much better than the rod. Capital punishment has been done away with in some States and will be ere long in all; the dark cell has everywhere been abolished, and the time will most assuredly come when jails and penitentiaries will have to go, as well. We doubt the wisdom of men turning themselves into a section of the Day of Judgment in order to punish other men, and to kill the murderer we find neither brings his victim back to life, nor does it prevent other crimes.

The best lawyers now are businessmen, who keep people out of trouble, instead of getting them in. The best doctors no longer treat symptoms—giving you something to cure your headache and settle your stomach—they seek the cause and tell you the truth. The preachers are everywhere acknowledging they do not know anything about another world— they are preaching social salvation here and now. The world is growing better, and that many people behold the chimera of Respectability through Conspicuous Waste, and are refusing to conform their lives to it, is very hopeful. Conspicuous Waste and Conspicuous Leisure do not bring health, happiness, long life nor contentment. Once we thought work was a curse; then it came to us that it was a necessary evil; and yesterday the truth dawned upon us that it is a blessed privilege. That the many are still blind to truth may be a fact, but the light is growing in the East. There is joy in useful effort.

We want to do what is best for ourselves, and we have made the discovery that what is best for ourselves is also best for others.

ALREADY we say, "That man is the best educated who is the most useful," and the true test of education will be in its possessor's ability to serve. And the day will surely come when the only man who is not Respectable will be the man who consumes but does not produce. Disgrace will then consist in living a life of Conspicuous Waste, and the greatest man in our midst will be the one who confers most benefits. The light is dawning in the East. We are living in eternity now just as much as we ever shall. God is right here now, and we are as near Him now as we shall ever be ﹡ He never started this world a-going and went away and left it—He is with us yet. There is no devil but fear, and nobody and nothing can harm you but yourself. We should remember the week-day to keep it holy, live one day at a time, doing our work the best we can. There is no more sacred place than where a man is doing good and useful work; there is no higher wisdom than to lose yourself in useful industry, and be kind—and be kind.

﹡ ﹡

IT is not necessary to see the man to know what sort of person he is. You know the farmer by the appearance of his farm—his character is written all over it. His cattle, horses, hogs and sheep—all proclaim him. A farmer is known by his team, not by the company he keeps. As a boy I could look at the horses tied in front of a country store and make a close guess as to the moral, mental and financial status of the owners, and I was not so awfully smart, either. The bridle and saddle of a drunkard always give him away. We know

Ragged Haggard by his clothes. This is the point: the family whose members work together succeed. And the success of this family is in exact ratio to the love that cements them into a Whole. Of course the more intellect you can mix with this mutual love, the better; but intellect alone is too cold to fuse the dumb indifference of inanimate things and command success. Love is the fulfilling of life's law.

﹡ ﹡

ONCE when bread and honey were up for discussion a little girl from the city asked her country cousin this question, " Does your papa keep a bee? " And that is all there is of the story. But let me here state a great, undisputed fact: A bee alone can make no honey. A bee alone is not self-supporting. ¶ In fact, a bee alone loses heart absolutely; its intelligence vanishes, it even forgets how to sting. And separated a distance of from three to five miles from its hive it will soon droop and die. Bees are successful only as they work with other bees ﹡ ﹡ A man alone will accomplish nothing. All of his thoughts and acts have a direct relationship with others. Men succeed only as they work together. Without companionship ambition droops; courage flags; reason totters; animation vanishes and the man dies. Nature puts a quick limit on the horrors of solitary confinement—she unhinges the reason of the prisoner, and he addresses comrades who have no existence, save in his fevered imagination.

﹡ ﹡

THERE are two kinds of literature: one, the literature of power; and the other, the literature of explanation and apology ﹡ ﹡

THE reason opinions are so diverse concerning every strong man is that most people fix their attention on some particular phase of his character—some mere external eccentricity possibly, that is of no value, one way or the other. The whole is what makes up the character—not these trivial parts.

SOLDIERS who are cowards when by themselves often fight bravely when placed on the firing line with others ✀ ❡ We succeed only as we band ourselves with others. Each man is a molecule that is needed to make up the All. Successful employers of labor recognize this full well, for they always allow their helpers to work in gangs where possible. A division superintendent in the employ of the Pennsylvania Railroad tells me that in painting railroad-stations he has found that four men working together will do at least five times as much work as one man working alone, and they will also do the work better. Teachers know the principle, and thus they teach in classes. The private tutor is never quite a success unless his scholar is a defective. Children will teach each other quite as much as they are taught by their teachers.

Healthy people like to work, play, eat, learn and live together. The Kindergarten Spirit (and no finer thing exists) is possible only through association ✀ A child absolutely alone would never evolve. A child deprived of the companionship of its own becomes abnormal. A great man is one who carries the Kindergarten Spirit right through life, and any one who carries the Kindergarten Spirit through life is great.

✀ ✀

THERE is a fallacy to the effect that plain and so-called ignorant people can not get into city society. This is a mistake; there is a shade and grade of society in every city that fits any and every class ✀ There are "fifty-seven varieties" of city society.

The grade of newly rich is a very important grade; it is hard to get into, if you do not belong in it, but deadly easy if you do. It imitates the foibles and follies of the grade above. Conspicuous Leisure and Conspicuous Waste start at the top with the Four Hundred, and run right down through to girls who head the Social Seven, and work in the Paper Box Factory.—*Respectability.*

✀ ✀

ONE of Nature's chief intents in sex is to bring about beauty, grace and harmony. ❡ The flowing mane and proud step of the horse, the flamboyant tail of the peacock, the song of the bird, the perfume and color of the flowers, are all sex manifestations, put forth with intent to attract, please and fascinate. ❡ Charm of manner is a sex attribute which has become a habit.

The creative principle in all art is secondary sex manifestation.

✀ ✀

DO not be disturbed about saving your soul—it will be saved if you make it worth saving. ❡ Do your work ✀ ✀ Think the good.

And evil, which is a negative condition, shall be swallowed up by good.

Think no evil: and if you think only the good, you will think no evil.

Life is a search for power. To have power you must have life, and life in abundance. And life in abundance comes only through great love.

✀ ✀

THE age is crying for men— civilization wants men who can save it from dissolution; and those who can benefit it most are those who are freest from prejudice, hate, revenge, whim and fear. Two thousand years ago lived One who saw the absurdity of a man loving only his friends—He saw that this meant faction: lines of social cleavage: with ultimate discord, and so He painted the truth large and declared we should love our enemies and do good to those who might despitefully use us.

It is not necessary for us to leave our tasks and pattern our lives after His, but if we can imitate His sublime patience and keep thoughts of discord out of our lives, we, too, can work such wonders that men will indeed truthfully say that we are Sons of God.

There isn't much rivalry here—be patient, generous, kind, even to foolish folk and absurd people. Do not extricate yourself—be one with all—be Universal. So little real competition is there in this line that any man, in any walk of life, who puts jealousy, hate and fear behind him can make himself distinguished ✀ All good things shall be his.

ERSONALITY reveals itself especially in headwear. Fashion decrees that all men who do not have their hair cut to a certain length, and in a certain way, shall be anathema and without the pale. Now, the man of spirit rebels against this universal attempt of society to make all men look and act alike ◦ Wild animals are alike, and with them there is no progression ◦ You can not tell one wild pigeon from another, and in jack-rabbits all personality is completely ironed out. This is what society is constantly trying to do for her members—make them revert to a type.

SMALL men are apologetic and give excuses for being on the earth and reasons for staying here so long. Not so the Great Souls. Their actions are regal, their language oracular, their manners affirmative ◦ ◦

But the strong man knows that progress is only obtainable by the exercise of individuality. He thinks as he pleases, writes as he feels, expresses himself in his own way, and confronts ossified social smugness by letting his hair grow long, when society's edict has ordered it short. Further than this he glorifies his dome of thought by covering it with a peculiar hat. To wear a hat just like everybody else is to outwardly acknowledge that your head thinks the same thoughts that all other heads think. If you have reason to believe you have a peculiar head, you adorn it in a peculiar way ◦ ◦

To wear a hat that is long out of fashion, or one devised by your own genius, is to throw down the gauntlet to the bourgeoisie, and say: "Behold! As I now cover my thinkery with a hat different from the one you prescribe, so do I think thoughts that are to you impossible."
❡ It is with the hat that we bestow homage, placate our enemies, or affront our foes. To attractive young women, pretty widows, or parties rated in R. G. Dun and Co., Z, or above, we raise our hat with a flourish and completely uncover the thinkery; to unattractive maidens, or married women who are known to be needlessly happy in their domestic relations, we just barely lift the hat; to vinegar-faced virgins and to all those on moderate salaries, we merely jerk the hand toward the hat brim, and let it go at that. Then, of course, there is a whole round of people at whom we merely stare, leaving the hat to sit firmly on our head. So, from Beau Brummel, who lifted his hat with great flourish to titled and illustrious nobodies, to William Penn who was born with his hat on and never uncovered, even to King George, we run the whole gamut of symbolism of heart-attitude with the hat.

Personality first reveals itself in the hat. Woman lures with her hat—a bonnet beckons. The hat is a purely secondary sex manifestation ◦ What the comb and wattles are to the cock o' the walk, the hat is to man. With the hat we signal, apologize, or defy. Strong men do not allow Mrs. Grundy to dictate when they shall have their hair cut, nor to select their hats.

◦ ◦

MEN are only great as they have sympathy. Imagination is sympathy in motion. And the writers in the United States who possess a universal sympathy, served by a winged imagination, can be counted on the fingers of one hand. We have purists by the score, stylists by the dozen, and advocates by the hundred who defend this, that and the other in strong and splendid English, but they are not men of all-round sympathy ◦

◦ ◦

All that tends to tyranny in parent manifests itself in slavish traits in the children. Freedom is a condition of mind, and the best way to secure it is to breed it ◦ ◦

HE way to learn to earn a living is to go at it and earn a living. And the man who can not and does not earn his own living is a parasite —a burden to society.

Moreover, the man who can not and does not support himself—producing more than he consumes—is not an educated man, no matter how many college degrees he may possess.

Herbert Spencer says, " the first requisite is to be a good animal." And we now say that the first requisite in education shall be to the end that the individual shall earn his own living. This for his own happiness and sweet content and moral uplift, and for the good of society

Marshall Field once gave this order to his Manager, " When you hire young men, give the preference to the High School Graduate, aged eighteen, over the University Graduate aged twenty-two. You can manage the boy of eighteen, while the other calls himself a ' man,' and will often protest, inwardly at least, against many of the things that you will want done."

Most of the " men " in the great colleges are there because their parents have the price—victims of misdirected parental love—eaglets, full fledged, carried by fussy old eagles, male and female, who set themselves against Nature, and have n't enough faith in God to let the youngsters drop

And the summing up of the argument is this—and it is a conclusion that can not be disproved, even by the partisan and prejudiced—i. e.: Your success in life does not hinge upon your having a college education.

THE business that begins small and grows is a safe business. The business that begins big is the one that goes by the board

And always before a failure in business occurs, there is moral degeneration of the men who manage it.

A man fails mentally, morally and physically, and then his business sympathizes with him, and together they go into the melting pot. Business nowadays is a constant readjustment, just as is the sailing of a ship, the running of an automobile, the driving of a team of horses.

The vast majority of businessmen are good business pilots. They know where they are going, and they know how to manage the machine so as not to land it in the ditch or make it climb a telegraph-pole.

THE spirit of Chicago demands the best. And now behold a curious fact, that the men at the top, the men who have the final word in making decisions among the railroadmen of the Middle West, almost without exception, came up from the ranks.

They were born on the farms, brought up to do things, to make things, to go without things, to wait on themselves. There was always hardship enough to put them on their mettle, and yet, if they worked, there was encouragement enough through the natural reward that followed, so that they were not repressed, depressed and cast down.

THE Middle West has produced a peculiar type of strong man. You will find these earnest, irrepressible, kindly, generous, intelligent, effective men, Middle West products, in all the big cities of America

They gravitate to where they belong— where they are needed.

In many instances they have snatched success from the teeth of failure. They know no such word as fail.

If they are whipped, they never are aware of it

IN this great transfer of services we have to trade quickly. There is no time for hate, much less for jealousy and fear

And so we have the new *Contract Social*, wherein we have all agreed to be decent. The man in business who does not tell the truth does not last as long as a snowball lasts in Juarez.

Truth was foreign to the old-time businessman, just as it is foreign in war

From the age of violence we drifted into

the age of palaver. Now we do business right out in the sunlight—we do business with our friends.

so so

WE now know that truth is an asset, and a lie is a liability.

There are too many of us here now to play the game on the haggle basis. The one-price system makes rapid trading possible. We eliminate friction and lubricate the whole proposition with reciprocity. That is to say, business is now on a human basis. We have imagination enough to see that the brotherhood of man is a paying principle.

We are parts and particles of one another. To injure another is to injure yourself. We thrive only as we bestow a benefit. All that we give away comes back to us. Cast thy bread upon the waters and it shall return to you shortly —buttered so so

Here we get a great Spiritual Law. And a Spiritual Law is a Natural Law. Natural Law manifests itself in the Science of Service. The laws of economics are eminently Nature's enactments.

Sentiment plays a big part in business today. Emotion, enthusiasm, good-cheer, affection, friendship—these are important factors in business.

so so

THE only way to make money is to render a service for humanity—to supply something that people want, and to carry things from where they are plentiful to where they are needed.

He who confers the greatest service at the least expense is the man whom we will crown with honor and clothe with riches so so

Any other policy is running its rim on the high clutch, headed for the cliff. ⟨ Success turns upon ability to produce the goods. A business built by bunkum beckons bankruptcy. We live in the age of business. Economics is fast becoming a science so so

There is only one sin, and that is waste; and disuse and misuse are both forms of waste. The best brains in the world are now at work, endeavoring to eliminate lost motion and take up the economic slack so so

YESTERDAY I came across a valuable Fact—and this is how it all happened.

For some time I have thought that the Roycroft Shop would not be just right until it had a huge fireplace, made from boulders—many-hued, grim and ancient, each with a message from the eons that were, even when man was not: boulders that had been ground and polished by Fate, with the glacier's help, just as experience grinds us.

And to the end that the fire-place might be built, as I tramped through the fields, I located good and suitable specimens. I tried each with a geologist's hammer: and my companion, Simon, a St. Bernard, barked and wagged his tail in expectancy whenever I would stop to examine a boulder, for Simon was sure we were on the track of game, when all I wanted was to see the quality and character of the nigger-head. Having selected my specimen, I would go and ask the Honest Farmer, who owned the land, if I could have it, and the answer was always a smile and willing assent. And once out of the tail of my eye, I saw the Farmer turn to his wife and motion at me, over his shoulder with his thumb, and then he tapped his forehead with his fore-finger, onimously. But never mind, I was given to understand that the boulders were mine for the hauling, for the dash-blame things were only in the way, no-how! So I would tell Ali Baba where the geological specimens were, and he would hitch Juliet, the spotted pony, to the wagon, and go with pick and shovel and crow-bar, and proudly the spoils would be brought home.

And thus it was that yesterday I walked across the farm of Deacon Hoshkins, which as all folks know is on the road that leads from Frog Pond to Wales Center, four miles northwest from East Aurora. The Deacon's farm is made up more of stone than soil, so when I discussed hard-heads, the owner said; "Take 'em, Neighbor, take 'em and welcome; and if you take all there are you can come back next year and get as many more."

Now Deacon Hoshkins is no joker, and so I asked him to explain his remark, and he told me this:

" No one knows just how boulders come. You plough a field and pick up all the stones, and when you plough the next year, you can pick up more stones than you did the year before. Something very mysterious about it!"

Then boulders increase in size—slowly, of course, but all stones that are partially on the surface, so the sun and rain strikes 'em, grow.

In the year 1853, Deacon Hoshkins carried a small stone in his overcoat pocket and tossed it into his front yard.

" Four men can't lift that rock now—come and see!" said the Deacon.

I went with him and looked the rock over. He was right: four men could not lift it ﻌ ﻌ

" But if stones grow," I asked, " how is it possible that when we use them in building a wall the wall does not swell and crack?"

" There, Neighbor, is where you show your ignorance," replied the Deacon, chewing a straw in a meditative way. " When you take a stun out of its native place and chuck it in solid with a lot o' stuns it never saw afore, why, it just loses heart and dies. It stays there, of course, but it's dead, dead as hay, dead as a tooth when the Doc has killed the nerve. All field stuns want liberty; they want to choose their mates—tain't natural, see? to chuck a good decent stun all over with mortar and put it where it never gits the sun or rain or dew! It dies, of course,—I guess you would too." ﻌ ﻌ

I did not dissent from the good old Deacon's philosophy—I never have since he called me to order at the Farmer's Institute when I expressed a doubt as to the world having been made in six days of twenty-four hours each. No, I only said mildly: " Goodness me! do tell! who would ha' thought it!" The Deacon told me I could have the boulder that had grown from a pebble in '53 to a boulder in '99. I thanked him heartily.

So this morning Ali Baba hitched up the pony, and got Uncle Billy Bushnell, and they have gone with pries and crowbars after the nigger-head that rests half-covered with soil, in Deacon Hoshkin's front yard. But before going Ali Baba assured me that it was a fact that all field stones increased in size if not too much molested, and if I doubted it I could ask By Gibson ﻌ ﻌ

BEFORE co-operation comes in any line, there is always competition pushed to a point that threatens destruction and promises chaos; then to avert ruin, men devise a better way, a plan that conserves and economizes, and behold it is found in co-operation ﻌ ﻌ

ﻌ ﻌ

MEN are only grown-up children. They are cheerful after breakfast, cross at night. Houses, lands, barns, railroads, churches, books, racetracks are the playthings with which they amuse themselves until they grow tired, and Death, the kind old nurse, rocks them all to sleep.

So a man on earth is good or bad as the mood moves him. The devils are not coal-black, nor the saints pure white, but generally we are all a sort of steel-gray ﻌ ﻌ

Caprice, temper, accident, all act upon man. The North wind of hate, the simoon of jealousy, the cyclone of passion beat and buffet him. Pilots strong and pilots cowardly stand at the helm by turn. But sometimes the South wind softly blows, the sun comes out by day, the stars at night; friendship holds the rudder firm and love makes all secure. ℭ Such is the life of man, a voyage on life's unresting sea.

American Plan: A scheme for shortening human life through overeating.

Anarchist: Any man who wears his opinion pompadour.

Atheist: Any man who does not believe in himself.

Bibliocuss: A Person who borrows books and never returns them.

Bughouse: 1. A condition of mind (see Boston). 2. The place where a person without funds is sent under certain conditions ✸ ✸

Charity: A thing that begins at home, and usually stays there. Bracing up Ralph Waldo Emerson's reputation by attributing to him literary mousetraps which he should have made, but did n't. (also cheese).

College: A place where you have to go in order to find out that there is nothing in it. (See Marriage).

Compliment: A sarcastic remark with a flavor of truth, or not, as the case may be ✸ ✸

Co-operation: Doing what I tell you to do, and doing it quick.

Devil: A god who has been bounced for conduct unbecoming a gentleman.

Discord: A guinea hen, a peacock and a blue jay singing a trio.

Divorce: One of the beneficent results of marriage ✸ ✸

Divorcee: Any lady who is a post-graduate in Love's correspondence school ✸ ✸

Education: A form of self-delusion by those who muff every good wheeze.

An Epigram: Is made up of wit and wisdom, flavored with surprise.

Epitaph: 1. Postponed compliments. 2. Postmortem bull con. 3. Qualifying for the Ananias Club.

Farmer: 1. A man who raises early feed for potato bugs. 2. One who supplies raw stock for vaudeville jokes. (Farms were first devised as an excuse for the Agricultural Department at Washington.)

Feathers: Secondary sex advertisements made of fibre and horsetails, and used on ladies' lids, as eye gougers and such.

Hand: A convention-sized bread hook.

Has-Been: Any man who thinks he has arrived ✸ ✸

Ignoramus: Any man who flatters himself that he is educated.

Immortality: 1. A reward given to infidels and atheists by a somewhat humorous God, for not groveling before Him and annoying Him with importunities. 2. A system of punishment for suicides which makes suicide impossible, thereby putting one over on the ingrate who was tired of the gift of life or compelling him to live forever, willy-nilly. 3. A valueless thing, because unlimited in quantity, which those, hotly intent upon achieving, will forfeit through the law which provides that that for which we clutch, we lose. 4. A condition sought by political office holders, where the incumbent never either dies nor resigns.

Infidel: One who defames his Creator and impeaches his own reason by believing in Orthodox Christianity.

Ingrate: Any person who has got something for nothing, and wants more on the same terms.

Irish Confetti: Brickbats.

Knocking: A slow but sure way of putting the skids under your prospects. Push in the door softly, and all things are yours—knock and nothing shall be opened unto you. From the autobiography of a Has Been.

Libelous: To be tactless in type.

Litigation: A form of hell whereby money is transferred from the pockets of the proletariat to that of lawyers.

Man: 1. A being that claims to be the highest work of God. 2. Any creature that creates a Creator in its own image.

Morality: The line of conduct that pays.

Nancy: A person of neither sex, who yet combines the bad qualities of both.

Optimist: A man who does not care what happens, so long as it does n't happen to him ✦ ✦

Oratory: Palaver in a Prince Albert.

Perfume: Any smell that is used to drown a worse one.
tracts the lively interest of lawyers, and warrants your being sued for damages

Prosperity: 1. That condition which attracts the lively interest of lawyers, and warrants your being sued for damages or indicted for something, or both. 2. That peculiar condition which excites the lively interest of the ambulance chaser.

Reciprocity: 1. The act of seconding the emotion. 2. When a widow teaches a clergyman how to tango, in return for his kindness in showing her how to swim ✦ ✦

Renunciation: The act of giving up your seat in a street car to a pretty woman, and then purposely stepping on an old man's toes.

Righteous Indignation: Your own wrath as opposed to the shocking bad temper of others.

Sanity: The ability to do team work.

Sorehead: A politician who has reached for something that was not his, and missed ✦ ✦

Total Depravity: The greatest idea for the acquisition of power and pelf ever devised ✦ ✦

Trouble: 1. A hallucination that affords great joy to the possessor. 2. Any interesting topic of conversation. 3. A plan of nature whereby a person is diverted from the humiliation of seeing himself as others see him.

The Unpardonable Sin: Neglecting to close the screen door.

Utopia: A place where you have but to suggest a thing to consider it done; a condition where all things are supplied on slipping a wish into a slot.

Vacation: A period of increased and pleasurable activity when your wife is at the seashore.

Villager: Any man laboring under the illusion that he is very wise and infintely clever ✦ ✦

Wealth: A cunning device of fate whereby men are made captive and burdened with repsonsibilities from which only Death can file their fetters.

Wit: The thing that fractures many a friendship ✦ ✦

Work: A plan of God to circumvent the Devil ✦ ✦

Metaphysics: 1. An attempt to define a thing and by so doing escape the bother of understanding it. 2. The explanation of a thing by a person who does not understand it.

Middleman: One who works both ends against the middle.

Music: 1. Anything that has charms to soothe a savage beast. 2. Unnecessary noises heard in restaurants and cheap hotels. 3. The only one of the arts that can not be prostituted to a base use. 4. An attempt to express the emotions that are beyond speech. 5. A noise less objectionable than any other noise.

Obstinacy: 1. To stick to your favorite lie or truth because you know you are wrong in either case. 2. The ego's peacock-plumes ✦ ✦

Public Opinion: The judgment of the incapable many opposed to that of the discerning few.

Philistine: A term of reproach used by prigs to designate certain people they do not like.

Roycroft: 1. *Roy* means " king;" and *croft* means " home or craft." Thus, Roycroft means King-craft; working for the highest; doing your work just as good as you can—making things for the King. 2. The dignity and the divinity of labor—peace, reciprocity, health, industry, persistency and endurance.

Repartee: Any remark which is so clever that it makes the listener wish he had said it himself.

HEN I write I never consider what will be done with the matter, how it will be liked, and who will read it ✧ ✧ I just write for myself. And the most captious, relentless critic I have is myself. When I write well, as I occasionnally do, I am filled with a rapturous intoxicating joy. No pleasure in life compares with the joy of creation—catching in the Cadmean mesh a new thought —putting salt on the tail of an idea. And a certain critic has said that I can catch more ideas with less salt than any other man in America. ❡ I am not sure whether the man was speaking ironically or in compliment, but since the remark has been bruited abroad, it has struck me as being fairly good, and so I here repeat it, for I am making no special attempt to conceal the fact that I am still on earth. ❡ In order to write well you require respite and rest in change. Ideas come to one on the mountains, while tramping the fields, at the woodpile. When you are in the best condition is the time to do nothing, for at such a time, if ever, the divine current surges through you.

If we could only find the cosmic switchboard when we want to think, how delightful it would be to simply turn on the current! But no, all we can do is to walk, ride horseback, dig in the garden, placing ourselves in receptive mood, and from the Unknown the ideas come. Then to use them is a matter of the workroom. ❡ In the course of each year I give about a hundred lectures.

Public speaking, if carried on with moderation, is a valuable form of mental excitation.

Ill-health comes from too much excitement, or not enough. Platform work keeps your mental pores open and tends to correct faulty elimination of mental dross ✧ ✧

To stand before an audience of a thousand people for two hours with no manuscript, and only your tongue and brain to save you from the ruin that may engulf you any instant, and which many in your audience hope will engulf you, requires a goodly modicum of concentration. I have seen the giving way of a collarbutton in an impassioned moment cross-buttock a Baptist preacher. I am always prepared for accidents in oratory, such, say, as a harmless necessary cat coming on the stage without her cue. In public speaking one shakes the brush-piles of thought and starts a deal more game than he runs down at the time, and this game which he follows up at his leisure, and the stimulus of success in having stayed the limit, make for mental growth.

✧ ✧

EACH of us imagines he is bigger than Fate—an exception to the rule. And out of the sadness we distil a kind of joy on account of the fact that we are alive. In the pains of others there is a certain satisfaction, and we mentally are congratulating ourselves on the fact that the tragedy is none of ours.

THE teacher is the child's other mother. In a pure state of nature the child would need no other teacher than its mother, but the economic demands upon the poor and the social demands upon the rich make a third party indispensable.

In the average home, there is a woful lack of love—everybody is so busy! So the child is sent to school, and the other mother gives her mother-love, her patience and her tact to bring about a pleasurable animation—a condition the average parent can not evolve, and without which mental and spiritual growth is impossible ✧ ✧

✧ ✧

Is it worth while to hate anything—even sin?

Y wife is my helpmeet, and I am hers. I do not support her; rather, she supports me. All I have is hers—not only do I trust her with my heart, but with my pocketbook. And what I here write is not a tombstone testimonial, weighted with a granitic sense of loss, but a simple tribute of truth to a woman who is yet on earth in full possession of her powers, her star still in the ascendent.

I know the great women of history. I know the qualities that go to make up, not only the superior person but the one sublimely great. Humanity is the raw stock with which I work.

I know how Sappho loved and sung, and Aspasia inspired Pericles to think and act, and Cleopatra was wooed by two Emperors of Rome, and how Theodora suggested the Justinian Code and had the last word in its compilation. I know Madame De Stael, Sarah Wedgwood, George Eliot, Susanna Wesley, Elizabeth Barrett. I know them all, for I can read, and I have lived, and I have imagination.

And knowing the great women of the world, and having analyzed their characters and characteristics, I still believe that Alice Hubbard, in way of mental reach, sanity, sympathy and all-round ability, outclasses any woman of history, ancient or modern, mentally, morally or spiritually.

To make a better woman than Alice Hubbard one would have to take the talents and graces of many great women and omit their faults. If she is a departure in some minor respects from a perfect standard, it is in all probability because she lives in a faulty world, with a faulty man, and deals with faulty folks, a few of whom, doubtless, will peruse this book.

HE youth loves his doxy in the mass; I analyze, formulate and reduce character to its constituent parts.

And yet, I have never fully analyzed the mind of the woman I love, for there is always and forever an undissolved residuum of wit, reason, logic, invention and comparison bubbling forth that makes association with her a continual delight. I have no more sounded the depths of her soul than I have my own.

What she will say and what she will do are delightful problems; only this, that what she says and what she does will be regal, right, gracious, kindly—tempered with a lenity that has come from suffering, and charged with a sanity that has enjoyed, and which knows because through it plays unvexed the Divine Intelligence that rules the world and carries the planets in safety on their accustomed way—this I know.

Perhaps the principal reason my wife and I get along so well together is because we have similar ideas as to what constitutes wit. She laughs at all of my jokes, and I do as much for her. All of our quarrels are papier-mache, made, played and performed for the gallery of our psychic selves. Having such a wife as this, I do not chase the ghosts of dead hopes through the graveyard of my dreams

HO can deny that the mother-heart of a natural and free woman makes the controlling impulse of her life a prayer to bless and benefit, to minister and serve?

Such is Alice Hubbard—a free woman who has gained freedom by giving it. But her charity is never maudlin.

She has the courage of her lack of convictions, and decision enough to withhold the dollar when the cause is not hers, and when to bestow merely means escape from importunity. To give people that which they do not earn is to make them think less of themselves—and of you. The only way to help people is to give them a chance to help themselves. ❡ She is the only woman I ever knew who realizes as a vital truth that the basic elements for all human betterments are economic, not mental or spiritual. ❡ Alice Hubbard is an economist by nature, and her skill as a financier is founded on absolute honesty and flawless integrity. She has the savings-bank habit, and next to paying her debts, gets a fine tang out of life by wise and safe investments. She knows that a savings bank account is an anchor win'ard, and that to sail fast and far your craft must be close-hauled to weather squalls.

In manufacturing she studies cost, knowing better far than most businessmen that deterioration of property and overhead charges must be carefully considered, if the Referee in Bankruptcy would be kept at a safe distance. She is a methodizer of time and effort, and knows the value of system, realizing the absurdity of a thirty-dollar-a-week man doing the work of a five-dollar-a-week boy. She knows the proportion of truth to artistic jealousy in the melodious discord of the anvil chorus; and the foreman who opposes all reforms which he himself does not conjure forth from his chickadee brain is to her familiar.

The employee who is a knocker by nature, who constantly shows a tendency to get on the greased slide that leads to limbo, has her pity, and she in many gentle and diplomatic ways tries to show him the danger of his position.

IN my wife's mind I see my thoughts enlarged and reflected, just as in a telescope we behold the stars. She is the magic mirror in which I see the divine. Her mind acts on mine, and mine reacts upon hers. Most certainly I am aware that no one else can see the same in her which I behold, because no one else can call forth her qualities, any more than any other woman can call forth mine. Our minds, separate and apart, act together as one, forming a complete binocular, making plain that which to one alone is invisible.

Every worthy theme and sentiment I have expressed to the public has been first expressed to her, or, more likely, borrowed from her. I have seen her in almost every possible exigency of life: in health, success, and high hope; in poverty, and what the world calls disgrace and defeat. But here I should

explain that disgrace is for those who accept disgrace, and defeat consists in acknowledging it.

I have seen her face the robustious fury of an attorney weighing three hundred pounds, and reduce him to pork cracklings by her poise, quiet persistence, and the righteousness of her cause.

I WOULD rather be able to appreciate things I can not have than to have things I am not able to appreciate.

SHE is at home with children, the old, the decrepit, the sick, the lonely, the unfortunate, the vicious, the stupid, the insane. She puts people at their ease; she is one with them, but not necessarily of them.

She recognizes the divinity in all of God's creatures, even the lowliest, and those who wear prison-stripes are to her akin— all this without condoning the offense. She respects the sinner, but not the sin.

¶ Wherever she goes her spirit carries with it the message, " Peace be still!" With the noble, the titled, the famous, she is equally at home.

I have seen her before an audience of highly critical, intellectual and aristocratic people, stating her cause with that same gentle, considerate courtesy and clearness that is so becoming to her. The strongest feature of her nature is her humanitarianism, and this springs from her unselfish heart and her wide-reaching imagination. And imagination is only sympathy illumined by love and ballasted with brains.

She wins by abnegation and yet never renounces anything. She has the faith that gives all, and therefore receives all.

SHE has proved herself an ideal mother, not only in every physical function, but in that all-brooding tenderness and loving service which is contained in the word Mother. She, of all mothers, realizes that the mother is the true teacher: that all good teachers are really spiritual mothers. She knows that not only does the mother teach by precept, but by every action, thought and attribute of her character. Scolding mothers have impatient babies and educated parents have educated children. ❡ That supreme tragedy of motherhood, that the best mothers are constantly training their children to live without them, is fully appreciated and understood by Alice Hubbard.

Those who are admitted into the close presence of Alice Hubbard are transformed into different people. This is especially true of budding youth—boys and girls from fourteen to eighteen. For them she has a peculiar and potent charm—Her vivacity, her animation, her sympathy, her knowledge of flowers, plants, trees, birds and animals delights them ❧ ❧

She carries with her an aura in which vulgarity can not thrive nor pretense flourish. She has a gentle and gracious dignity that contains not a trace of affectation, prudery, pedantry or priggishness. She has the happy faculty of putting people at their ease and making them pleased with themselves; so with her they are wise beyond their wont and gracious beyond their accustomed habit.

❧ ❧

SHE wins without trying to win, and if she pleases, as she always does, it is without apparent effort.

In moral qualities she has a steadfastness in the right; a sharp distinction as to *meum et tuum:* a persistence in completing the task begun; the habit of being on time and keeping her word, especially with servants and children and those who can not enforce their claims; an absence of all exaggeration, with no vestige of boasting as to what she has done or intends to do—all of which sets her apart as one superior, refined and unselfish beyond the actual as we find it, except in the ideals of the masters in imaginative literature.

In mental qualities she appreciates the work of the great statesmen, creators, inventors, reformers, scientists, and all those who live again in minds made better ❧ ❧

❧ ❧

TO those who disagree with her she is ever tolerant; in her opinions she is not dogmatic, realizing that truth is only a point of view, and even at the last, people should have the right to be wrong, so long as they give this right to others. She does not mix in quarrels, has none of her own, nor is she quick to take sides in argument and wordy warfare. ❡ She keeps out of cliques, invites no secrets and has none herself, respects the mood of those she is with, and when she does not know what to say, says nothing, and in times of doubt minds her own business ❧ ❧

She is patient under censure, just or unjust; and resentful toward hypocrisy, pretense and stupidity. Of course, she recognizes that certain people are not hers, and these she neither avoids nor seeks to please or placate. She holds all ties lightly, never clutching even friendship—growing rich by giving.

❧ ❧

PHYSICALLY she is strong as a rope of silk; she can outride and outwalk most athletic men, although her form is slender and slight. Those who regard bulk and beauty as synonymous, never turn and look at her in the public streets. In countenance she is as plain as was Julius Cæsar, and to his busts she bears a striking resemblance in the features of nose, mouth, chin and eyes.

In the moral qualities of patience, poise and persistence she is certainly Cæsarian, and in these she outranks any woman I have been able to resurrect from the dusty tomes of days gone by. This, then, is my one close companion, my confidente, my friend, my wife; and my relation with her will be my sole passport to Paradise, if there is one beyond this life. ❡ I married a rich woman—one rich in love, loyalty, gentleness, insight, gratitude, appreciation—one who caused me, at thirty-three years of age, to be born again ❧ ❧

❧ ❧

The fact that a man advertises does not prove that man's inability to do work of a high grade, any more than you can assume that because a man does not advertise he is safe and competent.

❧ ❧

It is the finest thing in the world to live—most people only exist.

THROUGH a sudden and terrible accident, a few weeks ago, the daughter of John Alex. Dowie was fatally injured. Half of the surface of her body was burned to a crisp—death was inevitable. In a few hours she passed away

I need not dwell upon the place which a beautiful and intellectual young woman of twenty-three fills in the heart of a father of sixty. The feeling is something essentially loverlike—Shakespeare has hinted at the tenderness of the relation in the story of King Lear and his daughter Cordelia.

A thousand people attended the funeral, and standing by the open grave Dowie delivered an address—an address tragically, fearfully self-contained, with that reserve which only a sorrow too great for tears can know. The breaking heart of the man would have hidden itself away, but the public position of all concerned made a private funeral out of the question. No daily paper mentioned the address—no religious periodical quoted it. I give the following short extract from the stricken parent's words:

She said, " Father, will it be long?"
¶ I said, " Not long, dear."
"Lord, take me," she said.
And we prayed for it at last, because we could not bear to see her suffer any more.
¶ Then I sang, " Lead Kindly Light."
¶ Then we repeated the Shepherd Psalm: " The Lord is my Shepherd"—She said it so strongly—" I shall not want. He maketh me to lie down in green pastures; He leadeth me beside the still waters."
¶ I could hear her murmur, " Beside the still waters."
The still waters were there. She was beginning to see the green pastures.
" Yea, though I walk through the Valley of the Shadow of Death, I will fear no evil."
And that was all we could hear.
She closed her lids and was sleeping.
¶ I would let none weep.
She opened her eyes and smiled and then she slept.
I sang to her the song I have sung so many times to those who were sleeping in Jesus, and when I had finished she departed without a sigh, without a tremor

My hand was upon her head and my hand was upon her body and I, felt no quiver

And now I stand here and I have no daughter on earth.

I had only one. You must all be my daughters, daughters of Zion. I have no daughter.—*Death of Dowie's Daughter.*

SEVENTY per cent of the members of all our law-making bodies are lawyers Very naturally, lawyers in making laws favor laws that make lawyers a necessity. If this were not so, lawyers would not be human.

Until very recent times, and in degree I am told it is so yet, laws are for the subjection of the many and the upholding of the privileges of the few. The few employ a vast lobby, while all the many can do is to obey, or be ground into the mire. All the justice the plain people have, they have had to fight for, and what we get is a sop to keep us quiet. The law, for most people, is a great, mysterious, malevolent engine of wrath. A legal summons will yet blanch the cheek of most honest men, and an officer of the door sends consternation into the family. The District Attorney prosecutes us— we must defend ourselves. " And if you have no money to hire a lawyer, you are adjudged guilty and for you justice is a by-word," says Edward Lauterbach, the eminent lawyer.

BUILDERS all come from a country that has weather as well as climate. On the equator, where Nature is too lavish, man simply lies down and depends upon the Dame to tuck him in and shake the friendly branches so that fruit will fall within his reach.

Where parents do too much for their children, the children will not do much for themselves. And when Mother Nature does too much for her family, the result is exactly the same.

¶ Is he sincere? Probably not, if he is always asking this question about others.

T was about the year Eighteen Hundred Fifty-seven that Henry Ward Beecher entered his pulpit one Sunday morning and announced to his congregation that he wanted a thousand dollars to buy Bibles for poor people in Kansas. He said the matter was absolutely imperative, and he would not go on with the services until the money was raised. ❧ The Plymouth Church congregation had faith in Henry Ward Beecher, so they simply raised the money as a matter of course ∾ ∾

And the next day Henry Ward Beecher took the thousand dollars, and bought Sharpe's rifles and shipped them to Old John Brown in Kansas.

One of these "Bibles" was given to Major Pond, and he, in turn, presented me the document, after he no longer had use for it. I have it now, with his initials cut on the butt, with several notches adjacent. Just what these notches stand for, I do not know.

∾ ∾

ORTHODOXY: That peculiar condition where the patient can neither eliminate an old idea or absorb a new one. 2. In religion that state of mind which congratulates itself on being absolutely right, and a belief that all who think otherwise are wholly wrong. 3. A faith in the fixed—a worship of the static. 4. The joy that comes from thinking that most everybody is lined up for Limbus with no return ticket. 5. A condition brought about by the sprites of Humor according to the rule that whom the gods would destroy they first make mad. 6. The zenith of selfishness and the nadir of egotism.

∾ ∾

TO love one's friends, to bathe in the sunshine of life, to preserve a right mental attitude—the receptive attitude, the attitude of gratitude—and to do one's work—these make the sum of an ideal life. To make a man exempt is to take away from him just so much manhood.

∾ ∾

BEFORE you are fit to give orders, you must be willing to take orders. The leader of the orchestra has always been a man who has played second fiddle ∾ ∾

∾ ∾

FRANKLIN'S dictum that Government would yet be educational, and nothing else, was backed up by the argument that it was cheaper to educate men than forcibly to restrain or compel them. To breed criminals and produce the incompetent is surely a costly and foolish plan as compared with educating boys and girls to use their heads and hands to help themselves by helping other people. The first intent of our American Government is not to compel people to do certain things and restrain them from doing other things; but it is to make the right life and the useful life the natural and easy one to live. To this end, as a people, we stand pledged to education. The Schoolhouse is our fortress and our hope. Moreover, we believe that all men and women should go to school as long as they live. There is no end to education. We are all in the Kindergarten of God.

∾ ∾

PARTIES pass, politicians die, but the people live on forever.

The most important thing in the world is business, and business is a matter of supplying human wants.

Business is the production and the distribution of the things that are necessary to life and its well-being.

The ability of the many to buy makes business good. If men are out of work, naturally they are not purchasing anything save the bare necessities of life. We build only when prosperity flows.

∾ ∾

IN an inventor's work there is required something similar to that which the artist brings to bear.

The artist must be a man of imagination. He must be able to close his eyes and see things which the world does not perceive. So the inventor must have the prophetic vision. The machine exists in his brain before he materializes it.

The great thing is the idea, and imagination is the greatest gift of God.

∾ ∾

Men are strong only as they believe in one another.

OW there is a certain kind of lawyer, a new kind, and this is the man who, when you lay a proposition before him, will not say, " My dear boy, you can't do that; I advise you to leave it strictly alone!" This is n't what he says. He says, " If you will be here tomorrow morning at ten o'clock, I will, in the meantime, formulate you a plan of action that I believe will work out to the advantage of everybody concerned."

❡ This is exactly what Judge Elbert H. Gary did for a whipped-out manufacturer of steel. Gary was County Judge of DuPage County, Illinois. He lived at Wheaton, a common everyday county seat, population two thousand, and a public square and a courthouse in the center, with a row of stores all round. Judge Gary was fairly prosperous; had served two terms as County Judge, and given up the job to a more worthy man, because he wanted a wider field.

The salary of the County Judge was four thousand dollars a year.

Gary thought he ought to make five thousand, anyway.

Then it was that the whipped-out ironmaster came to him. The ironmaster was on the verge of making an assignment; but out of the wreck he wanted to pull a few thousand dollars to save his family from starvation.

How to get this money out and let the business go to the devil was the question at issue ঌ ঌ

Right there is where the lawyer, of the kind that keeps you from getting into trouble, sees his chance. Lawyers are always interested in receiverships, bankruptcies, dissolutions. Did Gary show the ironmaster how to lie down and take the legal count? Not at all. He studied the case and he found that this man had assets of three hundred thousand dollars. His liabilities were over a hundred thousand dollars, and these were coming due, and the man had no money to meet them. From the standpoint of the ironmaster, the case looked very dark.

Gary discovered that there were two other manufacturers of iron in the same vicinity; and these three manufacturers were fighting each other fiercely. They manufactured pig iron, steel ingots, bar iron and sheet steel, all in hearty competition with each other; men on the road cutting prices, offering rebates, and the cost of selling cut seriously into the profits; overhead and deterioration took the rest. Judge Gary decided that if these three men could be gotten together, and the three companies combined in one, the problem would be solved. How to get enemies together was the question. These men did not speak to each other as they passed. They had threatened each other in the mails. Lawsuits had been carried on between them.

However, Gary took them one at a time and showed how the three mills should and could be owned by one corporation. Every man should be paid a proportionate amount of stock, in payment for his business. Then one mill should make the pig iron and the ingots. All of its product would be taken by one of the other mills, which should manufacture all of the rolled bars. And the mill that made the ingots should also supply the third mill, which rolled the sheet steel. This would cut out two-thirds of the sales force. Also, it would help to maintain prices. Bonds then could be issued on the entire business, and the creditors paid in these. This would clean up the floating indebtedness of the entire outfit, and the cash sale of a few of the bonds would give working capital.

Here was the work for a diplomat and a financier, and Gary was the man. He showed these fighting, competing individuals the silliness of economic warfare.

❡ The whole thing was consummated, and out of the idea grew the Federal Steel Company, an institution essentially sound, strong, productive.

HO are those who will eventually be damned?" "Oh, the others, the others, the others!"

Where did Judge Gary get his fee out of this getting three fighting competitors together? Oh, he simply took a certain per cent of the bonds. Nobody in particular paid him his fee; nobody was strained or overcharged. The service he rendered was worth the money; but Judge Gary's fee was—never mind the exact figures—call it one hundred thousand dollars ·⁕· ·⁕·

Not only had Judge Gary supplied these three competitors, all of them on the verge of bankruptcy, a big idea, but he also supplied himself one. Out of this transaction grew the United States Steel Corporation ·⁕· ·⁕·

A man who can take a complex situation, where good and able men are distressed, at their wit's end, not knowing which way to turn, and make friends of men who were before enemies, and transform bankrupt institutions into a paying enterprise, is a genius. And the simplicity and ease of the whole transaction is of such a commonsense sort that one is amazed to think that no one else had ever done the thing before.

Peace, to Judge Gary's mind, is n't the peace of Julius Cæsar, nor is his civilization that of Ferdinand and Torquemada. It is the antithesis of these.

He touched the rock of natural resources with the wand of his genius, and the welling waters gushed forth.

Judge Gary is now Chairman of the Board of Directors and Chairman of the Financial Committee of the United States Steel Corporation.

The President is James Farrell, a man who has come up from the ranks, having once worked as a laborer. Step by step, Farrell has climbed the steel ladder. ❡ Farrell and Gary form a great team. There is a complete understanding between them. They do not usurp each other's territory and each assumes that the other knows his business. When either of these men wants to do a thing, the other gives way and allows him to do it ·⁕· ·⁕·

The general offices of the United States Steel Corporation are plain, simple, unpretentious. There are no costly rugs, hangings or furnishings. There is no advertising of power by conspicuous waste; and certainly they do not advertise it by conspicuous leisure.

Anybody who has business with Judge Gary can see him.

He has set a new example for executives in office furnishings.

Judge Gary has no desk. He simply sits at the head of a long table, with chairs down each side, and for two or three hours every morning holds a continual reception. Any one who wants to see him is invited in and takes one of the chairs. Judge Gary sits at the head of the table, with pencil in hand and a pad before him, and talks or listens.

If you had never seen the man before, you would put him down as a Christian Scientist. He has the placid smile, the glow of health, the good teeth, the bright eyes, the patience, the hopeful attitude that marks a man who is on good terms with himself, with the world, and with his Creator.

With him nothing matters much, but everything matters a little. And as he visits with one after another, and gently disposes of them, each man going away pleased and satisfied, thinking that he has got something, all without jolly or josh, it grows upon you that the title of "The Great Pacificator" is eminently fit and proper.

Judge Gary is never irascible, peevish, fretful. He does not accuse. If any one makes accusations against others, Judge Gary always seems to be forming a defence. You hear him gently murmur in reply: " Oh, well, you know his intentions are right. He carries heavy burdens. You must remember how long his hours are. He copes with great difficulties. His tasks are very much greater than ours."

❡ Such simple phrases, interjected in the conversation, show the attitude of the man's mind. He is not militant, save passively. He wins through sympathy, through sociability, through knowing what he wants; and he does not want anything that is not within reach. His plans are eminently practical, and his business is to work from the complex to the simple ·⁕· ·⁕·

He thinks with pencil in hand and a pad before him. There are no letters in sight; no papers. One thing is brought to him at a time, and he gives a decision on it, as a wise judge should and that disposes of it.

His secretaries seem to be clairvoyant. They know his needs and move quietly on O'Sullivan rubber heels, entering into no disputes, understanding that their chief is a man who comprehends everything with a minimum of explanation ☙ ☙

Elbert H. Gary is a great democrat; he is one of the demos. His days of poverty, struggle, obstacle, trial are still before him, unforgotten. He has great respect for old people, and his love for the young is unfailing. His nerves do not play him false.

When you call on most of the so-called Napoleons of finance, you will find them fussy ☙ They monkey with papers; pick things up and lay them down; play with their watch-chains; cough, sneeze, and indulge in a deal of vacuity and sometimes verbosity. ℂ Judge Gary does none of these things. He gives his undivided time and attention to each visitor, to each project in hand, to every document that is laid before him. He does not try to anticipate you, nor run ahead of you. I would not put him in the class with Sir Isaac Newton and Alexander Humboldt. He is just the average man focused—the strong, able, practical, athletic type of Middle-West man—a man who in his youth constantly met with what the pampered sons of the East might have called misfortune.

All difficulties are comparative, and a man who has known trial and obstacle and loss early in life is doubly blest, in that the small misfits of life are accepted quite as a matter of course. And so I can not conceive of Elbert H. Gary reading a father-confessor into whose pliant ears he would pour a tale of woe ☙ ☙

Gary is an inspirer of men, and his attitude is one that gives courage and lends ambition.

☙ ☙

THE entire Christian doctrine of rewards and punishments, of vicarious atonement and the substitution of a pure and holy man for the culprit, is a vicious and misleading philosophy.

☙ ☙

ANY individual who uses the word "commercial" as an epithet, who regards business enterprise as synonymous with graft and greed, who speaks of certain men as "self-made" and others as "educated," who gives more attention to war than to peace, who seeks to destroy rather than to create and build up, is essentially un-American.

The word "education" sometimes stands for idleness, but the American Philosophy symbols work, effort, industry. It means intelligent, thoughtful, reasonable and wise busy-ness—helping yourself by helping others.

The world's greatest prizes in the future will go to the businessman. The businessman is our only scientist, and to him we must look for a Science of Economics that will eradicate poverty, disease, superstition—all that dissipates and destroys. The day is dawning!

THE weaknesses of the many make the leader possible—and the man who craves disciples and wants followers is always more or less of a charlatan.

The man of genuine worth and insight wants to be himself; and he wants others to be themselves, also.

Discipleship is a degenerating process to all parties concerned ☙ ☙

People who are able to do their own thinking should not allow others to do it for them.

PHILOSOPHERS of the Far East have told us that man's deliverance from the evils of life must come through the killing of desire; we reach Nirvana — rest — through nothingness. But within a decade it has been borne in upon a vast number of thinking men of the world that deliverance from discontent and sorrow was to be had, not through ceasing to ask questions, but by asking one more. The question is this, "What can I do?" And then doing it.

When man went to work, action removed the doubt that theory could not solve. ❡ The rushing winds purify the air; only running water is pure; and the holy man, if there be such, is the one who loses himself in persistent, useful effort. The saint is the man who keeps his word and is on time. By working for all we secure the best results for self, and when we truly work for self, we work for all. The self-assumed superior class evolves naturally into being everywhere as man awakens and asks questions. Only the unknown is terrible, says Victor Hugo. We can cope with the known, and at the worst we can overcome the known by accepting it.

❧ ❧

I THINK I'll start a crusade for the reformation of reformers. I am fully persuaded that our besetting sin, as a people, is neither intemperance nor grafting, but plain pretense.

We are not frank and honest with ourselves nor with each other.

The disposition to cheapen and adulterate and get the start of our fellows by Number Six Bluff and Guff is the universal habit of Church and State. ❡ We are copper cents trying to pass for half-dollars.

My suggestion is that for a whole year we let the heathen rest, resign all public work in the Personal Purity League, and declare a vacation in the W.C.T.U.

❡ Then let each man and woman set a guard over his own spirit and try to be greater than he who taketh a city. ❡ In other words, just do our work and practise the old, plain, simple virtues of gentleness, charity and honesty, doing unto others as we would be done by *❧ ❧*

WE shall never get the right idea of work until we see at the bottom of it is public service.

By this method we should not have to talk so much and do so much, and so could think and rest, and dream and love. I'm sure it would be better for our nerves — that are getting outside of our clothes — and possibly just as well for the heathen and drunkard *❧ ❧*

Stop this violent running to and fro, and be simple and honest — only for a year! And then possibly at the end of that time we could sit in the presence of each other and be silent without being uncomfortable *❧ ❧*

Let us try being gentle in our judgments —just kind—and see if we can't reform more wrongs than by going after folks who have made mistakes, with comealongs and the loud ballyhoo and a brass-plated bazoo. Let us be kind— something the world has really never tried *❧ ❧*

❧ ❧

MEN hotly intent on making money are not apt to make much money, because the dollar is a rolling disk, and when you chase it, it attains a terrific velocity.

It exceeds the speed-limit, and many a man has chased it clear into the penitentiary-walls and heard the gates click behind him before he realized what he was doing.

❧ ❧

THE longing for perpetual bliss, in perfect peace, where all good things are provided, might well seem a malevolent inspiration from the Lords of Death and Darkness. We grow only by enduring and overcoming.

❧ ❧

Art is only the best way of doing things.

EFT alone and uninstructed, no one would ever imagine he was conceived in sin and born in iniquity. Neither would he say that we are born to trouble as the sparks fly upward, and that sickness was sent from God. Naturally we slough trouble, we shed sorrow, we sleep and awake refreshed. In six months the grass grows over all graves.

Much of our sickness is caused by fear, and fear is an importation *so* Our very existence turns on being happy. Misery affects the circulation, fear means congestion, and congestion continued means disease, and disease continued means *rigor mortis*.

¶ Diseases are symptoms. To cure a disease or cut out a diseased part is not to make the man well—it will catch him somewhere else. You have to reach the cause *so* *so*

Bad collections and inability to meet a note will give you cold feet and then a cold in the head. A quarrel will cause tonsilitis. A threat will give granulated eyelids. Overeat, underbreathe, fill life full of fear, jealousy and hate, and Bright's Disease follows, and Bright's Disease is simply a contamination of the water-supply by the sewage. *so* *so*

NIGH aims are good things, we are told, and doubtless, like the mariners, we should steer our courses by the stars. Still there is good game which lies close to the earth if we knew how to hunt for it—and there is the fun of hunting anyway, game or not.

so *so*

Hot air is all right, but see that it is well compressed before you use it.

so *so*

ALL strong men begin by worshiping a shrine, and if they continue to grow they shift their allegiance until they know only one altar and that is the Ideal which dwells in their own hearts.

THE worst effect of vivisection is not, I believe, the fact of the cruelty to the animal, but the evil reactionary effect on the man who practises the business. Work is for the worker, art is for the artist, love is for the lover, and murder is for the murderer. The victim dies— the one who does the deed lives on.

¶ That poor wretch in the stocks suffered, but not so direly as did the children who were given opportunity to pelt him with mud. All cruelty and inhumanity reacts to the detriment of society *so* Nature is kind— she puts a quick limit on suffering—perhaps the vivisectionist is right, that the animal does not really suffer much. But the fact is, the vivisector suffers, whether he knows it or not. He has immersed his hands in innocent blood, and instead of being the protector of the helpless, he has taken advantage of the animal's helplessness to destroy it, by a means slow, complex, refined, prolonged and peculiar. Life has become to him cheap and common. Something divine has died out of his soul.

so *so*

THE business of government is to make all government unnecessary, just as wise parents are bringing up their children to do without them *so* *so*

VERESTCHAGIN, the great painter, who knew the psychology of war as few men have, and went down to his death gloriously, as he should, on a sinking battleship, once said: " In modern warfare, where man does not see his enemy, the poetry of battle is gone, and man is rendered by the unknown into a quaking coward. Enveloped in the fog of ignorance, every phenomenon of Nature causes man to quake and tremble—he wants to know. Wonder prompts him to ask, and greed for power, place and pelf replies." *so* *so*

so *so*

Armistices are agreed upon only for the sake of getting into the other's camp to find out what is going on.

so *so*

Remember the week-day to keep it holy.

T was once considered a wonderful thing to agitate the catgut, pound the piano, and toot the B-flat horn, while folks were feeding.

The introduction of London Music-Hall features in hotel dining rooms is only about fifteen years old.

The innovation came in with the bizarre, the loud, the blatant. It matched the Plaster-of-Paris, gold-leaf figures on the wall

All of the modern hotels about that time had a balcony built for the musicians. We gulped our soup to waltz time, did the entree to a two-step and disposed of pie to Chopin's Funeral March. You bawled to your vis-a-vis across a three-foot void, and if the music stopped suddenly, you found yourself addressing the audience

It was a wonderful thing. We got the concert free, and we had to have a dinner anyway! The concert was given as a sort of premium, and at that time the air was full of the idea of getting something for nothing

The hotels and restaurants advertising music at meals caught the great unwashed, who hypnotized themselves into the belief that they had broken into good society with a social jimmy.

THE first protest that I know of came from Richard Mansfield who walked into the Grand Central Hotel at Oshkosh. Behind him was his valet, carrying two big grips.

The tragedian took four strides from the door to the desk, and leaning over in one of those half-confidential stage-voice asides that reach to the topmost gallery, said, " Ah, have-you-music-at-meals?"

And the clerk adjusted the glittering glass on his bosom, smiled serenely, and said, " Oh, yes, surely so; yes, we have music at all meals."

And Mansfield turned to his valet, who was resting his hands from carrying the heavy valises, and said, " Oho, oho, James! Look you to our luggage! To our luggage!" And four more strides took him to the door, and the actor and the valet disappeared, engulfed by the all enfolding night.

SOCIABILITY at meals is right and natural. We talk as we eat, and exchange confidences. Friendship is hygienic. But music is, or should be, a collaboration between the listener and the performer. Music demands an atmosphere. But it is impossible to get an atmosphere in a public dining-room to a jingle of dishes and a buzz of conversation. And not to listen to music is an insult to the musicians.

In the music-halls, people eat, drink, laugh and talk, while the singing is going on, or a man is making a speech. Nero fiddled while Rome burned, but surely we do not want to fletcherize to fireworks, or to be fiddled at while we feed.

Just note the musicians and see how they bang it off in true union-labor style, and hand us back the indifference that we have given them. They play not for the love of it, but for fifty cents an hour, and to get even with capitalism —darn it!

Music at meals is all right for convicts, where the silent system prevails. But in hotel dining-rooms, there should not be too much display of art, either mural or musical. Neither should there be either gaudy or noisy things in sleeping-rooms, devoted to rest, sweet peace and dreams.

There are bookworms who prop a book up in front of them, as they nibble; and we are all familiar with the sociable party who eats breakfast and hides behind the morning paper at the same time. These are merely individual preferences, but if art in the mass is to be fired at people as they dine, then by all means let some one read aloud from the *Essay on Silence*

ALL denominations are needed—they fit a certain type of temperament. Down in Pennsylvania they break up the coal and send it tumbling through various sieves, and each size finds its place in a separate bin. If sects did not serve mankind they would never have been evolved—each sect catches a certain-sized man.

HEN Judge Lindsey decides that it is best to send a boy to the Reform School at Golden, he does not send an officer with the youngster. No, he just makes out the commitment papers, gives the lad thirty-five cents to pay car fare, shakes hands with him, and away he goes. Of a hundred boys sent in this way, not one has proved disloyal to the trust reposed in him. Judge Lindsey believes in the boy, and the boy believes in Judge Lindsey, and when you get a boy in that frame of mind where he responds to a trust, proving true, even going to prison alone and unattended, that boy is on the way to reformation, for he is reforming himself.
¶ Judge Lindsey is one of the modern saviors of the world.

∿ ∿

BEFORE Co-operation comes in any line, there is always competition pushed to a point that threatens destruction and promises chaos; then to avert ruin men devise a better way, a plan that conserves and economizes, and behold it is found in Co-operation.

Civilization is an evolution.

Civilization is not a thing separate and apart, any more than art is.

Art is the beautiful way of doing things.

Civilization is the expeditious way of doing things.

And as haste is often waste—the more hurry the less speed—civilization is the best way of doing things.

As mankind multiplies in number, the problem of supplying people what they need is the important question of Earth. And mankind has ever held out offers of reward in fame and money—both being forms of power—to whomsoever would supply it better things.

Teachers are those who educate people to appreciate the things they need.
¶ The man who studies mankind, and ascertains what men really want, and then supplies them this, whether it be an Idea or a Thing, is the man who is crowned with honor and clothed with riches *∿ ∿*

What people need and what they want may be very different.

To undertake to supply people a thing you think they need but which they do not want, is to have your head elevated on a pike, and your bones buried in a Potter's Field.

But wait, and the world will yet want the thing it needs, and your bones may then become Sacred Relics.

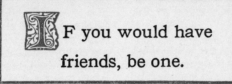

F you would have friends, be one.

¶ This change in desire on the part of mankind is the result of a growth of intellect *∿ ∿*

It is Progress, and Progress is Evolution, and Evolution is Progress.

There are men who are continually trying to push Progress along: we call them "Reformers." *∿ ∿*

There are others who always oppose the Reformer—the mildest name we have for them is "Conservative."

The Reformer is a savior or a rebel, all depending largely upon whether he succeeds or fails. He is what he is, regardless of what men think of him.

The man who is indicted and executed as a rebel, often afterward has the word "Savior" carved on his tomb; and sometimes men who are hailed as saviors in their day are afterward found to be sham saviors—to wit, charlatans. Conservation is a plan of Nature. To keep the good is to conserve. The Conservative is a man who puts on the brakes when he thinks Progress is going to land Civilization in the ditch.

Brakemen are necessary, but in the language of Koheleth, there is a time to apply the brake and there is a time to abstain from applying the brake. To clog the wheels continually is to stand still, and to stand still is to retreat.

Progress needs the brakeman, but the brakeman should not occupy all of his time putting on the brakes.

The Conservative is as necessary as the Radical. The Conservative keeps the

Reformer from going too fast, and plucking the fruit before it is ripe. Governments are only good where there is a strong Opposition, just as the planets are held in place by the opposition of forces ❧ ❧

And so civilization goes forward by stops and starts—pushed by Reformers, held back by Conservatives. One is necessary to the other, and they often shift places. But forward and forward forever civilization goes—ascertaining the best way of doing things.

❧ ❧

DRINK in the ozone, bathe in the sunshine and out in the silent night, under the stars, say to yourself again and yet again, "I am a part of all my eyes behold!" And the feeling will surely come to you that you are no mere interloper between earth and sky; but that you are a necessary particle of the Whole.

❧ ❧

Happy is the man who conserves his God-given energy until wisdom and not passion shall direct it.

❧ ❧

If pleasures are greatest in anticipation, just remember that this is also true of trouble.

❧ ❧

Mutual favors do not cancel each other.

❧ ❧

The widow who marries again does not deserve to be one.

❧ ❧

I THINK I know what love is for, although I'm not quite sure. I think love is given us so we can see a soul. And this soul we see is the highest conception of excellence and truth we can bring forth. This soul is our reflected self. And from seeing what one soul is, we imagine what all souls may be—and thus we reach God, who is the Universal Soul ❧

❧ ❧

DON'T be selfish. If you have something that you do not want, and know some one who has use for it, give it to that person. In this way you can be generous without expenditure or self-denial, and also help another to be the same ❧ ❧

ON the walls of the Louvre for nearly four hundred years has hung the "Mona Lisa" of Leonardo da Vinci. This picture has been the exasperation and inspiration of every portrait-painter who has put brush to palette. Well does Walter Pater call it, "The Despair of Painters."

There is in the face all you can read into it, and nothing more. It gives you what you bring, and nothing else. It is as silent as the lips of Memnon, as voiceless as the Sphinx. It suggests to you every joy that you have ever felt, every sorrow you have ever known, every triumph you have ever experienced.

❡ This woman is beautiful, just as all life is beautiful when we are in health. She has no quarrel with the world—she loves and she is loved again. No vain longing fills her heart, no feverish unrest disturbs her dreams, for her no crouching fears haunt the passing hours—that ineffable smile which plays around her mouth says plainly that life is good. And yet the circles about the eyes and the drooping lids hint of world-weariness, and speak the message of Koheleth and say, "Vanity of vanities, all is vanity." ❧ ❧

La Gioconda is infinitely wise, for she has lived. That supreme poise is only possible to one who knows. All the experiences and emotions of manifold existence have etched and molded that form and face until the body has become the perfect instrument of the soul.

Like every piece of intense personality, this picture has power both to repel and to attract. To this woman nothing is necessarily either good or bad. She has known strange woodland loves in far-off eons when the world was young. She is familiar with the nights and days of Cleopatra, for they were hers: the lavish luxury, the animalism of a soul on fire, the smoke of curious incense that brought poppy-like repose, the satiety that sickens—all these were her portion; the sting of the asp yet lingers in her memory, and the faint scar from its fangs is upon her white breast, known and wondered at by Leonardo who loved her. Back of her stretches her life—a mysterious purple shadow. Do you not see the palaces turned to dust, the broken columns, the sunken treasures, the creeping mosses and the rank ooze of fretted waters that have undermined cities and turned kingdoms into desert seas? The galleys of pagan Greece have swung wide for her on the unforgetting tide, for her soul dwelt in the body of Helen of Troy, and Pallas Athene has followed her ways and whispered to her even the secrets of the gods. Aye! Not only was she Helen, but she was Leda, the mother of Helen. Then she was Saint Ann, mother of Mary; and next she was Mary, visited by an Angel in a dream, and followed by the Wise Men who had seen the Star in the East. The centuries, that are but thoughts, found her a Vestal Virgin in pagan Rome, when brutes were kings, and lust stalked rampant through the streets. She was the bride of Christ, and her fair, frail body was flung to the wild beasts, and torn limb from limb while the multitude feasted on the sight. True to the central impulse of her soul, the Dark Ages rightly called her Cecilia, and then Saint Cecilia, mother of sacred music, and later she ministered to men as Melania, the Nun of Tagaste; next as that daughter of William the Conqueror, the Sister of Charity who went throughout Italy, Spain and France and taught the women of the nunneries how to sew, to weave, to embroider, to illumnate books and make beauty, truth and harmony manifest to human eyes. And so this Lady of the Beaitful Hands stood to Leonardo as the embodiment of a perpetual life; moving in a constantly ascending scale; gathering wisdom, graciousness, love, even as he himself in this life met every experience half-way and counted it joy, knowing that experience is the germ of power. ℂ Life writes its history upon the face,

MAN has constantly grown in power, wisdom, excellence and worth. If he has ever fallen, it has been upstairs, not down

so that all those who have had a like experience read and understand. The human face is the masterpiece of God

IF ANY aspiring college youth wishes a subject for a thesis, I commend this—*Pamphlets and Pamphleteers*. The theme is old, but it is not hackneyed. When you write of pamphleteers, you will touch history at a thousand points
He who knows the history of pamphleteering knows the record of the rise of human rights. ℂ The pamphlet is the weapon of the thinker. By the pamphlet he extends his mental antennæ and reaches millions that otherwise could not hear his message. The pamphlet has been an arsenal of arguments for the common people and was in circulation long before the age of printing

From the Roycroft Dictionary

Romance: Where the hero begins by deceiving himself and ends by deceiving others

Righteous Indignation: 1. Hate that scorches like hell, but which the possessor thinks proves he is right. 2. Your own wrath as opposed to the shocking bad temper of others.

Righteousness: 1. Only a form of commonsense. 2. Wise expediency.

Revival: Religion with a vaudeville attachment

Self-reliance: The name we give to the egotism of the man who succeeds.

School: A training-place—mental, physical, moral. Good boys are boys at work. Bad boys are good boys who mis-direct their energies.

Self-Control: The ability to restrain a laugh at the wrong place.

HE business of Robert Burns was love-making. All love is good, but some kinds of love are better than others.

Through Burns' penchant for falling in love we have his songs. A Burns' bibliography is simply a record of his love affairs, and the spasms of repentance that followed his lapses are made manifest in religious verse.

Poetry is the very earliest form of literature, and is the natural expression of a person in love; and I suppose we might as well admit the fact at once that without love there would be no poetry. Poetry is the bill and coo of sex. All poets are lovers, either actual or potential, and all lovers are poets. Potential poets are the people who read poetry; and so without lovers the poet would never have a market for his wares.

If you have ceased to be moved by religious emotion; if your spirit is no longer surged by music; if you do not linger over certain lines of poetry, it is because the love instinct in your heart has withered to ashes of roses.

It is idle to imagine Bobby Burns as a staid member of the Kirk. Had he a' been, there would now be no Bobby Burns ৯ ৯

The literary ebullition of Robert Burns, he himself told us, began shortly after he had reached the age of indiscretion; and the occasion was his being paired in the hay-field, according to the Scottish custom, with a bonnie lassie. This custom of pairing still endures, and is what the students of sociology call an expeditious move. The Scotch are great economists —the greatest in the world. Adam Smith, the father of the science of economics, was a Scotchman; and Buckle, author of *A History of Civilization,* flatly declares that Adam Smith's *Wealth of Nations* has influenced the people of Earth for good more than any other book that has ever been written—save none. The Scotch are great conservators of energy.

The practice of pairing men and women in the hay-field gets the work done. One man and one woman going down the grass-grown path afield might linger and dally by the way. They would never make hay; but a company of a dozen or more men and women would not only reach the field, but do a lot of work. In Scotland the hay-harvest is short: when the grass is in bloom, just right to make the best hay, it must be cut. And so the men and women, girls and the boys, sally forth. It is a jolly picnic-time, looked forward to with fond anticipation, and gazed back upon with sweet, sad memories, or otherwise, as the case may be ৯ ৯

But they all make hay while the sun shines, and count it joy. Liberties are allowed during haying-time that otherwise would be declared scandalous; during haying-time the Kirk waives her censor's right, and priests and people mingle joyously. Wives are not jealous during haying-harvest, and husbands are never fault-finding, because they each get even by allowing a mutual license. In Scotland during haying-time every married man works alongside of some other man's wife. To the psychologist it is somewhat curious how the desire for propriety is overridden by a stronger desire—the desire for the shilling. The Scotch farmer says, "Anything to get the hay in;" and by loosening a bit the strict bands of social custom the hay is harvested ৯ ৯

In the hay-harvest the law of natural selection holds; partners are often arranged for weeks in advance; and trysts continue year after year. Old lovers meet, touch hands in friendly scuffle for a fork, drink from the same jug, recline at noon and eat lunch in the shade of a friendly stack, and talk to heart's content as they Maud Muller on a summer's day.

℄ Of course, this joyousness of the haying-time is not wholly monopolized by the Scotch. Have n't you seen the jolly haying-parties in Southern Germany, France, Switzerland and the Tyrol? How the bright costumes of the men and the jaunty attire of the women gleam in the glad sunshine!

But the practice is carried to a degree of perfection in Scotland that I have not noticed elsewhere. Surely it is a great economic scheme! It is like that invention of a Connecticut man, which utilizes the ebb and flow of the ocean tides to turn a grist-mill. And it seems queer that no one has ever attempted to utilize the waste of dynamic force involved in the maintenance of the Company Sofa ﾟﾟ

In Ayrshire, I have started out with a haying-party of twenty—ten men and ten women—at six o'clock in the morning, and worked until six at night. I never worked so hard nor did so much. All day long there was a fire of jokes and jolly jibes, interspersed with song, while beneath all ran a gentle hum of confidential interchange of thought. The man who owned the field was there to direct our efforts, and urge us on in well-doing by merry raillery, threat and joyous rivalry.

OME men succeed by what they know; some by what they do; and a few by what they are.

The point I make is this: we did the work. Take heed, ye Captains of Industry, and note this truth, that where men and women work together, under right influences, much good is accomplished, and the work is pleasurable.

Of course there are vinegar-faced philosophers who object to the Scotch custom of pairing young men and maidens in the hayfield; and I 'm willing to admit there may be danger in the scheme. But life is a dangerous business anyway—few indeed, there be, who get out of it alive.

ﾟ ﾟ

JOSIAH WEDGEWOOD has been called the world's first modern businessman; that is, he was the first man to introduce factory betterments and to pay special attention to the idea of beauty. His factory was surrounded by ample space, so as to insure proper light and ventilation. Also, he had flowerbeds and an extensive garden, where many of his people worked at odd hours. Josiah Wedgewood gave prizes for the best gardens and for the most beautiful back-yards; and this, please remember, was nearly a hundred years ago ﾟ ﾟ

Unfortunately, the times were not ripe for Wedgewood's ideas as to factory building and factory surroundings; nevertheless, he left his mark upon the times ﾟ ﾟ

One thing sure, he influenced profoundly another great businessman, Robert Owen who, in degree, followed the Wedgewood idea and endeavored to make his factory not only a place for manufacturing things, but a place where men and women would evolve and grow and become. Robert Owen's factory was also a school. A product of Robert Owen's factory idea was John Tyndall the scientist, known to the world as one of the "big five." The other four are Herbert Spencer, Thomas Huxley, Alfred Russel Wallace and Charles Darwin. And a daughter of Josiah Wedgewood was the mother of Charles Darwin. Charles Darwin's book, *The Origin of Species,* has influenced the world more profoundly than any other book issued within three hundred years. But in this year of grace, Nineteen Hundred Fourteen, the ideas of Aristotle, Pliny, Leonardo, John Wesley, Josiah Wedgewood and Robert Owen are to be found in many towns, villages and cities of the United States and Europe.

For instance, the Oregon plan of teaching gardening in every public school is a literal following out of the suggestions of Aristotle. Wedgewood and Robert Owen were businessmen, and never claimed to be anything else.

Business is supplying human wants. It is carrying things from where they are plentiful to where they are needed. Business is human service, and the good businessman today is essentially a public servant.

ﾟ ﾟ

HERBERT SPENCER was once beaten at billiards by a smart young man. Spencer proved his humanity by making a testy remark to this effect: " Young man, to play billiards well is an accomplishment, but to play billiards too well is proof of a misspent youth." In Plutarch's life of Pericles he has King Philip say to Alexander, " Are you not ashamed to sing so well?"

And Antisthenes, when he was told that Ismenias played excellently upon the flute, answered, " Well he is good for nothing else; otherwise he would not have played so well."

MARK TWAIN said there are only six original stories, and four of these were unfit for ladies' ears, and that all six of these stories trace back to Rameses the Second who had the felicity to live ninety-six years

This remark of Mark Twain traces a direct pedigree to Plutarch, who said the Egyptians lived life in its every phase; and anything that could happen to any man or woman happened in Egypt, therefore all stories of misunderstandings, tragedies, comedies and such can be traced to Egypt.

ON a simple little granite column in Nancy Hanks Park, Lincoln City, Indiana, is the Inscription:

NANCY HANKS LINCOLN
Mother of Abraham Lincoln
Died October 5th, 1818
Aged 35 years

" Died, aged 35," runs the inscription.

❡ The family had come from Kentucky only a half-day's journey distant as we count miles today by steam and trolley.

❡ But in Eighteen Hundred Seventeen it took the little cavalcade a month to come from LaRue County, Kentucky, to Spencer County, Indiana, sixteen miles as the birds fly, North of the Ohio River

Here land was to be had for the settling. For ten miles North from the Ohio the soil is black and fertile.

Then you reach the hills, or what the early settlers called " the barrens." The soil here is yellow, the land rolling. It is picturesque beyond compare,

NO doubt Browning was partially right—"God's in His Heaven," but fortunately, He does n't remain there all the time.

beautiful as a poet's dream, but tickle it as you will with a hoe it will not laugh a harvest. At the best it will only grimly grin

It is a country of timber and toil.

Valuable hardwoods abound—oak, walnut, ash, hickory.

Springs flowing from the hills are plentiful, wild flowers grow in profusion, the trees are vocal with song of birds, but the ground is stony and stubborn

Here the family rested by the side of the cold sparkling stream. Across the valley to the West the hills arose, grand, somber, majestic.

❡ Down below a stream went dancing its way to the sea.

And near by were rushes and little patches of grass, where the tired horses nibbled in gratitude.

And so they rested. There were Thomas Lincoln; Nancy Hanks Lincoln, his wife; Sarah Lincoln aged ten; and little Abe Lincoln, aged eight.

The family had four horses, old and lame. In the wagon were a few household goods, two sacks of cornmeal, a side of bacon. Instead of pushing on Westward the family decided to remain. They built a shack from logs, closed on three sides, open to the South.

The reason the South side was left open was because there was no chimney, and the fire they built was half in the home and half outside.

Here the family lived that first, bleak, dreary Winter. To Abe and Sarah it was only fun. But to Nancy Hanks Lincoln, who was delicate, illy clothed, underfed, and who had known better things in her Kentucky home, it was hardship.

She was a woman of aspiration and purpose, a woman with romance and dreams in her heart. Now all had turned to ashes of roses. Children, those little bold explorers on life's stormy sea, accept everything just as a matter of course.

❡ Abe wrote long years afterward: " My mother worked steadily and without complaining. She cooked, made clothing, planted a little garden. She coughed at times, and often would have to lie down for a little while. We did not know she was ill. She was worn, yellow and sad. One day when she was lying down she motioned me to come near. And when I stood by the bed she reached out one hand as if to embrace me, and pointing to my sister Sarah said in a whisper, ' Be good to her, Abe!'" The tired woman closed her eyes and it was several hours before the children knew she was dead.

SYMPATHY and sentiment in right proportion are all right and are needed, but both must be used as the warp and woof of the practical

❧ The next day Thomas Lincoln made a coffin of split boards. The body of the dead woman was placed in the rude coffin. And then four men carried the coffin up to the top of a little hill near by and it was lowered into a grave.

A mound of rocks was piled on top, according to the custom of the times, to protect the grave from wild animals.
❧ Little Abe and Sarah went down the hill, dazed and undone, clinging to each other in their grief. But there was work to do, and Sarah was the " little other mother."

For a year she cooked, scrubbed, patched the clothing, and looked after the household

THEN one day Thomas Lincoln went away, and left the two children alone
He was gone for a week, and when he came back he brought the children a stepmother—Sally Bush Johnston, a widow with three children of her own but enough love for two more.

Her heart went out to little Abe, and his lonely heart responded. She brought provisions, dishes, cloth for clothing, needles to sew with, scissors to cut. She was a good cook. And best of all she had three books.
Up to this time Abe had never worn shoes or cap. She made him moccasins, and also a coonskin cap, with a dangling tail

She taught Abe and Sarah to read, their own mother having taught them the alphabet. She told them stories—stories of George Washington and Thomas Jefferson. She told them of the great outside world of towns and cities where many people lived. She told them of the Capitol at Washington, and of the Government of the United States. And they learned to repeat the names of these States, and write the names out with a burnt stick on a slab

And little Abe Lincoln and his sister Sarah were very happy.
Their hearts were full of love and gratitude for their New Mother, and they sometimes wondered if anywhere in the wide world there were little boys and girls who had as much as they.
" All I am, and all I hope to be, I owe to my darling mother!" wrote Abraham Lincoln, years later.
And it is good to know that Sarah Bush Lincoln lived to see the boy evolve into the greatest man in America. She survived him four years.

WHEN Abe was twenty-one, the family decided to move West.
❧ There were four ox-carts in all. One of these carts was driven by Abraham Lincoln. But before they started, Abe cut the initials N. H. L. on a slab and placed it securely at the head of the grave of his mother—the mother who had given him birth.

IN Nineteen Hundred Five certain citizens of Indiana bought the hilltop, a beautiful grove of thirty acres, and this property is now the possession of the State, forever.
A guardian lives there who keeps the property in good condition. A chapel,

roofed, but open on all sides, has been built, the trees are trimmed, the underbrush removed. Winding walks and well-kept roadways are to be seen. The park is open to the public. Visitors come, some of them great and learned.

And now and again comes some old woman, tired, worn, knowing somewhat of the history of Nancy Hanks, and all she endured and suffered, and places on the mound a bouquet gathered down in the meadows. Abraham Lincoln can never die. He belongs to the ages. Memories of him will be passed on from generation to generation—the blessed heritage of all mankind.

And here alone on the hilltop sleeps the woman who went down into the shadow and gave him birth.

Biting poverty was her portion; deprivation and loneliness were her lot. But on her tomb are four words that express the highest praise that tongue can utter, or pen indite:

MOTHER OF ABRAHAM LINCOLN
    —The Mother of Lincoln.

THERE is only one thing worth living for, writing for, working for, dying for—and that is freedom.

On the way to the gallows, a mother held up her baby boy, and John Brown stopped long enough to kiss the cheek of the little black baby. John Brown could not take the baby in his arms, for his hands were tied behind his back. Happy l'il coon—Mammy's pet! kissed by Ol' John Brown on his way to launch his soul upon the River Styx.

To be kissed by a man who was on the way to the Ferry, going because he tried to make men free, is no small matter. It has been denied that John Brown kissed the black baby, but I guess, and I also reckon, that it was so, for I've seen that painting depicting the scene, by dear Tom Hovenden, who died rescuing a child from in front of a moving train.

¶ John Brown was a fanatic, certainly, that is true. His methods were wrong—but the man himself was right, as every man is who lifts up his voice for freedom, and flings away his life that others may have liberty. The path of progress winds by the thorn-road, and all along one can trace it by the tracks of bleeding feet

IT is coming across the best minds in America that if we had sent missionaries to Japan in order to learn of the Japanese, instead of trying to convert them to our social and religious system, it would have been just as well for the Japanese and a good deal better for us.

¶ Nations must get acquainted with one another, just as individuals should, in order to have a fair and proper understanding. Electricity and quick transportation have practically made the world one.

EACH soul is a center in itself, and the mistakes of others—the follies of wife or child, husband or parent—are none of ours. We are individuals—we came into the world alone, we live alone, and we die alone; and we must be so girded round by right that no fault of another can touch us. God is on our side —nothing can harm us but ourselves. Let us make sure that we are right, and then the follies of others will pass us by unscathed. And above all, remember it is not for us to punish. " Vengeance is mine: I will repay, saith the Lord."

Two necessities in doing a great and important work: a definite plan and limited time.

To try many things means power: to finish a few is immortality.

To act in absolute freedom and at the same time realize that responsibility is the price of freedom is salvation.

The Divine Economy is automatic and very simple: we receive only that which we give.

Men do not vary much in virtue: their vices only are different.

A few conquer by fighting, but it is well to remember that more battles are won by submitting.

INDEX

ii

v

SO HERE ENDETH THE NOTE BOOK OF ELBERT HUBBARD
NOW PUT INTO PERMANENT FORM BY THE ROYCROFTERS
๑ THE BORDERS, INITIALS AND BINDING BY ROYCROFT
ARTISTS AND CRAFTSMEN ๑ THE WHOLE PRODUCED
BY THE ROYCROFTERS AT THEIR SHOPS, WHICH ARE
LOCATED AT ROYCROFT-TOWN, EAST AURORA, ERIE
COUNTY, NEW YORK STATE, ANNO DOMINI, MCMXXVII